AMERICAN TOGETHER

A JOURNEY TO THE LAND
OF SECOND CHANCES

Gayle;
     Immigrants didn't give us the
melting pot. They gave us a beautiful
mosiac called Americans!
              Ricardo Anzurya
              05-18-21

AMERICAN TOGETHER
A Journey to the Land of Second Chances

ISBN #978-1-938842-53-5

Copyright © 2020
by Ricardo Inzunza, PhD
CEO, RIA International Ltd.

Cover design by Chrisbel Cortez and Andres Salazar
Interior layout by Bardolf & Company

Appreciation and Inspiration

With a deep sense of appreciation, this book is dedicated to immigrants. Those intrepid pioneers, who ventured into the unknown to stake their claim, to do what must be done to gain a foothold, a start on the creation of a life of freedom and happiness for themselves, their families and for the countless generations to follow. How could they know how their dreams would flourish and endure?

While much has changed since the nation's founding, our immigrant ideals have not. The United States is still a country with a mission and a desire for greatness on the world stage. America's openness to people, who want to build the life of their dreams, in the nation of their dreams, is still the fuel for our nation's greatness and diversity.

AMERICAN TOGETHER

A JOURNEY TO THE LAND
OF SECOND CHANCES

Ricardo Inzunza, PhD

Bardolf & Company
Sarasota, Florida

CONTENTS

PROLOGUE

My name is Ricardo Rogelio Inzunza Jr.

It took me many years to come to terms with that name. Growing up on the wrong side of the proverbial tracks in San Ysidro, California, I learned early on that being a Mexican was somehow "less" than being an American. Being the bull-headed kid that I was, I decided I didn't want to be "less" than anyone. (Can you blame me?) So instead, I learned how to hide my Mexican identity and pretend to be American until life in the real world made that impossible.

I have been many things during my 80-odd years on this planet: an illegitimate son, a ward of the state, a troublemaker, an airman and a veteran, a baseball player, a PhD candidate, a family man and a father (all with varying levels of success, depending on who you ask). I've served in Senior Executive Service postings under two Republican administrations, I've acted as an independent consultant for foreign governments and conglomerates, and I've launched and relaunched my own company several times.

Through it all, from my troubled teens stealing pennies at abandoned gas stations to my years working at the Pentagon and being responsible for the actions (and inactions) of 40,000 U.S. Government employees, one thing has stayed the same: I, Ricardo Rogelio Inzunza Jr, have been a fierce proponent for immigration and an even fiercer believer in second chances.

And that, in a way, is what this book is all about.

In this book, I'll be talking a lot about the second chances I've been given to turn my life around, second chances that have brought me to where I am today (to the amazement of many and to the vexation of others, including myself). I'll also be talking a lot about a second chance at reforming our immigration system in order to help millions of deserving families and individuals who want nothing more than to be able to live happy and peaceful lives in the United States. And people like me. A Mexican American, who directed the first immigration legalization program in 1986 and still to this day thinks about all the things he could have done better to help even more people.

I'll also be talking a lot about America, and how I've seen it change throughout the years: from its political parties and the way they approach immigration issues to the social struggles and ever-persisting problems of inequality, racism, sexism and xenophobia; from what it means to declare wars we have no business declaring to what it means fighting in those wars as devoted and loyal patriots and military men and women; and from having blind faith in our government to seeing through the lies and the propaganda.

But I'll also be talking a lot about all the good stuff: the visionary people who changed our country for the better; the everyday people who choose to lift each other up instead of bringing each other down; the America that's helped people when they needed her and ultimately won their hearts forever.

In his farewell address to the nation in 1989, President Ronald Reagan (a man I admire deeply and under whose administration I had the privilege of serving in the '80s) spoke about the America of our dreams, the "shining city upon a hill." His speech, considered by many a love-letter to immigration, has stayed with me through the years. President Reagan envisioned this shining city, this America, to be "teeming with people of all kinds living in harmony and peace: a city with free ports that hummed with commerce and creativity." If there had to be city walls, President Reagan said, "The walls had doors, and the doors were open to anyone with the will and the heart to get here." (Hear, hear!) He saw an America that's "a magnet for all who must have freedom, for all the pilgrims from all the lost places who are hurling through the darkness, toward home."

The reason I wrote this book was to instill hope in people who are wondering about their future, about what their next move should be. I'm hoping by telling my story, the story of someone who grew up with an identity crisis, feeling like he was a foreigner living in a foreign land even though he was living in the country of his birth, that people will feel less alone. Hopefully, they will realize there are folks out there who genuinely care about them, folks who can help us all to be American Together.

So, in this book, I'll be talking a lot about this America President Reagan dreamed of, a place of inclusion, not exclusion. A land of second chances, open to anyone who wants to call it home.

I won't be doing it out of nostalgia (certainly not out of a nostalgia for the '80s and those haircuts!). But out of my unwavering certainty that now more than ever, this inclusive America is the America we need. And all these "pilgrims from all the lost places," are and should be the New Americans. We should be American Together.

My name is Ricardo Rogelio Inzunza Jr. and this is the story of my life and my country.

Part I

FROM PENNIES
TO THE PENTAGON

Chapter 1

HOW MANY MOTHERS DOES IT TAKE?

People often use the expression, "It takes a village to raise a child." Whenever I come across this African proverb (usually in some article about the importance of community when it comes to shaping well-rounded individuals), my immediate thought is, "Yeah, but how many *mothers* does it take?"

Mothers are incredibly special people. I believe that even the worst of mothers have a unique charisma about them. And I don't mean "worst" in the sense that they are evil. Rather, in the sense that these are women who've had a hard life and were, perhaps, ill-equipped to handle the challenges motherhood threw at them.

That motherly charisma is something no child can ever resist. It's something no lovelorn adult, who's been yearning for affection all his life, can resist either.

In my troubled and frequently lovelorn life, I have to acknowledge that I've been lucky enough to be blessed with not one, not two, but three mothers! Each and every one of them, in her own special way, shaped me into the (well-rounded, I want to believe) man I have become today.

It didn't take a village after all.

My First Mother Was Anita Sanchez

She was not my biological mother, but she raised me during the early childhood phase of my life: the time when the most important physical, mental, emotional, social and language development takes place. (Most studies agree that the major portion of this development happens by the age of five.) So, although she did not give birth to me, Anita was the one who built the foundation on which the rest of my life would stand.

Anita Sanchez and me,
San Diego, 1939.

To this day, it is a bit unclear to me exactly when I was given to Anita. Later, I heard stories that it happened when I was just two weeks old. I think she and my mom were friends. I don't know exactly how they met and what their association was, but I believe Anita knew my father's side of the family. I'm not sure if she was married to my father's brother or lived with him but there was some connection there, I think. In one of these hazy, early childhood memories that could as well have been a dream, I remember Anita going to visit somebody on Coronado Island (a suburb of San Diego) and that, although she took me with her part of the way, she couldn't take me with her inside that house.

I believe now that it was my father's house. And I wasn't allowed in.

Perhaps I should explain, before you get all confused by the many intricacies of my family situation, that my parents were not married. Not to each other, at least. My father, Ricardo Inzunza, was a ranch hand on a ranch that my grandfather managed, the Timken Ranch in Holtville, California. When he met my mother there, he was already married with children. My birth in April of 1938 was on the Timken Ranch and it was an illegitimate one.

My father, Ricardo Inzunza Sr,
circa 1951.

Which brings me back to Anita Sanchez.

Although she couldn't take me inside that house, Anita would take me close to it whenever she visited. She had this little bag of food she'd leave with me, and she'd tell me to sit under a nearby tree. So, there I sat for hours on end, a child alone under a tree, waiting for the only woman whom I knew as my mother to get back from her mysterious visit. I wasn't alone for long, however. While I waited, some kids would usually appear and come talk to me. Now that I think about it, I have to assume that these children, some of them at least, were my siblings.

My adult self, now able to rationalize, understands why I wasn't allowed inside my father's house. I can't imagine his wife having a yearning for the illegitimate son to darken her doorway. But it still stings a bit. At least Anita (or somebody in the family) must have told these children to go talk to the weird kid, sitting all alone under that tree. My adult self thanks them.

Me, age 4, San Diego.

I was too young to recall much from my time with Anita Sanchez. I do remember, though, that she was a deeply religious woman who only spoke Spanish and a seriously devout Catholic, who made sure to baptize me (this will be important later). She also made sure that I attended church religiously. To be doubly certain I didn't stray from the faith, she had a crucifix blessed at the Metropolitan Cathedral of the Assumption of the Most Blessed Virgin Mary into Heaven which is the seat of the Catholic Archdiocese in Mexico City before she hung it around my neck on a gold chain. She admonished me to never take it off. It still hangs around my neck today, mostly for sentimental reasons.

So, my first memory of myself as a child revolves around Anita and, in a way, religion.

Somehow, I'd gotten myself into a car; I am unsure exactly when that event took place. I remember I hadn't started school yet, so the fact that I managed to sneak into a car at such a young age is both impressive and disconcerting, I suppose. Everyone seemed to be amused about it afterwards. In any case, the car was parked by our apartment with the engine running, so I managed to put the transmission into reverse and the car shot backwards until it was stopped by a crash into a chain link fence that was part of a lumberyard across the street from Anita's apartment.

As I recall, it was raining that day, unusual for San Diego. I remember Anita coming out of the house holding something over her head to protect her hair from the rain. It could have been a blanket; it looked more like a shawl. In Mexican culture, Our Lady of Guadalupe (who some view as an alternative version of the Virgin Mary) is the Patroness Saint of Mexico. Everyone has a picture of her in their home somewhere. I still carry a picture of her and the "Most Sacred Heart of Jesus" in my wallet today, mostly for sentimental reasons. As I mentioned earlier, Anita was pushing me really hard to attend church, so I had become familiar with religious imagery.

In my little kid brain that was probably in shock from the car accident, when I saw her running to save me in the rain, I thought she was the spitting image of Our Lady of Guadalupe. At that moment,

Anita looked like a saint to me. Of course, when I told her as much, she whacked me. Perhaps she thought I was being blasphemous (or she wanted to make sure I didn't sneak into any more cars).

I often think that, had I been able to spend more time with Anita Sanchez, I would have turned out to be a completely different person. But our time together was cut short in the most violent of ways.

Anita's next-door neighbor was a Navy seaman from the Philippines. Back in the day, men from the Philippines could join the U.S. military. This happened a lot during the WWII years, although they usually served in low-ranking Navy placements (such as valets and waiters). But his ethnicity doesn't matter. At least it doesn't matter to me now because, if I'm being honest, the incident did color my perception of Asian people for quite some time until I was able to visit Asia myself, meet more people, and know better.

At this point of the story though, what matters is that the man next door decided to sexually assault my godmother Anita.

Anita's daughter and I had gone out somewhere and, by the time we returned, it was dusk. I wasn't allowed to go inside the house since it was a crime scene, so they made me sit and wait in the car. I sat there for as long as I could but I just couldn't help myself; I wanted to see what had happened. I got out of the car and ran to the back of the apartment to peek through the windows. I remember I could see blood spread all over the floor, but I couldn't see anybody. Later on, I found out what happened. Not the particular horrors of it, mind you, but I do know that Anita was close to death. Her assailant stabbed her quite a few times.

The wounds she suffered weakened her heart to the point she could no longer care for me. Under doctor's orders, Anita reluctantly gave me back to my second mother, my biological one.

Although our time together was too short, Anita Sanchez managed to instill quite a few beliefs in me, a few constants, rather. Those were, in no particular order: everyone in the world had brown eyes and black hair; everyone spoke Spanish; everyone had a Hispanic surname; there was only one religion, Catholicism. That was it. Most of these constants held up for quite some time, affirmed by the environment I grew up in. In the fourth grade, for example, we had seven girls named Maria Gonzales in my class, and they had to be given nicknames to prevent confusion for them and our classmates. It wasn't until we were bused to Junior High School, away from the border, that I met folks who were different. Non-Catholics, imagine that!

Anita, and others after her, tried hard to pull me into the flock of Catholicism. In my mid-twenties I even took a catechism class. After I completed the class, another was starting, but I was still confused; so I enrolled in the class again. After the first session concluded, Father Cornelius, who taught the class, asked for a word with me. "Everything in religion is based on faith," he said. "It is the foundation that everything stands on. If your foundation is weak, so is your faith. Faith comes from inside of you. I cannot pour faith into you with a funnel. You must want it bad enough to make it real in your heart. You don't have faith. You are looking for proof and we can't provide it; that's why we call it faith. You must believe. I tried to motivate you to seek faith within your heart, but you are wasting your time here. Go forward seeking faith. Don't give up. When you find faith, everything will become clear for you." With that, he turned and walked away. The hand off was complete.

He was not wrong. Here I am, many years later, still looking for my faith. If there ever was hope for me to find it, it certainly isn't in today's Catholic Church. I believe there is no right way to do the wrong thing. Until the church gets that message and purges all vestiges of pedophilia from within its ranks (because the problem is real and it is pervasive), there is no way I can be associated with it. Sorry, Father Cornelius, I know you were probably a good guy.

Now, I may not be an expert on faith, but when it comes to high-risk behavior, I know what real fear is. I've learned how to deal with it in my life. Without that inner power, I am certain I would be looking to some external source to bolster me. For a big part of my young life, I believed the bonds of family and blood would ignite and sustain the inner power I so desperately sought.

Thus started my complicated relationship with my second mother.

My Second Mother Was Also My Biological Mother

Her name was Antonia Figueroa. Her nickname was Toni. The first time I laid eyes on her, she was standing on National Avenue, in Logan Heights, a San Diego Mexican neighborhood.

I think I was in kindergarten then, perhaps five or six years old. I thought she was the most beautiful woman I'd ever seen! Toni looked like an angel or at least like my Mexican-colored understanding of what an angel should look like. She had long black hair, brown skin and brown eyes. I think she might have been five feet tall, and I seriously doubt she weighed more than a hundred pounds. To me, though, she was the epitome of beauty.

My mother was born on the same ranch I was, in Holtville, California. She had many siblings, perhaps seven or eight (Alicia, Margarita, Alejandro, Carlos, Erlinda—I'm always forgetting someone), and she was the second oldest of that group. Her father, Thomas Figueroa, was married to a woman by the name of Carlota—my grandmother. Having a large family was a necessary element of farm life. In those days, the more children you had, the easier life was. Essentially you had more hands to help work the farm.

My mother, Antonia Figueroa,
19 years old, circa 1953.

I guess you could say my mother had a troubled life. In November 1936, my mother's mother (Carlotta) and 3 of my mother's siblings (Tommy (7), Delia (4) and Johnny (2) burned to death in an automobile accident. I never heard my mother mention the accident so I have no idea what impact it had on her but it must have left some residue. She gave birth to about a dozen children and was only married to the man who fathered her last three. But then again, those were troubled times for us all, with World War II looming over people's heads. When the war started, my mother left the ranch in the Imperial Valley and ended up in San Diego.

San Diego was, and continues to be, a Navy town. Back then, everything was about the war effort. Everybody was pitching in. America was humming along, supporting the war. San Diego had large shipyards that were busy, day and night, building ships for the war effort. My mother was hired as a riveter, putting the rivets in a lot of the Navy ships. I don't know if that job wasn't enough to pay rent or if it didn't satisfy her, but she also worked as a bartender.

At the time, two of my siblings were living with my mother, my brother Gilberto (or Gilbert) and my sister Eileen. This is where things started getting a bit confusing for me and my notions of family and identity.

My sister's name was Eileen Songer. My brother's name was Gilbert Fierro. My name was—I realized then, for the first time, that I didn't know what my surname was. Of course, at the age of five or six you don't really worry about things like surnames and lineage. They called me Richey (the Hispanic version of Rickie or Richie), so I assumed, or sub-consciously wanted my name to be Richard and not Ricardo. My brother was two years older than me and his last name was Fierro, so I also assumed my surname was Fierro. Even then, I had a keen sense of the obvious.

Richard Fierro. That's the name I enrolled in school with, and the name I went by until I turned seventeen. But we'll get to that later.

Since she was working both at the shipyards and as a bartender, my mother slept during the day and was not to be disturbed. She slept until she had to go to work. Then, she'd go from one shift to another. When she'd come home again, she would go back to sleep. At least, that's the routine I remember. Whether she worked seven days a week or five, whether she ever had days off, I don't remember. I do recall we didn't see too much of her. Eileen, Gilbert and I were pretty much on our own. We set our own course and made our own rules, with little adult supervision or boundaries.

As a result, we didn't go to school very often (even though we were enrolled). We weren't very clean either.

Just a few blocks from where we lived on National Avenue was a market called Amador's. Gilbert and I used to go there to try to steal candy or something to eat. The owner apparently took pity on us and, when we went there looking like little ragamuffins, he would tell us that if we went home and took a bath, he'd give us ice cream cones. He didn't have to tell us twice. I can imagine we were a sight to behold.

Thinking about it, Gilbert and I must have looked like poster siblings for multi-racial families. He was very dark, and I was light skinned. Gilbert's nickname was "Chanate," a slang term referring to a "blackbird" and used by ex-prisoners, of which there were many, in the "barrio." In today's slang it refers to how you like your coffee. That's how dark his complexion was. As soon as folks saw us, they must have assumed we were from different races and that one of us was adopted. I always hoped they saw him as the adopted one.

Gilbert, me behind him, Eileen behind me, and three neighbor's kids,
Oceanview Blvd, San Diego, circa 1943.

We lived in Logan Heights, which was the "Chicano" barrio of San Diego. It still is. In those days it was euphemistically called "Barrio Logan," a neighborhood on the wrong side of the tracks, but it wasn't always that way. Its transformation began in 1910 with the influx of refugees from the Mexican Revolution, who soon became the majority ethnic group. For this reason, the southern part of the original Logan Heights neighborhood came to be called "Barrio Logan." (Barrio is a Spanish word for "neighborhood".)

This barrio was the bottom rung of the poverty ladder in San Diego, populated predominantly by ethnic Mexicans, some Anglos who were down on their luck, and some Mexican Nationals. We went to school at Lowell Elementary school (now named Perkins Elementary School). I don't remember much about my teacher except that she didn't speak Spanish and she kept saying, "Well, there he is. He doesn't speak English, and the worst part is that he will be back tomorrow." I realize now her vitriol was directed more at my bad behavior than my language capability. Still, it smarted.

But I guess she wasn't wrong. I didn't fit in, and language played a part in that.

My mother and siblings' first language wasn't Spanish but mine was. They were English dominant, but I wasn't. Switching suddenly from Spanish only to mostly English at home took its toll on me. The thoughts would come to my brain in Spanish faster than my limited English vocabulary could find the words to express them, so I developed a stutter in English. As you can imagine, I wasn't eager to do any public speaking in English. I was a left-handed, freckled faced, Mexican, from the wrong side of the tracks, from what looked like an interracial family, unclean, with a stutter and a behavior problem. Boy, did I need that inner strength.

Nowadays, because I haven't spoken Spanish in so many years, I stutter in Spanish. It's a very interesting experience, to stutter in two different languages at different times or even at the same time, if I am switching from one language to another. It goes to show how complicated our brains are, how interconnected our speech is with our psychological state and whatever is going on in our lives.

In the barrio most of my classmates were Spanish-dominant, so I was able to communicate with them. Unfortunately, I had already started to talk with the group that accepted me, and it was the wrong kind of group.

I guess I was a pretty unruly student. Back then, San Diego didn't have air conditioning. Our classroom was on the ground floor, so the windows were usually open, except during inclement weather. I used to jump out of the window if I didn't want to stay in class. The class had a snack break every day, where the kids would sign up for lunch and the school would give them a little container of milk and a snack of some kind, but it cost money, so I couldn't participate in that. I remember vividly that I used to rock in my chair and create such a ruckus that, out of desperation, the teacher would provide me with a snack so she could restore order. As soon as she did, I would quiet down. Unfortunately, she was rewarding my worst behavior.

With my mother either working or sleeping, I really had little or no adult supervision. I could pretty much do as I pleased when I pleased. Our small, two-bedroom apartment in the Barrio Logan was situated between two bars. (The house is still there, but the bars are not.) One of the bars was called "Clancy's" and was owned by an elderly man who stored his empty bottles out back until he could return them to the cooper. The bottles were protected from theft by a storage shed he proudly built, fenced in and with a roof. It was quite adequate, but the fence didn't go all the way to the ground for some reason. There was space for a little person to crawl under, although not enough space for an adult. When Gilbert and his friends needed money, they would get me to crawl under the fence and steal bottles for them.

I was good at stealing bottles, and soon it became routine for me. In some perverse fashion, it provided me with a feeling of belonging.

Until one night, as I was crawling out of the storage area a waitress grabbed me by my feet and started hollering, "Clancy, Clancy, I caught a boy stealing your bottles!" When Gilbert and his friends heard her shouting, they scattered. The police made a report of the incident and took me home to my parents, but, since no parents were available, they took me to the juvenile detention center until my mother could fetch me. Quite naturally, she was not pleased.

The beer bottle incident is memorable because, for years afterward, Gilbert made me the butt of the "Clancy" joke by mimicking the waitress to get a laugh. It's also memorable because it brought my mother to the attention of Children's Protective Services (CPS).

One day, after I'd lived with her for, I don't know how long, Gilbert, Eileen and I were picked up by the state of California and made wards of the court. This brings me to my third mother.

My Third Mother, Mrs. Leone

She was my most important foster mother. In many ways, Mrs. Leone was the one who shaped me the most, the one who better equipped me with the tools I'd need in the future to face all the challenges life would throw at me. Although, being a selfish, troubled teenager, I wasn't very grateful to her for it at the time.

I sure am now. Believe me, the irony that her surname means "lion" in English is not lost on me.

To tell you more about Mrs. Leone though, I need to talk about some bad things that happened to me first. Some bad things that had to happen in order to get me to her doorstep.

It all started with a California Social Services car.

Chapter 2

FOSTERING HOPE

The first time I saw the car that would change my life, it was parked by our apartment.

I didn't know what that car was, only that it meant trouble. It had a very distinct design: the insignia of the state of California was emblazoned on the front doors, on both sides. Very soon, I learned that the car belonged to California's Child Protective Services and it was there, courtesy of the city of San Diego, to take my brother Gilbert, my sister Eileen and me away from our mother's care and custody.

That car would officially begin my journey as a ward of the court.

We were out that day, as we so often were, out of school, out of touch, and out of control. But our days of being out were about to end. As we were approaching home, I remember seeing a woman waiting next to that ominous car. To her, we might as well have had neon signs above our heads flashing "Children out of order." She immediately recognized us as the kids she was looking for. She scooped all three of us up and drove us to a place called the "Boys and Girls Aid Society," a place that provided preventive services or direct care to abused, neglected and at-risk youth in San Diego County. Of course, they also provided services to kids who had either psychological or family problems. Looking back, it's easy to see how we could have fit into most of those categories.

The first thing that happened to us in our soon-to-be status as wards of the court, was to have our heads shaved. It wasn't meant as punishment; apparently, we had some sort of scabies. Our heads were full of open sores from not being clean enough and us scratching them all the time. They shaved us and smeared smelly ointment all over our bald heads which, I remember, smelled so bad it made me throw up. It wasn't all doom and gloom though. I had my own bed, and for the first time, I didn't have to share it with Gilbert and Eileen. The bed had clean sheets that smelled wonderful and not at all like urine. Imagine that! (Our bed at home only had a mattress, and Gilbert was a bed wetter.)

Soon after, we were to appear before an Administrative Law Judge for a hearing. Our mother was also there; she was required to attend. I remember how strong my mother was. Not once did I see her cry, not even when the judge determined that she was unable to "discharge her parental duties," which was a fancy way of saying she was an unfit mother. We were deemed to be at risk. The judge decided that our mother should be stripped of her parental rights, and just like that, we were made wards of the court for protection and placed into the foster care system. That was the last time I saw my sister Eileen for many years. Back then, the foster care system didn't much care for blood relations. Biological siblings were split up and placed in different foster homes. I understand that most state foster care systems have improved since then.

By some twist of fate, however, my brother Gilbert and I were the exception to that rule. Throughout the years, we were kept together like a matching (or a mismatched) set.

A Set That Changed Way Too Many Hands

I don't remember exactly in how many different foster homes Gilbert and I were placed. My recollection has been dulled by the passage of time. I don't remember the names or addresses of our early placements either, just some disembodied images of some of the foster mothers' faces. I do vaguely recall two instances when I wanted to stay but Gilbert wanted to run. That was a bit distressing to me, who'd already lost two different mothers but we ran anyway.

What I do recall is that the foster homes were several and that our stay in most was brief.

This was during WWII. Many families clearly needed the extra income provided by foster care, so potential parents were in abundance. But none of them seemed good enough for Gilbert. As soon as we'd get into a new foster home, he would tell me we needed to run. To this day, I don't know what made him feel that we shouldn't stay there. But I'd learned not to question my big brother, even if the foster home seemed okay to me. "We're running," he'd say, and so we would. In most places, we didn't last more than a couple of days.

As I've already mentioned, we looked very different, my blackbird of a brother and me. I have no idea how this played out when it came to Gilbert feeling uncomfortable in our various foster homes, but it must have had some effect.

I realized at a young age that I was smarter than Gilbert. Despite being aware, I still took my cues from my brother, but I also manipulated him a bit. If I wanted him to think or feel a certain way, I knew I could nudge him in that direction (I understand it sounds horrible now, but these are the kinds of things you do when exploring your limits and your group dynamic as kids.) So, he may have been the one declaring we should run away, but I was the puppeteer. In all honesty, if I didn't like a place, I knew I could plant the run away seed in his mind. Even if he liked it at first, pretty soon he would say "let's run," and I would happily oblige. That way, all the blame could be put at his feet. It was a good system. I guess you can say my brother had me right where I wanted him.

My brother Gilbert, Eileen Songer, and me,
Tijuana, Mexico, circa 1949.

And so the cycle continued: Gilbert and I would run away from a foster home, the state would find us and place us in another. The abundance of willing foster families due to the war notwithstanding, we quickly developed a reputation as hard to place brothers. The brothers Gilbert and Richard Fierro, the troublemakers. Even at school, where we were enrolled by the state and forced to attend, we had to wear t-shirts that denoted our status as belonging to the "Boys & Girls Aid." I remember that, whenever I acted out during class (which was not a rare occurrence), the teacher would point at me and say, "See, it's those kids from the Aid. They're troublemakers." It seemed to be the norm for my early teachers. They weren't kind, although they probably were acting more out of frustration than anger. It wasn't all mean-spirited.

By then, I had grown into a troublemaker. Two recurring themes were shaping my behavior: petty theft and hoarding.

The two were often intertwined. I would pilfer small amounts of food from our foster homes and hide it somewhere within the house. I would do the same with small amounts of money, usually change. This was never done with malice or for personal gain; I just needed the sense of security it provided me. Even with the food. The food I was hoarding was of absolutely no use to me. My comfort derived solely from knowing it was there and that it was mine.

I remember an instance in a new foster home where I had crawled under my bed looking for hiding places. I discovered that if I tore a hole in the box spring ticking, it was possible to hide things on the slats that held up the box spring and mattress set. The slats became perfect shelves for hiding my loot. To this day, thinking about my discovery still makes me feel secure.

I realize, of course, how extremely insecure and afraid I must have been.

That fear created a pattern in my psyche, a need for material security that follows me to this day. It still makes me feel good, for instance, to have something I am craving in the refrigerator. (Even if I keep it until it spoils, it doesn't matter. Just having it gives me the warm fuzzies.) I do the same thing with clothing: I will buy something I'll convince myself I really want or need, and it will hang in the closet with tags still in place for years, always making me strangely content and secure. Every time I see those tags, I know the stuff is new and it's mine. More warm fuzzies!

I guess it makes sense, considering for how long our lives were filled with other people's things. I wanted to have a corner of the world to call my own. Still do.

A feeling of abandonment also persisted, at a subconscious level, during my foster years. And because of that, I developed a high approval need. I wanted to be liked by everyone. I think this stems from a belief that I wasn't really wanted by anyone. In my mind, my godmother gave me away, then my biological mother gave me away, and then foster mothers gave me away, willingly. I saw myself as a "drag and drop kid," and because of that, I was always fighting a fear of rejection.

Some of this has carried into adulthood. Later in the Air Force, when I was stationed in England, I wouldn't even ask USO ladies (women who worked for the United Service Organizations, specifically there to help boost the morale of the US military) to dance because if they said no, even for perfectly valid reasons, I knew I would feel rejected. So, I insulated myself by avoiding situations where I didn't believe I could control the outcome. You could say I protected myself from living. Unless I was drinking, then I didn't have enough sense to care.

But let's get back to our foster home saga. After running away from enough of them, we were returned to the care and custody of our mother for a short time. Her situation had improved by then.

While Gilbert and I (and, I suppose, Eileen) were bouncing around the foster care system, my mom had a few more children.

I remember a sister named Penny, another sister whose name I don't recall, a brother whom I called Tommy and a brother named Carlos. But then the state removed us from my mother's care again and put us back into the foster care system, so I never saw these new siblings again. All my life I've wondered about them.

That is until recently, when I decided to do an ancestry test. According to my DNA results, a couple of women and some guy, whose names didn't mean anything to me, turned out to be my sister Penny, my brother Carlos, and my sister Gloria. I also found out that my brother Tommy died in Vietnam. As it turns out, in our family, the name Tommy is unlucky. One died in an automobile accident and another in war.

My mom had a lot of kids. And then, there was my dad's side of the family. If I were to count all my siblings from both sides, I would need to use the fingers of both my hands more than once. I have twenty-one siblings in total. With some of them I am close, others I've never met, and still others I have started getting to know recently because of that DNA ancestry test. It seems my family tree is turning into a forest!

Back then, however, it was basically me and my brother for many years.

Then, Along Came Mrs. Leone

When Gilbert and I were put back into the foster care system, we eventually ended up in San Ysidro, California.

San Ysidro is a true border town. It's a gateway city to Mexico and home of the busiest port of entry in the World. When you enter Mexico from San Ysidro you are in Tijuana, Baja California, Mexico. Tijuana is more or less a resort city that's known for bullfighting, crime and racetracks. During Prohibition and after

WWII it was a popular destination for American Servicemen seeking tequila and other things that were on the prohibited list north of the border.

We were placed in a foster home on Averil Road, within sight of the Mexican border (it was probably three or four blocks), not from the Port of Entry, but from the border itself, the place where you're not supposed to cross. Being able to see Mexico from that house also meant I could see the border patrol policing the area. San Ysidro was a special place I have to say. It was populated by a rich mix of Mexicans, some born in the United States and some born in Mexico. Unlike in Barrio Logan, these folks were a few rungs higher on the poverty ladder, still poor, but not as poor as folks from Logan Heights. In those days, the population of San Ysidro was less than eight thousand souls.

It was an improvement for Gilbert and me. An improvement in every sense.

Our new foster mother was an older, stern, Mexican American woman named Emilia Leone. Her husband, Frank Leone, was a junk collector. It didn't take long for Gilbert and me to realize that this foster home came with rules, boundaries, high expectations and the power of "do right" on Mrs. Leone's part. That was a game changer for us. But it was also difficult to accept boundaries, so we ran away the same day we arrived (probably a record time for the Fierro brothers). We were picked up by the police at the plaza in downtown San Diego and our probation officer took us back to Mrs. Leone's home the next day to retrieve our belongings. When we arrived, Mrs. Shelton, our probation officer, exchanged greetings with Mrs. Leone and explained why we were there. To say we were surprised hearing Mrs. Leone object was an understatement. "Unless you are required to return them, I would like them to stay here," Mrs. Leone said, quite unperturbed. The tone of her voice said it all. Mrs. Leone was not a quitter. The power of "do right" was about to descend on us. Finally, someone cared enough not to give us away willingly, or at all. It was simultaneously touching and terrifying: we knew our goose was cooked. This woman would make us do right.

From right: Mrs. Leone and her two daughters, Blanca and Julietta Figueroa, and two grandchildren, circa 1946.

And so, Gilbert and I remained in Mrs. Leone's foster care until we were in our teens. My brother had trouble adjusting to her rules and boundaries, but I, with my high-approval need, was willing to accept everything. And throughout our years with her, although we had both good and bad days, Mrs. Leone never gave up on us. My third mother dedicated her life to our well-being, and I will be eternally grateful to her.

It turned out to be the first phase of my salvation.

Mrs. Leone was a proud woman. She spoke English at a simple, third or fourth grade level, but intellectually she was incredibly astute. As a Spanish dominant speaker, she had a great command of the Spanish language, something that was both helpful and inconvenient for me. As I pointed out earlier, I was raised by my godmother who didn't speak English, so Spanish was the first language I learned. But Gilbert grew up with my mom, who was English dominant, so Gilbert spoke English. I was able to understand Mrs. Leone while Gilbert couldn't and suddenly, my "no entiendo" response when I didn't feel like doing something fell woefully short.

This was the first foster home where I recall being clearly understood when I spoke. It was a blessing and a curse.

Mrs. Leone wanted us to be independent, to be self-sufficient. She taught us (and expected us) to do household chores and clean up after ourselves. She would say, "Look, there won't always be a woman around to clean up after you. You have to learn to do it yourselves." At first, we would jokingly say she was abusing us by making us wash our own clothes and do the dishes. But we had to accept that's how it was going to be living with her. Every night, one of us had to help her cook dinner and the other had to set the table or do the dishes; we took turns between those two tasks on a daily basis. Before we went to bed, each night, we had to kneel beside the bed and pray out loud so Mrs. Leone could be certain we were actually praying. We had to learn how to wash, sew and iron our own clothes, all important life skills that would turn out to be more useful to my future self than I could have ever predicted back then.

But sewing was not the only thing Mrs. Leone taught me. Her most important lesson was instilling me with a sense of national pride.

Mrs. Leone immigrated to the United States from Mexico, although I don't know the exact circumstances behind her move. Ah, but that woman was so proud to be an American! As she was very fond of saying, she was born on June the 14th, Flag Day. She believed that everything she wanted to realize in her life was going to be available to her in America. Mrs. Leone tried to instill that feeling, that love for America, in us by frequently reminding us that our own biological family hadn't taken such good care of us, as America had. "America has clothed you, fed you and is trying to educate you," she would say. "You owe America a great debt of gratitude and you always have to be mindful of that fact. You need to remember where you came from and how you got there, and that it was this country that gave you the opportunity." That was not a notion that was wasted on me. It made good sense that the fact that I had any opportunities in life at all, was made possible because the state of California took care of me.

Me, 3rd grade, San Ysidro, 1946.

But despite all of Mrs. Leone's teachings and her attempts to make me a better person, I still got into trouble a lot. Trouble seemed to follow me around back then.

My penchant for petty theft and food hoarding hadn't subsided. When I was fourteen or fifteen years old, Gilbert and I were caught stealing watermelons from the freight yards in San Diego, where trains loaded and unloaded their cargo. When the boxcars from the Imperial Valley were unloaded, whole or parts of watermelons were very often discarded and left behind. We used to help ourselves to the remains. Of course, we were on railroad property, and in those days railroads were still having problems with homeless vagrants riding the rails. So, Gilbert and I were caught plundering discarded watermelons, which the security guards did not view as childhood pranks and they turned us over to the juvenile authorities, who also took a dim view of our behavior.

We were placed in the Anthony Home until Mrs. Leone could send someone to collect us. I didn't relish the thought of facing her, but what happened next was even worse.

The part of the Anthony Home I was in was called "The Max" (short for "maximum security"). Gilbert and I were put there not because we represented flight risks, but because of the simple fact that the place was overcrowded. Still, it was a violation of the rules: delinquents and non-delinquents cannot be housed together. During daylight hours, kids in "The Max" were permitted to be in a well-secured, exercise area outside of the main structure. The exercise yard was divided by a chain link fence: one side for the boys and the other side for the girls.

Because I was the new guy, I was standing alone by the dividing fence when a girl started a conversation with me. Gilbert didn't come out to the yard, so I welcomed the chit-chat but, as we talked, a guy came up to me and told me to leave his girl alone or he would "cut my dick off!" When the guy turned and walked away, the girl said she didn't know him; she wasn't "his girl." So, we continued chatting through the fence. Suddenly, out of the corner of my eye, I caught a glimpse of someone charging at me. It was the same guy, shouting, "Now, I am going to cut your dick off!"

He didn't though, but he stabbed me three times.

Fortunately, the County hospital was nearby. I was rushed there, operated on and placed in intensive care for a week and then I spent another fifteen weeks in the hospital recuperating. I was terrified during that time, because I knew that before I could be released to Mrs. Leone, I had to be returned to the Anthony Home as a formality. The fear of me running into the guy who stabbed me was overwhelming; it consumed me completely. I tried desperately to find a way to not have to go back to the Anthony Home, but to no avail. Thankfully, by the time I was returned, the guy was no longer there; he had been moved to a more secure facility. The relief that swept over me was astonishing!

That guy managed to put fear in my heart. Prior to that day, I knew about fear, I talked about fear but I had never experienced true fear up close and personal. Anyone who has been truly terrified will know exactly what I am talking about. Even today, I still have a great deal of respect for knives, and I use them only when I must. I also turn away from any stabbing or knife scenes depicted in movies . . . I can't look. It arouses bad feelings.

"Serve Your Country . . . or Serve Time"

Eventually, I was returned to Mrs. Leone where Gilbert and I stayed until our late teens.

When Gilbert was around seventeen, he had an opportunity to go live with our mother once again. He took it. I never knew why he left. Gilbert never shared much with me. He didn't have to; he was my older brother, so he had an exalted position in my life.

Me in 10th grade, 1954.

By that time, my mother had married a gentleman named Paul Mundell, a Navy Chief, and had three more children with him. While living with them, Gilbert became a member of a trio that played local gigs around La Jolla California and, after a while, he volunteered for the Air Force. Gilbert served four years in the Air Force, three of which he spent in Japan. Once he completed his enlistment, he moved to Waukegan, Illinois, to live with our Mother again.

My brother worked at Johns Manville for many years. He married and had three daughters before his marriage ended in a divorce. After a few years, he remarried and became a truck driver and lived in Russellville, Alabama. I think Gilbert found happiness there. He became a "Mexican Redneck" and had a surprisingly good network of friends. (His friendships have always struck me as a bit unusual, since he was so dark skinned and because Alabama has such a sordid racial history.)

Gilbert died several years ago. But in some ways, he's still with me.

Thanks to that DNA test I took a few months ago, I discovered two more sisters I didn't know about and one brother. That brother is Gilbert's full brother, Chuck, who'd gone through his whole life believing he was an only child. We are slowly introducing Chuck and his family to the rest of the clan; he's already met Gilbert's daughters.

Back then though, Gilbert leaving broke Mrs. Leone's heart. She never had children of her own, so she saw us as her children. She gave us unconditional love peppered with rules and boundaries, which was exactly what we needed. Still, it wasn't enough to keep me content at the time. And with my big brother gone, I managed to get into even more trouble.

When you live in an economically depressed area like the one we lived in, you tend to identify with the other people who live there. And if those people are angry or rebellious, you have to adapt until you become more like them than you'd think possible. It was easy for me to get into trouble because I was trying to identify with the local group of youngsters. We did all sorts of idiotic stuff. Once, we even tried to rob a service station.

It did not take long for me to show up in a court of law.

It wasn't much of a crime, really. A one-pump gas station, closed, with nobody there. They didn't even sell gas anymore, but there was a cash register in the office, so our criminal masterminds thought that we'd go in and take some money. As I recall, we knocked out a windowpane to get in. Not the whole window mind you, which had about nine little panes. Just one of them in order to be able to put our hands through, unlock the window from the inside and push it up. Once inside, we realized the cash register was empty but for about 25 to 30 pennies; so, we took them. I know it doesn't sound like a lot of money now, but in those days a gallon of gas cost about 12 to 13 cents. You could get two gallons of gas with that money and still have a nickel to spare for a coke.

Anyway, we took the pennies. As we were making our get-away somebody saw us and reported the crime to the police.

I was arrested and had to appear in Juvenile Court, before a man called Judge Shoemaker. I think he'd been on the bench for a while, perhaps seen his share of stuff. He didn't have a lot of sympathy for teenage delinquents, but Mrs. Shelton who was still my probation officer (apparently these people multitasked a lot) thought she saw something in me, some redeeming quality.

She went to talk to Judge Shoemaker on my behalf and convinced him to allow me to test for the military. Apparently, his response was something along the lines of "If his feet don't touch the ground between here and the induction center, yes that will be fine." So the deal was, if I passed the Armed Services Vocational Aptitude Battery (ASVAB) test, I would be permitted to join the military in lieu of reform school. The ASVAB examination is used to determine a potential recruit's enlistment eligibility and to assign recruits to military jobs. If I didn't pass the ASVAB, I would be sent to a juvenile detention reform facility near Fresno, California. Today it's called the Juvenile Detention Center in Tulare County, California.

In those days, you could get into the Army with no high school diploma and with a low ASVAB score. The Army drafted recruits. The Navy and Marines required high school diplomas and a lower passing ASVAB score than the Air Force. If you didn't have a high school diploma but you had a high enough ASVAB score, you could get into the Air Force in rare instances. The Air Force was an All-Volunteer Force. They didn't participate in the draft.

Still, Mrs. Shelton arranged for me to test for the Air Force. So I took it.

I'm not sure what my test score was exactly, but apparently I did quite well because the Air Force agreed to take me. I don't know if it was because they had trouble recruiting or because my test score was that high, although I do recall one of my teachers one time asking me if I knew how high my IQ was. (She'd said something to indicate that it was either the highest in the school or one of the highest.) All that matters is that I was accepted in the Air Force. When Judge Shoemaker told me I would be allowed to join the Air Force, he added, "I'm giving you a choice son, serve your country or serve time."

I chose to serve my country. I like to think that's what Mrs. Leone would have wanted me to do.

Me at Parks Air Force Base, 1956.

Chapter 3

A "LITTLE MAN" BECOMES AN AIRMAN

The year was 1956. Dwight D. ("Ike") Eisenhower was President, and everyone was still in a post-war haze. I was in a haze myself: nobody had prepared me for my upcoming transition to military life.

Later on, I would learn that my brother Gilbert had also joined the Air Force at some point. But back then, since he'd left Mrs. Leone to go back to living with our mother, I didn't have anybody at the time to tell me, "This is what happens when you get in." Then again, no one knows exactly what they're getting into when first joining the military, even if they've chosen it themselves and no judge ever told them, "Serve your country or serve time!"

So I went in blind. And the first thing I stumbled upon, as I was making my way into this new chapter of my life, was a surreal realization: apparently, I was not who I thought I was.

The name I carried for the first seventeen years of my life wasn't my name at all.

I Had Been Calling Myself Richard Fierro

"Fierro" because it was my big brother Gilbert's last name; "Richard" because we spoke English at home with my mother and we believed the translation of "Richey" from Spanish to English was "Richard." But in all honesty, for me the name "Richard" was more American, thus more attractive to me. No one ever corrected us, so quite naturally, we never figured my assumed name was really assumed. So, my identity was never questioned until I had to produce a birth certificate to join the military.

Prior to my birth and prior to WWII, capturing delayed vital statistics was not important. But as the nation shifted into a wartime industrial economy, America suddenly became aware of birth certificates. And back then, U.S. law specified that aircraft companies must only hire U.S. citizens. Despite the importance of being able to prove one's citizenship, about forty-three million Americans (that's nearly one-third of the working-age population) didn't have birth certificates. Many native-born Americans faced difficulty proving that they were, in fact, citizens by birth.

The possibility that any particular person might be issued a state birth certificate depended heavily upon the person's age, whether they were born in a rural area or a city and whether they had white, English-speaking parents. This was particularly true for those who sought work in the aircraft industry in San Diego. California allowed delayed birth registration through a convoluted process which tried to make fraud more difficult for Chinese, Japanese and Hispanic immigrants. Applying for a delayed birth certificate in California could rack up to $100 in court costs and legal fees. This was a sizable percentage of any worker's monthly wages, making a birth certificate inaccessible for most Californians whose birth was not registered. Unfortunately, the cost of registering my birth was beyond our means.

That birth certificate opened a whole can of worms. As it turned out, my birth was not recorded in California, but it was recorded in the Catholic Church. The woman I like to call "my first mother," Anita Sanchez, had me baptized, like the devout Catholic she was. I don't know if that saved my soul as she intended, but it certainly saved the day. I was able to use the baptismal certificate for my induction to the Air Force.

This series of events also made me realize that I knew little about who I actually was.

Up to that point, I had never dwelt on all the things I didn't know regarding the circumstances of my birth. Even the knowledge I had about the place of my birth was quite hazy. I knew I was born in the Imperial Valley of California, for instance, but I didn't know if it was in the city of Holtville, or on the Timken Ranch where my mother was born and lived before moving to San Diego.

But the biggest shock was my name. The name on the baptismal certificate was not Richard Fierro. It was Ricardo Rogelio Inzunza Jr., and his birthday was April 16th, 1938. The birthday I had been celebrating all my life was different. Richard Fierro never really existed! Nothing I had was really mine. That hurt.

I was in a state of disbelief and denial. Intellectually, I always knew my cultural legacy came from Mexico, but I didn't want to be defined as Mexican. Nonetheless, for the longest part of my youth, when people referred to me as Mexican, I passionately denied it. I was with people when they talked about folks entering the country without permission and I knew they saw them as inferior. I simply wanted to be accepted as American. That wasn't in the cards though. Consequently, I've spent a good part of my life trying to convince folks that my ethnic affiliation was Irish, Italian and even American Indian; anything but Mexican. "Richard Fierro" at least offered that possibility, as the name sounded ethnically ambiguous enough. But there was nothing ambiguous about the ethnicity of "Ricardo

Rogelio Inzunza Jr." Just like that, a good chunk of my hope of ever becoming American (at least in my mind) was dashed. I was dumbfounded.

So much so, that after my enlistment I was too embarrassed to allow my school mates to know about my confirmed Mexican status. Before I enlisted I gave them my new mailing address. They would write to me, and during mail call, letters would be pulled from the mail sacks addressed to Airman Basic Richard Fierro. I would grit my teeth as they were placed in the return to sender pouch. I believed I couldn't ever look back again. That was hard to take.

I recognize now that I had been running from myself ever since I was a kid.

I remember Gilbert and I being referred to as "the Mexican brothers." The brother's part was okay, but I resented the Mexican moniker. As I look back now though, I can't help but think that the "brothers" part was actually more fascinating. It must have been difficult for people to see Gilbert and me as brothers. We were as different as day and night! Gilbert was considerably taller than me, very dark skinned (hence his nickname, "blackbird") and could easily be identified as Mexican, but he spoke no Spanish. I, on the other hand, with my light skin and freckles (and quite small for my age), could pass for American, but I spoke little English; and I stuttered. We must have looked like the products of a genetic experiment gone horribly wrong.

Growing up on the Mexican border, for me, was a double-edged sword. It permitted me to become intimate with border life, border issues and immigration problems which I would have the honor and privilege to tackle head-on in a variety of my subsequent job postings. But as a kid, it was a hassle. Gilbert and I were hauled off to the border patrol station at the port of entry more than once. Initially, it was because of how Gilbert looked, coupled with my lack of fluency in English and my stutter. They thought we were Mexican nationals. As we grew older and I became English dominant, we were stopped strictly as a matter of profiling Gilbert's looks. I was never stopped when Gilbert was not around. To be released, Mrs. Leone had to come to the port of entry to vouch for us. I was never able to get comfortable with being identified as a Mexican. Who knew one day I would have an opportunity to improve that system.

Mrs. Leone had family on both sides of the border, so I visited Tijuana frequently. Several of her relatives were in the midst of immigrating to the United States and they would ask me to translate documents they received from immigration into Spanish. Sometimes the documents contained good news and at other times bad news. Even then, I was struck by how deeply people were affected by immigration. Mrs. Leone's family told their friends who were immigrating that I could translate documents into Spanish. Soon I was the "go to guy" to translate immigration stuff. I must admit I enjoyed being seen as more American than Mexican.

During the summer months I had a part time job just across the border at the Agua Caliente Racetrack in Tijuana, Mexico. They raced horses on Saturday and Sunday during the day and Greyhound dogs at night. I was a stable boy with the foolish notion that I wanted to be a jockey. After I was thrown off the horse a couple of times the idea lost its luster. While working at the track I met young men who were from the interior of Mexico on their way north. They took part-time work at the track in order to save enough money to get them to Los Angeles or to pay the "Coyotes" to guide them safely across the border. They would ask me a million questions about life in America. Not only did the fact that they saw me as American make me feel good about myself but it helped me develop a deep sense of empathy for people entangled in the migration process.

Because we were on the border, every day I would see Mexican nationals transiting San Ysidro heading north looking for work. They were referred to as "wetbacks," "border jumpers" and "illegal aliens" among other pejorative terms. Everyday Americans on this side of the border reminded me that I was Mexican and by association the same as the north-bound Mexicans. On the Mexican side of the border I was told I was not really Mexican. In their eyes, I was American. I was stuck between two cultures. I wasn't white enough to be American or brown enough to be Mexican and neither one of them claimed me.

My desire to shed my Mexican identity was amplified daily and the lion's share of my frustration derived from the fact that people around me (who were ethnic German, Polish, Irish and Italian) managed to shed their ethnic affiliation. They were referred to as Americans. Why couldn't I? It was maddening. Sadly, in my heart I knew that's the way it was and that was the way it would stay. I didn't measure up in either culture. Nothing could change that. But with the name Richard Fierro, I could at least try to bury my shame. For Ricardo Inzunza, there was no way out of the trap.

I hadn't learned yet that being ethnic Mexican and American could be a winning amalgamation. That would come later with maturity, education and attitude change. The more I studied what Hispanics were and weren't, and what their contributions to America's defense were, the more I felt the opposite of shame in who I was and where I came from. I started to feel a sense of pride in being Hispanic. I enjoyed belonging to the same group as these great Americans, learning all the things they had sacrificed and done for our country. I think that was the beginning of the long process of accepting and eventually liking myself.

This brings me back to that name on my baptismal certificate: Ricardo Rogelio Inzunza Jr.

One of the many things that surprise me about my family is that three of my mother's sisters (Alicia, Erlinda and Margarita), as well as two of her brothers, were also living in San Diego and they knew about me and the circumstances of my birth. And yet nobody, not one of them, ever bothered to reach out to me and say, "Hey, you know, your name is not Richard Fierro. Your name is Ricardo Inzunza." I don't know how all of them could keep the secret so well. But as soon as they found out that I enlisted in the Air Force and the cover had been yanked off me, everyone was willing to share stories: how my dad was a hired hand on the Timken Ranch, how my mom was a typical farmer's daughter. Where had all these stories been before?

It's not hard to see that the feeling of displacement I had was not just ethnic; it also stemmed from my complicated relationship with my mother. It would take many years for this relationship to come to some sort of resolution but enlisting in the Air Force and leaving San Diego was actually the first step in my salvation. I was now free to change. This may not sound like much but for me it was huge. I was a Mexican, there was no getting around it, but I didn't have to be the cliché Mexican of the time, that underage delinquent who ran with the wrong sort of people and engaged in petty crime just to feel accepted by his peers. In the Air Force I was free, encouraged even, to reach for the highest level my ability would support.

So, after the shock of induction, Richard Fierro was forever gone. I was now Ricardo Inzunza with a brand-new birthday! I would be lying if I didn't admit that it was distressing.

Basic Training at Parks Air Force Base

My journey in the military didn't start as a breeze. Nobody's journey does. I had to learn to accept rules and boundaries, and we didn't have any of those while growing up with my mother. It was Mrs. Leone who taught us everything we knew about accepting and understanding limits, the things we could say and the things we could do.

And that paved the way for my life in the military.

In the military, the rules and limitations start the very moment you arrive, when you're still a wide-eyed civilian. They bring you to the base on a bus and you start to learn how to be a military person from the moment you exit the bus.

People are yelling at you to fall in, "Tallest up front, shortest to the rear! They want you to create a column of fours based on a descending order of height (which means, if you are taller than the man in front of you, move up. It was always me at the back, as I was always the shortest). Everyone in charge keeps giving you instructions and rushing you. "This is your barracks, you have five minutes to go in, drop your bags, shit, shave, shower, shampoo, shine your shoes and be back out here in formation! Is that clear gentlemen?"

Oh, it was clear. Clear that this wouldn't be a walk in the park.

I remember it was after midnight when we arrived at Parks Air Force Base. Our squadron was composed of guys, from all over the country who were quite tired. But late arrival for basic training is not by accident. It's by design.

They took us to eat at what the Air Force now calls a "dining facility," but was then called the "chow hall." (Food is "affectionately" referred to as "chow.") There, they served us from metal trays, most of them so warped that they would start rocking the moment you set them on the table. In basic training, you're not given a lot of time to eat; it's all part of your training. In our case, the tables were configured by groups of four. If you were the first to get to the table with your tray, you had to stand at attention until three more people arrived before you could sit down to start eating. If your table didn't receive four people, tough luck. You had to stand there with your tray until time was up, and then you had to put your tray into the clipper so it could be washed. Believe me we learned to fill the tables up quickly.

After chow, we were marched to our barracks, where they gave us instructions on where and how we were going to bunk. One of the Tactical Instructors (they were called TI's) asked anyone who brought pajamas to surrender them immediately. They were not permitted. He then warned that tomorrow would begin early; "so get plenty of sleep ladies." He also said, "Lights out in five minutes," and they were. Of course, they were back on at 4:00 AM when we were required to fall out in five minutes. "Five minutes" would become a recurring order.

In the Air Force, as I learned soon enough, your uniform has to be pressed every day. The guys who didn't know how to do that had to send their clothes to the laundry and have them pressed and starched. They had to pay for that service; whereas I could simply do it myself, thanks to Mrs. Leone and her insistence that my brother and I participate equally in the household chores. Sewing is a bit of a ritual in the Air Force. When you are promoted, for instance, you have to sew your new stripes onto your uniform yourself. Thanks to Mrs. Leone, I could also do that when I was finally promoted.

Tidiness and cleanliness, in general, are habits (if not values) you need to cultivate in the military. You must shine your shoes every day, a task I excelled at. Our TI was fond of shouting, "A man that doesn't shine the back of his boots doesn't wipe his ass." I never really understood the significance of the saying but I heard it frequently. You have to know how to make your bed, how to clean your area, how to fold and hang your clothes, how to set up your footlocker, how to line up your shoes and boots up in the proper order.

We had a community bathroom that had to be in spick-and-span order for daily inspections. Mrs. Leone's voice echoed in my ears back then: "Don't make round corners!" That Spanish expression meant that when sweeping the floor, you can't just sweep around the corner of a room in a circular motion; you have to clean inside the corner properly, from every angle. "You've got to have sharp corners," she would say. Like Mrs. Leone, the military believed in sharp corners too.

On my second day at Parks Air Force Base, we were introduced to the barbers.

In Air Force Basic Training, "reveille" (from the French word for "wake up") sounds at 4:00 am. In our case, it was a bugle call used to wake military personnel before sunrise. Maybe five minutes after reveille sounds, the TI's come into the barracks making a tremendous racket. When they enter you must be out of your rack (military name for a bed). If you are still lounging trying to wake up you are immediately branded as a "goldbricker" and singled out for special attention. Believe me, in the Air force you don't want to be on the receiving end of special attention.

4:00 am in San Francisco is quite chilly, and all we had to wear was what the TI's called "field jackets," issued to each of us when we arrived. Everyone was required to wear one and every jacket button had to be buttoned up. They made sure we understood the word "uniform" was revered and received special attention in the Air Force.

We had to fall out of the barracks into the cold morning air and fall-in in front of the barracks. We were marched to the "chow hall" for breakfast and then marched again to the barber shop. There, just to mess with us, they'd ask, "Do you want to keep your hair son?" If you fell for it and said, "Yes," the response was always, "OK then, put your hands in front of you and your hair will fall into your hands in a minute." Of course, they cut everyone's hair just the same: high and tight.

I know it all sounds a bit inhuman, perhaps, to an outsider. But the purpose of all this wasn't to torture us. The military has to break you down from your civilian persona. They have to remove all vestiges of your civilian self before they can raise you up again as a military person. You need to develop a military bearing, self-respect, confidence and team spirit while military customs and courtesies are being ingrained in you. You need to learn how to march, how to be respectful of each other, and how to salute your superiors in the appropriate manner.

Basic training at Parks Air Force Base lasted eleven weeks, but basic training is such an intense time that you usually make some memories and have friends you're going to remember for the rest of your life. It also has to be said that the people who train you don't put up with a lot. They'll bounce you out of there in no time if you misbehave. But you really don't have a lot of time for that, as most of your time is already taken up by all the things you need to do or learn. Those who do misbehave were probably not adaptable to military service and they didn't make it through basic training. For those of us who did make it, it was on to the next phase of our evolution, technical school.

Last Basic Training Flight at Parks Air Force Base

It would be fun if I could claim it was because of me that training ended, but the truth is that these types of consolidation operations are programmed far in advance. Basic training was also ended at Sampson AFB in New York, so all Air Force Basic Training was consolidated at Lackland Air Force Base in San Antonio, Texas.

At Parks AFB, I volunteered for flight training but I was disqualified because of a stutter and assigned to technical school at Lowry AFB in Denver, Colorado, to undergo technical weapons training. There I received training for ten months as a weapons release technician, euphemistically called an "Armor." Our job was to prepare and mate all manner of tactical weapons to weapons release platforms (aircraft.) We were learning about weapons release systems and munitions of all types: iron bombs, guided bombs, nuclear weapons, heat-seeking and radar missiles, rockets, napalm, you name it. We were responsible for assembling these weapons, mating them to the aircraft, maintaining the weapons release systems, and arming the weapons just prior to aircraft lift-off on strike or training sorties. We had to de-arm aircraft when they recovered with unexpended or "hung" ordinance and we were required to "safe" all ejection and jettison safety systems prior to personnel performing any type of service on the aircraft.

As the duties became more technical and complex, the Air Force reorganized. Under the reorganization, weapons release technicians were only responsible for maintaining the aircraft weapons release systems and for mating ordinance of every type to Air Force weapons platforms. Responsibility for munitions maintenance and assembly was left to the weapons maintenance technicians.

If a weapons system failed to operate properly, we were required to troubleshoot the problem and make necessary repairs. In short, we had to make sure those weapons would do exactly what they were supposed to do, when they were supposed to do it. There was always a friendly tension between air and ground crews—both joked about whose job was most important. The truth was, "One fail, all fail!" Either the mission was 100 percent successful or it was a total failure.

Truth was, I didn't mind being part of the ground crew. I suffered from motion sickness ever since I was a kid. It didn't matter if I was on a bus, a train, a ship, a plane, or just spinning around while standing on the ground, I got sick. I was the worst!

I recall one of my later deployments, where we were scheduled to fly from Wethersfield, England, to Chaumont, France, refuel and then leap off to Casablanca, Morocco. After we loaded up in England and the first propeller of our C119 aircraft started to rotate, I felt the motion sickness coming on. I threw up practically all the way to France. When we landed at Chaumont, the guys set me on the tarmac next to the plane while they readied the plane for the next leg of our flight, and they loaded me back on when it was time to leap off. But as soon as the first propeller started rotating, I became ill again and barfed all the way to Casablanca. It was horrible and I didn't get much sympathy from the group. (They told me that if I needed "sympathy," I should look between "shit" and "sorry" in the dictionary. It turns out it's not there either.)

I wasn't the only Airman having problems with flying though.

I remember another time, when we were headed back to Portland, Oregon, from Travis AFB after competing in a "William Tell" missile-firing competition. There were about 25 of us loaded up in a Douglas C-47 Skytrain military transport. The C-47 or "Gooney Bird" as it was nicknamed during WWII was preparing to land at Klamath Falls Air Force Station to refuel. It was dark, and, just as we were about to touchdown, the pilot made a hard landing. We blew a main gear tire. As the pilot powered to 100 percent to get us airborne again, the plane shook and roared like it would fall apart. The plane was configured for paratroopers so we were sitting side by side in jump seats not making a sound. You would be surprised how quiet a plane becomes when you believe you're about to die. In his silent panic, the guy sitting next to me grabbed my thigh and held on to it for dear life. I didn't feel a thing, but the next day my thigh was black and blue. What matters is we managed to get airborne. We climbed to altitude to dump fuel to lose weight, while the runway was foamed for a wheel's-up landing.

The main gear on the "Gooney Bird" retracts but it has a fixed tailwheel. As it turned out the tailwheel was not a problem and we skidded to a smooth stop, but it was scary. As they say in the Air Force, "If you walk away from it, it was a good landing." Everything else is window dressing. According to the Air Force ours was a good landing.

Flying, like everything else in life, is a challenge. Challenges carry risk. You must make up your mind, when you take these risks, that you will be okay.

You must be a special kind of crazy to get on a plane if you believe it will crash. The people who buy life insurance just prior to boarding a flight amaze me. They are betting the insurance company the plane is going to crash and the insurance company is saying "Our actuarial tables are telling us you and the flight will be okay. Give us your money!" Insane . . . but I digress.

After graduating, I was ordered to Wethersfield RAF Station in the United Kingdom to begin my first Air Force assignment. I was assigned to the 3rd Air Force, 20th Fighter Bomber Wing, and 77th Fighter Bomber Squadron.

When I received orders advising me that I would be shipping overseas on a 3-year unaccompanied tour, I was authorized seven days travel time to get to McGuire Air Force Base in New Jersey. I was already in California so my intention was to return to San Diego to say goodbye to Mrs. Leone and friends and then go directly to my port of embarkation. I shared my plan with Mrs. Leone and she was excited and promised to cook some of my favorite Mexican dishes. I was excited too. But as the story goes, the road to hell is paved with good intentions and bad execution.

I know, all too well, in moments of selfishness it's easy to make decisions we come to regret. I live with that knowledge daily. It eats me up. On the day I was supposed to visit Mrs. Leone, I called her to confirm my arrival time. She told me she was busy cooking my favorite dishes and couldn't wait to see me. I said I was going to make a quick stop in Imperial Beach to tell some of my buddies I was shipping overseas. Then I would come straight to her home. Well, when it came time to leave my friends begged me to stay a little bit longer, which I did. I called Mrs. Leone and told her I would be a bit late. She said OK. Then other friends arrived and wanted to visit. The result was that I didn't visit Mrs. Leone. I didn't even have the decency to call to tell her I wouldn't be there.

I was booked on a Greyhound bus the following morning which was leaving San Diego at 5 AM. I was guilt ridden but I knew I had to call Mrs. Leone to apologize. She said it was OK, but I could feel the hurt in her voice. This made my guilt worse. I had a three-day bus ride ahead of me to stew in my own juice. To this day the memory of having hurt her, the remembrance of what I lost distracts and torments me. How could I have been so ignorant and thoughtless? For me, real regrets are not bad things that have happened to me but about things I have done. Real regret is a deep sorrow. It's an inward directed anger at my selfishness for having had enough information to have made the right decision, but then making the wrong call. With the exception of a few letters we exchanged, Mrs. Leone and I never communicated again. She passed before I rotated out of England. Now, I find myself permanently mired in the land of "if only."

A Change of Attitude

I had been in the Air Force longer than some people who outranked me, and that's simply because they behaved better than I did. Whenever I would misbehave, and I did so frequently, in lieu of a Court Martial I would elect punishment under Article 15 of the UCMJ, which usually resulted in a reduction in grade or a fine. I would then have to start from scratch, climbing the rank ladder again. I remember someone told me one time I should put my stripes on "with zippers" so I could zip them off and on instead of sewing them back on all the time. Hilarious. But I guess I deserved it.

Every day was a struggle for me when it came to certain chores that needed to be done routinely. Not because I didn't know how to do the chores, but because I didn't like to. I felt it was beneath me. In this instance, it was the repetitious housekeeping that pushed my buttons. There were three shifts daily. Normally, an hour before each shift ended, the shop had to be cleaned before it was accepted by the incoming shift supervisor; coffee cups washed, ash trays emptied, floors swept, mopped and buffed. Usually, hours before we were scheduled to start shift change, I would start working myself up in anticipation that I would have to clean up. Well, I was always the lowest-ranking guy, so I knew they would start with the "Little Man," as they called me. "Little Man, get started on those cups!" This made me bristle!

I would start getting angry around noon. By mid-afternoon I was like a bear with a sore ass. People didn't want to be around me. Then one day something happened. I just got fed up with being fed up as the saying goes. So, without prompting, scolding or being ordered, I started cleaning the shop around 3 pm. I emptied ashtrays, washed coffee cups, swept and mopped the floor. It was like lightning flashed! As soon as my attitude changed, my whole life changed; everything started falling into place. I started getting and holding promotions and I was asked to join some of the best temporary duty assignments. Most importantly, I felt respected. From being stationed in locations such as Casablanca in Morocco and Tripoli in Libya, I was suddenly sent to countries such as Norway, Finland and Sweden. Climbing the ladder of success, as it turns out, was all about that mental switch.

I guess the reason they didn't throw me out of the military, despite my constant mishaps and grade reductions, was that I was always a good worker. And this was thanks to Mrs. Leone.

When I lived with her, we had to do farm work every day. We had chickens, cows, goats, and a mule that needed to be fed, we had two acres of land with corn, beans, potatoes, radishes, and lettuce that we had to tend to on the weekends. So I'd learned not to be afraid of work, especially manual labor. And I was a quick learner;

I picked things up very quickly. I guess I was also a good team player. So although my supervisors could have moved against me and would have had little difficulty separating me from the service, they didn't. They always came to my defense, always gave me another chance, even when every few months, like clockwork, I would do something stupid. One supervisor who stuck with me when he didn't have to joked about my doing so much manual labor. He would say, "You must have joined the Air Force because you thought manual labor was a Mexican!"

Once my attitude changed; however, I was able to further my career in the military and have some fun while doing it.

Chapter 4

A "YANK" IN EUROPE

The first time I really allowed myself to have fun was in England.

I was 18 when I arrived at RAF Station Burtonwood. This was 1957 and Burtonwood, England, was the American Aerial Port of Debarkation (POD) for troops rotating into England by air. It was also the port of embarkation (POE) for troops rotating home. I say Aerial Port even though most of the troops assigned to the United Kingdom in those days arrived by ship. The primary seaport of debarkation for England was Liverpool. (Transatlantic air flights were new and I was one of the early passengers). Our flight plan took us to Thule AFB on the Northwest corner of Greenland where we refueled. Then we leaped off to Shannon, Ireland, where we landed to refuel again. Finally, we landed at Burtonwood in the United Kingdom.

This was my first Air Force permanent duty assignment after graduation from technical school in Colorado. Normally, between graduation and arrival at your first duty station, a 30-day leave was authorized. I didn't have any place to go, or anyway to finance it, so I volunteered to be assigned directly from tech school to the 20th Fighter Bomber Wing (FBW). I didn't know it then, but the 20th FBW was slated to become the world's first fighter outfit with a nuclear capability. We were the vanguard of combat units, scheduled to introduce nuclear weapons to the European theater under the auspices of NATO during the Cold War. RAF Station Wethersfield was the new headquarters for the 20th FBW and the first European base to receive nuclear weapons.

Me at Wethersfield Air Base, England, 1958.

Three Fighter Bomber Squadrons (55th, 77th and 79th) were assigned to the 20th FBW. I was assigned to the 77th FBS. Major Anthony Blanchard was our squadron commander. Some of you may know him better as Doc Blanchard, the West Point football player. He was the first ever junior to win the Heisman Trophy, Maxwell Award, and James E. Sullivan Award, all in 1945. Need I say more about the reputation of the 77th?

The Wing's mission was new. Most of the personnel were recent inductees to the military, and even though we were well-trained in the care, maintenance and deployment of nuclear weapons and their delivery platforms in technical school, we received zero hands-on experience with actual special munitions. Our first priority was to develop experience working with actual special weapons and to then develop training standards and certifications for the NATO forces we would be training in turn on handling, storage, transportation, delivery and safety of real nuclear weapons. During that initial period, the Wing flew training air operations in Morocco, Libya, Norway, Spain, Italy, and Sardinia.

Nouasseur Air Base, Morocco, Practice Bombing, 1960.

Leaving the States and being on a different continent for the first time was both liberating and challenging for me. I knew I was alone in the world, and that aroused quite a bit of trepidation, but I also felt a new-found sense of liberation. I always wanted to be considered American, not Mexican. Being with the armed forces in England, I finally achieved that distinction.

I First Felt Like a "Yank" at a Pub in Braintree, Essex

There was an incident involving a couple of beers (well maybe more than a couple) where, apparently, I offended a young lady. I remember she looked at me and said, "The problem with you Yanks is that you are oversexed, overpaid, and over here." I know she was trying to insult me, but I felt exalted. She'd called me a Yank! No one had ever done that before. Indirectly, this wonderful woman was calling me an American! Someone, without reservation, finally saw me as an American, even if she didn't think of my "Americanness" as such an appealing quality.

Me in London, England, 1959.

For a guy like me, who spent a good portion of his youth running from himself, this was golden. I could have hugged and kissed her (although as I recall, my earlier attempts to do so may have been what got me in trouble with her in the first place). Of course, then she went on to say, "Why don't you go home and grow up a little bit and then come back and join the Air Force," which stung a little bit but didn't diminish the warm glow of being called a Yank. Finally someone saw me as an American.

But it wasn't all sunshine and roses.

There was another occasion where I was talking to a young man in Piccadilly Circus on the West End of London, and he asked "what" I was. Without thinking, I said, "I am Irish." Old habits die hard. (I may even have said my name was Richard Shannon or something like that, to make it more plausible.) Then he rained on my parade. "Oh, Irish huh?" he responded, not entirely convinced. "By looking at you, I could have sworn you're some sort of Latin." Now that knocked me back.

As dumb as it sounds, it was the first time in my life I realized that people could just look at me and decide who I was (or who they thought I was), based on how I looked without ever talking to me. People could be staring at me and thinking to themselves, "Ah, a Mexican," and I would never know. I didn't want that, but there was nothing I could do about it. I was defenseless. Unknowingly, that guy wire brushed me.

But that's just how it was in Europe or in the UK at least. I was an American to most, even if not to everyone. That made it possible for me to hide, more easily than before, the part of myself I wasn't yet ready to face. Until I was ready to come to grips with my true identity, I was determined to be the best American these folks would ever meet.

I remember that Piccadilly Circus incident as one of the turning points in my life, when I knew I couldn't stay in that headspace. I had to move off dead center, get over it, and be who I was. Part of the difficulty was that I was a stranger to most of me, so part of the

fix called for a great deal of reflection, introspection and acceptance. As social and civil unrest was starting to boil over in America, I was becoming aware of the realities and plights of certain
people. That propelled me in the direction of social actions later.

However, at that point in England, I may have been 19 and
I didn't know anything about anything. A friend used to say to
me, "Americans have a right to be stupid, Little Man, but you're
abusing that right!" I was selfish, self-serving, egotistical and they
were the Brits, with hundreds of years of history. I enjoyed their
culture. (Although, predictably, I did not enjoy their food. I don't
think it's a coincidence that in America, where we have eateries
serving ethnic food from every corner of the world, we have so
few British restaurants.) The accent thing was also funny: they
thought I had an American accent, which pleased me. I thought
they had beautiful British accents, which led us to a place of mutual admiration.

I guess I was all about mutual acceptance back then.

The Second World War had recently ended, England was getting back on its feet, and we were there to stand up for the nuclear
option for NATO. It was an important mission that the Dutch
also picked up, then the Swedes. Soon, all the forces in NATO
became nuclear equipped. Of course, if any of them had dropped
just one bomb, it would have ushered in destruction of the world
as we knew it then. But thankfully, the world didn't end then.
And, after my three years in England were up, I moved on to my
next assignment.

The German Air Force In NATO

By this time, the Germans had a nuclear mission as did all other NATO participants. At that point, the Luftwaffe (German Air

Force) and Marineflieger (German Airborne Navy) were all flying the 104G (G for German) Starfighter. The Lockheed F-104G was dubbed by the company as the "missile with a man in it," but it was known in the Luftwaffe as the "widow maker."

At their peak, more than 900 Starfighters were in the Luftwaffe and Marineflieger inventory. The first futuristic-looking F-104G Starfighter flew in early 1956. With its long, circular fuselage, sharply pointed nose, and tiny, thin wings, it looked every inch the best fighter in the world. But it was a terrible plane. It kept crashing. The result was a horrific number of accidents. By mid-1966, a total of 61 German F-104's had crashed, with a loss of 35 pilots. The crashes continued despite a variety of fixes. Between 15 and 20 German 104G's crashed every year between 1968 and 1972 and continued at a rate of about 10 F-104G's per year until the aircraft were finally replaced.

Like all NATO participants, the Luftwaffe had a nuclear alert commitment. This meant that they were responsible for maintaining two 104G Starfighters, configured for nuclear strike missions, on constant "Victor Alert," and five properly configured backup birds on secondary alert. This responsibility required the "Victor Alert" birds to be airborne on strike missions within five minutes of notification of release by proper authority. Secondary alert birds had to be ready to launch within thirty minutes of proper notification. Our job, as Weapons Control Officers, was to maintain custody and control of the weapons until we received a properly authenticated release code from an authorized authority.

Because of inspection and safety requirements, weapons could only be mated to the aircraft for seven consecutive days. Then they had to be returned to the weapons maintenance facility for inspection and dry out. There was a delicate balance between the availability of aircraft that could stand alert and good flying weather necessary to keep flight crews certified. Because of the frequent inclement weather in Germany, most training of flight crews was conducted in Africa and Sardinia, where we could have more than 300 days of good flying weather a year. In the Eifel Mountains where we were based, there was snow on the ground from October through April. In essence, we had all-weather fighter planes with fair weather pilots. Aircraft crashes and weather played havoc with our work schedules. If, for any reason, we failed to maintain two birds standing "Victor Alert," NATO's battle targets and objectives were degraded and the Pentagon had to be notified immediately. It dawned on me quickly that this was serious business.

American nuclear weapons were being married to German aircraft. We were charged with the responsibility of supervising the up- and downloading of our weapons by the German military weapons technicians, to make sure there were no deviations from established nuclear safety protocols. Adhering to safety standards was deadly serious business. There are no "do overs" in nuclear accidents. Once the weapon was mated and the aircraft accepted for "Victor Alert," we had to provide security to preclude any unauthorized launch. We did this by placing a physical barrier in front of that aircraft with two American security guards. The barrier was constantly staffed. When the launch sequence began, the German pilot would sit in the cockpit waiting for the release command from the German Government, while our security guards along with a Weapons Control Officer waited for a release command from the Pentagon.

The launch sequence was called "R hour" (the "R" stood for Release). When the pilot and the government verified each other's security codes and were satisfied that we were not acting under duress, the bird was ready to launch. Security guards would then remove the barrier from in front of the aircraft while we were dialing part of the weapon arming code into the positive action link system. I must say, "It was an intricate dance." While en route to the target, the pilot would receive a notice from Washington to engage the weapon arming mechanism, so that Washington could enter the remainder of the arming code. Once armed, the weapon was ready for a nuclear detonation, and there was no turning back. In the event the mission was going to abort prior to arming, there was no threat of a nuclear detonation. At least, that is what we were told. I am glad we never tested that notion.

A bit of an interesting story here: You know how people will often ask, "Where were you when Kennedy was shot?" Well, I know exactly where I was and for how long. I was embedded with the German Luftwaffe. We were stationed with the JABO 33 squadron on a German Air Force Base in Buechel, a village in the Eifel Mountains, 18 km outside of Cochem. When the news of President Kennedy's assassination reached us, we immediately went to DEFCON 5 (Cocked Pistol), meaning nuclear war was imminent. We had to be in a maximum state of readiness. In this instance, we had to physically stand by the aircraft waiting for an immediate launch command. We were on the alert pad for almost 21 days before we downgraded to DEFCON 1 (Fade Out). At that point, we returned to normal and were allowed to depart the alert pad for much needed hygiene! Those are 504 hours I will never forget.

Looking back now, I think this was one of those cases where "an ounce of prevention is worth a pound of cure." The military and specialized units like ours with access to nuclear weapons, had to be fully prepared in case anybody thought that the assassination of the U.S. President meant they could make a move against America or against NATO (or against Europe, even). Our base wasn't the only one at DEFCON 5. All NATO air bases were. Everyone went through a similar situation, waiting for the same release order, hoping it wouldn't come and glad when it didn't.

Of course, things didn't really "get back to normal" in the broader sense. President Kennedy's assassination ushered in a new era of military and social discord. Lyndon B. Johnson was sworn in as the President on November 22, 1963, and the Gulf of Tonkin incident happened on August 2, 1964. The Tonkin incident was the international confrontation that led to the United States engaging more directly in the Vietnam War.

The Vietnam conflict was a horribly divisive time for America. The war sowed seeds of discord that threatened to split the nation. It cost 58,220 American lives. Importantly, before these events transpired, Air Force Special Ops Teams were already engaged in Vietnam. On Oct. 11, 1961, President Kennedy in National Security Action Memo (NSAM) 104, directed that the Defense Secretary "introduce the Air Force 'Jungle Jim' Squadron into Vietnam for the initial purpose of training Vietnamese forces." I didn't know it then, but NSAM 104 was destined to impact me directly.

But that, as they say, is a story for another time. Or for another chapter, at least.

Setting the "Victor Alert" experience aside, I never felt unsafe during my twelve years in Germany. I liked the German people. And it's interesting because I grew up at a time when Germans were vilified and criminalized in America. They were portrayed as monsters and warmongers who wanted to take over the whole world, as the people who perpetrated the Holocaust. Actually, meeting German people was a revelation for me. All the images and beliefs I had about them were completely wrong; I had to rethink everything I thought I was taught to believe about Germans.

That was the first time that something like that happened to me, but it wouldn't be the last. I was to go through a similar experience in Vietnam.

I was never posted any place where I didn't meet people I liked. I'm not saying this to be nice or politically correct. I've always enjoyed meeting new people in different countries through my assignments. For instance, I liked the people in Norway a lot. We were at an air base called Sola Air Station, in Stavanger. I felt close to the people there. I also enjoyed the people in the Netherlands; they always came off as non-judgmental to me. I don't know exactly why I needed to like people so much. Maybe my upbringing played a part, my ingrained fear of abandonment coupled with a need for approval. Meeting and liking people might have been a way to avoid rejection. I certainly didn't need any more rejection. I'd felt enough during my childhood and early foster years to last me a lifetime.

Perhaps that's why I played a lot of baseball during my military years. It was a way to belong and make connections.

I played baseball for the Air Force in the Netherlands. There was a Dutch team in Utrecht that played American baseball and liked to play against Americans, so we scheduled games against them in several cities: Utrecht, Rotterdam, and Amsterdam. Most Air Force bases sponsored a base team that represented them in tournaments. The Air Force participated in an annual world-wide baseball tournament similar to the World Series. The winner had the distinction of being the best team in the Air Force and subsequently represented the Air Force in a world-wide inter-service competition to determine which branch of the military had the best team. For us, winning an inter-service tournament, which we did twice, provided the Air Force with tremendous bragging rights. But each year, when tryouts for the base team were underway, I noted that the guys competing were younger, stronger and better-rounded players. I knew my baseball days would soon be over.

A Conscious Decision
to Better Myself in Any Way I Could

While I was stationed in Germany, I earned an undergraduate degree in sociology from the University of Maryland on its Heidelberg campus. It only took me twelve years! And I didn't even get to do my graduation walk, as I was in Tripoli supporting air-to-air rotational gunnery missions. But hey, it was still worth it.

The undergraduate degree took me so long to complete because we were always stationed in some remote place or other. So, all my studying happened in night classes. I never spent one day on any college campus while there was still daylight (apart from when I had to buy books). And distance learning was new back then, barely in its infancy. In some cases, because we were working shifts with the German Air Force, I would have to drive from where we were stationed to the nearest American base to take a class, an 80-mile, one-way trip in a mountainous area, the Hunsrück mountains. So, if I was working a swing shift (that's the middle shift), I would have to trade shifts with somebody because classes were from 18:30 to 21:30 (military time). Or, if I worked in the morning, I would have to drive to class and then drive all the way back to work my shift. It was an effort. You had to want that degree pretty badly to stick with it. I had a supervisor who was fond of saying, "You must convince yourself that you need the degree like a dead man needs a coffin." I guess I did, because I eventually managed to get my undergraduate degree, and then started graduate school.

Initially, that took place at Maryland's Heidelberg campus, too, but then I was reassigned to the Pentagon. After I relocated to the United States, I completed my graduate degree, an MBS in "Pure Behavior," from the Catholic University of America. The decision had little to do with religion and very much to do with happenstance. Just like Georgetown happened to be a Jesuit institution, this one happened to be a Catholic university. The Shrine of the Immaculate Conception was on campus, but I never saw any overtly religious people around me. Then, I proceeded to earn my PhD in Behavioral Psychology from Portland State University. But it wasn't just the academia giving me an education. The world was changing, and we were all learning valuable lessons from it. Or we should have.

While I Was Serving Overseas, America Was Changing

President Lyndon B. Johnson's "War on Poverty" was making significant changes in America's psyche and society. Some of the change was positive and some wasn't. More importantly though, the civil rights movement was finally gaining momentum. To understand its importance and effect on me, I probably need to backfill the story.

In the late 1960s and early 1970s, the Air Force went through a very disturbing time in its social history. It was suffering the same growing pains as the rest of our country and had to adjust as well. Racial disturbances at Minot, Travis, and Laredo Air Force bases, which resulted in multiple injuries and mission degradation, made Air Force leaders realize that the problem was real and larger

79

than they thought. All of the military departments were affected. During and after the Vietnam War, drug and alcohol abuse grew to a service-wide problem. Supervisors failed to take corrective action or simply ignored these problems, and, as a result, they became a problem themselves.

Although the country survived those turbulent times, problems in society persisted. Drug and alcohol abuse continued to rise, both in and out of the Air Force (AF), as did racial unrest. Several things became abundantly clear. The AF understood that mission could only be as good as the people. Many of the recruits came from drug affected areas of society. But it was race riots among Air Force personnel, which resulted in multiple fatalities that proved to be the last straw. The Pentagon knew it was time for an immediate and massive intervention throughout all military branches. In the AF, the answer was the "Social Actions Program."

A new AF specialty code, or new career area, called "Social Actions" (SA) was created to support commanders. The SA program took the position that in the AF there was no room for discrimination for anything other than someone's performance. Regardless of race, gender, or religion, equal opportunity for all AF personnel and their families was the new program's goal. SA was charged to deal with matters of military equal opportunity seriously and to ensure that human relations between all AF personnel were free from any type of harassment. The SA program believed these were important qualities for a successful workforce. Moreover, AF believed success of the program was a mission imperative. All hands were expected to support this effort.

While the AF was integrating the SA program into its infrastructure I was cooped up in Europe, trying to find out who I was. When the call went out for volunteers for the new SA program, I stood forth. Even though this was a new job within the AF, it was not an entry level position and it had to be filled by more senior and experienced personnel. To qualify for entry, SA officers were required to demonstrate a thorough understanding of the complexities that could occur within the newly created military equal opportunity and human relations education programs (vital components of the SA program). I was selected to become a drug and alcohol abuse control officer, which was yet another component of the SA program.

It took a while, but the AF recognized that substance abuse (alcoholism and drug addiction) was a progressive and preventable disease that affected the entire family. The Air Force believed that substance abuse was degrading its mission so they developed a policy to prevent it among Air Force personnel and their family members. To do this, substance abuse control officers had to be recruited, trained and deployed Air Force-wide. I was one of those enlisted officers. I attended a special 30-week intensive training course in San Antonio, Texas, which met daily for more than seven months. We were trained in the use of psychodrama as a form of group therapy, in the use of Transactional Analysis for head-to-head counseling and in group dynamics for large and small group therapy. We also had to do a two-month internship in an Air Force regional "In Patient" rehabilitation facility. When I graduated, I returned to USAFE headquarters in Germany. The training, which enabled me to help others, was as helpful to me personally as well. I was finally gaining insights into who I was.

From the previous paragraphs, I hope you can see the Air Force was deadly serious about creating an environment that was free of discrimination and provided a place where each airman had an equal opportunity to rise to the highest level his/her ability could support.

To pull this off, in addition to trained and qualified personnel, the SA program required enlightened leadership.

That came in the form of General David C. Jones.

General David C. Jones

General Jones was the Commander and Chief of the United States Air Force in Europe (CINC-USAFE), whose headquarters was located at Ramstein Air Base. Ramstein is a United States Air Force base in Rhineland-Palatinate, a state in southwestern Germany. Today, the base serves as headquarters for the United States Air Forces in Europe, Air Forces Africa (USAFE-AFAFRICA) and also for NATO Allied Air Command (AIRCOM). When I was assigned to Ramstein it only supported USAFE. General Jones believed in the mission of the Social Actions program and he pushed hard to ensure that it was fully operational and successful throughout USAFE. He was the right guy, at the right time, in the right place.

The Social Actions program required every member of the AF, including generals, to receive forty hours of classroom race relations training. Because I was the only Hispanic on the headquarters SA staff, I was assigned the additional responsibility of teaching the race relations block for Hispanic history in America, in general, and the contributions of Hispanics to America's defense, specifically. That was one of the most enlightening experiences of my life. As I was doing research for the class, I was discovering so many wonderful facts about Hispanic history, culture, and contributions to American society. They filled me with pride, a sense of fulfillment, and a burning desire to tell our story. More importantly, the urge to tell others I was Mexican was starting to grow in me. I couldn't wait to teach my first class.

As the strongest proponent of the SA program, General Jones attended the first race relations seminar we taught in Europe. I was as nervous as a sinner in church because a 4-star general was in my class. Not just any general, but our commander in chief. When I completed my lecture and asked if there were any questions, General Jones raised his hand. Of course, I immediately recognized him. The General rose, turned to face the class and said, "I want to take this opportunity to personally thank the instructor. His presentation was clear, concise, colorful and a delight. Every Hispanic should be proud of their contributions to the development of and defense of our great nation. I salute you, sir." That said, he picked up his hat and walked out the door. There may have been a happier moment in my life up to then, but honestly I can't remember when.

CINC-USAFE was happy with the contributions of Hispanics to America, and for the first time ever I was proud to be a Mexican. My voyage to discover my true identity was complete, and a new voyage was about to begin.

In 1974, General Jones was nominated to be Air Force Chief of Staff. He came by my office to ask me if I wanted to join his team. He was planning to create a new enlisted position on the Air Staff called "Superintendent of Social Actions" and he wanted me to fill the billet. I didn't know if he was serious, at first. In the Air Force, you can't go any higher than the Air Staff. It has its home in the Pentagon and is considered the pinnacle of success for Air Force personnel. Of course, I accepted. I would have been crazy not to!

That concluded my twelve years in Germany. It was time to get back home. Now, I was ready.

Chapter 5

A TIME FOR MILITARY ACTIONS

Before I tell you what happened when I returned stateside for my final Air Force assignment as the Superintendent of Social Actions, I should probably talk about racial bias and prejudice and about how I experienced it.

Unconscious biases are social stereotypes about certain groups of people which individuals form outside their own conscious awareness. We all hold these unconscious beliefs about various social and identity groups and these biases stem from our tendency to organize social worlds by categorizing or grouping things. Make no mistake about it, these biases are important. They shape our worldview and our expectations of others. And as I mentioned we all carry them and we don't even know it. The disconcerting fact is that those unconscious biases can be contrary to our conscious beliefs, as they were in my case.

The Japanese sneak attack of December 7, 1941, on Pearl Harbor was almost more than America could stand. Japan "sucker punched" us and had to pay. Up to this point, America had tried to stay out of World War II, but we wanted retribution and we were galvanized as never before in our history. Every American believed the Japanese were the scourge of the earth. Even Hollywood joined the fray. Through the clamor of the build-up to a war footing, we'd constantly heard stories (propaganda, really) and saw movies about those inscrutable Orientals. Hollywood vilified them in movies like *Operation Pacific, They Were Expendable,* and *The Sands of Iwo Jima,* all starring my personal hero, John Wayne. The audiences would squeal with delight as our "Leathernecks" would crush Japanese soldiers. I was one of the squealers. I didn't realize it at the time, but a strong anti-Asian bias was being inculcated in me. Although I'd never met an Asian, I grew up disliking them.

World War II build-up was well underway as I was growing up. The war effort transformed San Diego into a mega-military city, the home port for the Pacific Fleet. The harbor filled with all types of Navy ships. Hundreds of raw recruits arrived in San Diego every day to enter a boot training regimen that would transform them into United States Navy and Marine recruits, ready to give their all for God and Country (and giving their all at the bars on Broadway, at night). The San Diego shipyards were humming around the clock building new Navy ships and refitting and upgrading older ones for combat duties in the Pacific theater. Once sea trials for the new and rehabilitated vessels were complete and the Navy accepted them, newly minted sailors and Marines were assigned to the new weapons of war. After a short training period, the ships would set sail for the Pacific to engage the Japanese "war mongers."

I knew, of course, that Vietnam was in Southeast Asia. And, like so many military people of my generation, I volunteered to go there. When I was notified that I had been selected, my knee-jerk reaction was, "Uh oh, I'm going to be among Asians for a year. I guess I'll just have to tolerate them." What a lousy way to view an entire group of human beings you have never met! Especially when they form the primary groups in over forty countries and make up sixty percent of the world's population. (Thinking back, the fact that the person who raped and tried to murder my godmother was a Filipino probably didn't help matters. Although, I don't think I knew enough about the issue to see Filipinos as Asians. I saw them as a distinctly separate group. (Of course, the fact that they were under Spanish rule for 333 years and most had Hispanic surnames may have played a significant role in how I viewed them.)

Being assigned to Asia taught me that our learned social behavior is not under our conscious control, at least not completely. Advances in neuroscience and other social sciences have helped me to understand that people can consciously believe in equality while simultaneously acting on subconscious prejudices they are not aware of. Isn't that bizarre? Bias even made me hate who I was, and I didn't even know it.

I now understand that the majority of our biases, both positive and negative, are based on vicarious experiences normally relayed to us through other people, stories, books, movies, media, culture, and even John Wayne. As human beings, I don't believe we will ever reach our full potential until we are able to muster the courage to own and correct our negative, unconscious biases.

It wasn't just a sign of the times I grew up in. People hold unconscious biases in this day and age; notably, in the vitriol that is being directed at immigrants. People who know better insist on referring to non-immigrated residents as "illegal aliens," "narco-terrorists," "rapists," "criminals," "murderers," and whatnot. In some convoluted way I suppose this vilification of immigrants might be acceptable if what is being said about them were true, but it's not. Most of it is made-up, bandwagon propaganda being used to further political ends.

It's not difficult to see how logical fallacies have caused some Americans to form negative biases against people they have never met. Not only are they negative, but they are incorrect. I can attest to how easy it is for persistent instruction to surreptitiously instill a bias in someone's mind. Thankfully, in my case, that feeling dissipated the moment I actually met Asians and realized that as human beings there was not a "nickel's worth of difference" between us.

But that's the power "bandwagon propaganda" has over people; it can make you despise things you don't even know you are loathing. Countless times, a faction of humanity has gone to war with another faction because of some bias based on a logical fallacy.

I should know. I went to war twice. Three times, if you count my war against who I was.

My First Time in Vietnam Was in 1964

In the long history of the Cold War, early 1961 stands out as particularly tense. The Soviet Union had shot down U-2 pilot Francis Gary Powers a few months earlier. In the divided city of Berlin, pressure was building. Then, on January 6, 1961, Nikita Khrushchev gave a speech that truly inflamed the East-West political conflict. In response to the threat, President Kennedy directed the Defense Secretary to develop an elite counterinsurgency force (which included the Air Force), capable of counteracting Russian aggression around the world. The call for qualified volunteers went out.

I volunteered to go to Vietnam because I thought that's what I'd been trained for. To spread American ideals across the world, to fight the good fight for the right reason. By then, I'd been in the service for eight years. I had experience with training, with working with weapons, and with other military services and psychological operations. but not so much with how world politics really worked. I was still a young guy, you see, just 23 years old. And I believed, back then, in the righteousness of our efforts "to help the Vietnamese help themselves."

The Air Force mission is to fly, fight, and win. However, the difficulty in that era was that the Air Force didn't have personnel who specialized in combat roles outside the specialty codes assigned to them, as the Navy Seals and Green Berets do. In the Air Force, special operations assignments were accepted and executed as mission requirements dictated. The experience gained from these specialized missions were documented in Air Force records as "special experience identifiers." After the missions concluded, volunteers returned to their normal responsibilities. When the need for another unique special experience arose, the first place the Air Force looked to for volunteers was in the special experience identifier codes. Mine was in weapons and weapons release systems. My special experience identifiers were nuclear weapons loading, storage and transportation, and intra-service training experience (domestic and foreign).

As military conditions in South Vietnam deteriorated, Secretary of Defense Robert S. McNamara began to consider dispatching military forces to test the utility of counterinsurgency techniques in Southeast Asia. It was against this backdrop in 1961 that President Kennedy directed the Defense Secretary to introduce the Air Force "Jungle Jim" mission into Vietnam for the initial purpose of training Vietnamese forces and resisting the inroads of Soviet-backed guerrillas. The unit was to proceed as a training mission and not for combat. It was during this time that I was summoned to Randolph AFB in San Antonio, Texas, for a "close hold" interview with Air Force personnel.

The Jungle Jim mission was to be covert and composed exclusively of volunteers. In anticipation that the training mission might deteriorate, each volunteer had to answer two questions in the affirmative before being considered for this mission. The first question was, "Would you be willing to fly and fight in support of a friendly foreign nation in situations where you could not wear the U.S. uniform?" And the second was, "Would you be willing to fly and fight on behalf of the U.S. Government and to agree to do so knowing that your government might choose to deny that you are a member of the U.S. military, or even associated with this nation, and thus might not be able to provide you with the protection normally afforded to American citizens?"

This subterfuge was necessary. Dispatching air advisors to South Vietnam came close to violating the Geneva Accords of 1954 that established the two Vietnams. American leadership wanted to be able to plausibly deny that it had military forces operating in the South. I answered in the affirmative; I was a volunteer and my Air Force experience credentials were in order. I was not selected for the advance party insertion but I was selected for replenishment or expansion stand by (as the mission dictated). I was slated to be in the second rotation with an EOD (enter on duty) date of April 1964. Travis AFB was our port of embarkation.

Before we were briefed as a team, we received individual instructions and were scrubbed down. Volunteers, who had significant and distinctive scars or tattoos of any type, size, or shape, were ineligible for the mission. The most important rule: "Do not, under any circumstances, use your real name even with other team members. Make up a single name, only one, starting now!" The mission was later briefed in total community there were about 50 of us and we launched from Travis on April 15th to what was then Hickam Air Force Base in Hawaii. (It has since been re-named Joint Base Pearl

Harbor.) We landed at Hickam around 9:00 p.m. After refueling we leaped off to Bangkok, Thailand.

Funny story: we lifted off from Hickam around 11:00 p.m. on April 15th. At midnight, the date changed to April 16th, my birthday. Thirty minutes or so later we crossed the International Date Line and it was April 17th. Just like that, poof, my birthday was gone! To this day, I don't believe I should have to count that year.

Don Mueang Air Force Base was then and is still owned by the Royal Thai Air Force. The facility had a dual mission in 1963. It served as Bangkok International Airport for all civilian commercial air service activities on one side of the runway, and, on the other, as the gateway airport for all American military ingress and egress to the Vietnam theatre of operations. After landing at Don Mueang, U.S. Air Force personnel cleared us for travel to Vietnam. Thai Air Force personnel then escorted us to the military side of the base where a C-130 aircraft, with no American markings, waited to transport us to Saigon. In Saigon we changed mode of transportation. We traveled by truck to Bien Hoa air base, about 20 miles North of Saigon. The 2.5 ton, six-by-six truck was a 6-wheel drive, standard class, medium-duty vehicle, designed at the beginning of World War II for the U.S. Armed Forces. I didn't know there were any left in the world. I hadn't seen one since the mid-1950s, when I was in North Africa.

My first interaction with Asians occurred at Don Mueang, as Thai Air Force personnel escorted us and cleared us at various checkpoints, going from one side of the airport to the other. This was the first time I saw Asians outside the United States. My initial reaction was that someone has been lying to me all my life. There was nothing wrong with Asians; they seemed perfectly nice. They had good military bearing and were very polite. In fact, they were not at all like the caricature depictions I had been exposed to. I realize that the deeply rooted effects of World War II propaganda had a lingering and profound effect on me. Truth was starting to seep into my conscious brain.

That was my first foray into Southeast Asia and my first time as a member of a covert operation.

Once in country, we were to maintain a low profile and avoid the press. Mission aircraft were configured with South Vietnamese Air Force insignia and all personnel were required to wear plain flight suits or BDUs (Battle Dress Utility) minus all insignia and name tags that could identify us as Americans. Jewelry that might help identify the individual as an American or loved family member had to be removed (I reluctantly took off my crucifix and left it behind). Refusal to do so canceled your volunteer status, thus rendering you ineligible to join the team. We were also required to sanitize our wallets. We were not permitted to carry personal mementos or Geneva Convention cards. We were not allowed to display weapons and could only use them in defensive actions. I should add that, when shots are fired, it isn't easy to distinguish between an offensive bullet and a defensive bullet. What you do know is that you don't have a lot of time to decide which is which. If you're wrong, you could be dead wrong.

Ostensibly we were Air Advisors to the Republic of Vietnam Air Force, helping them prepare aircraft for combat sorties, initially flown from Bien Hoa air base. In addition, the base also flew helicopter, transport, and patrol sorties. The patrol sorties were coastal watch for invasion by North Vietnam from the South China Sea.

In those days, the Vietnamese Air Force had two types of aircrafts, both of them Russian. We supplemented them with our aircraft. We taught them how to configure the aircraft to receive the munitions we provided. Those munitions included air-to-air missiles, air-to-ground rockets, general purpose iron bombs. Those were 500- and 750-pounders and a 15,000-pound fat boy affectionately called a "daisy cutter." Daisy cutters could be armed with proximity fuses which caused an aerial burst that could flatten a whole section of forest, turning it into an instant "chopper landing zone." Fortunately, not too many were expended. They were primarily used for extraction of downed aviators or trapped ground forces.

Our general-purpose iron bombs were armed with "non-tamper" fuses with different delays built in. This made them extremely dangerous. Once armed, any attempt to tamper with the fuse would cause a detonation. With varied delays in the fuses, the bombs did not necessarily detonate upon impact. They unexpectedly detonated at predetermined intervals. This kept the enemy out of the bombed site for at least 24 hours while ordinance "cooked off." The lion's share of my time in Vietnam was spent trying to teach the Vietnamese that you will live much longer if you take safety seriously. I was constantly preaching that in the munitions business, "short cuts can and will kill." Nonetheless, there were still too many accidental detonations.

I made some durable friendships at Bien Hoa. One in particular was with an Electronic Counter Measures specialist named Tran Van Duc (who you will hear more about later). He was having difficulty understanding the abstractions in some of the psychological operations I was teaching. I had to spend extra time getting him to understand the utility of using non-combat techniques during war, to reduce an opponent's morale or mental well-being. Initially, he thought taking the enemy out was faster and safer. Tran was always upbeat and expressed a great love for Vietnam and for America. He wished democracy would flourish in Vietnam so he could raise his family there in peace. When my final rotation came about, we promised to stay in touch but we never did.

I rotated out in April 1965, after my replacement signed in. This time Travis AFB was our port of disembarkation. It was a relatively easy return but after we landed things got a bit weird. Apparently, there was already some unrest in many universities and colleges back in the United States. The students probably knew more about what was really going on politically in Southeast Asia than we did, and they were beginning to make their positions known to the government. Although we would normally have been required to travel in uniform to our next duty station, we were advised to wear civilian clothes instead. They didn't want us to create any undue concerns in anybody's minds if we were seen traveling in uniform.

That was my first inclination that something was not right. However, in August 1964, the Gulf of Tonkin incident happened and everything changed.

We were told, America was told, that the North Vietnamese had fired on two U.S. warships in the Gulf of Tonkin. As we discovered later, that wasn't actually what took place. The situation was far more complicated. But at that point, I believed what I was told by my government. See, this is where bias comes in, again. I may not have had a bias against the Vietnamese at that point since I'd met many and gotten along fine with them for a year. But my bias for believing everything my government told me was still strong and abiding. I believed we were doing the right thing. Weren't we, always?

Immediately, I felt that I should go back again. Perhaps it was a good thing that I didn't.

I was stationed in Germany then, well into my assignment with the German Air Force in NATO (being the technical monitors for their nuclear mission). Even though I volunteered for another tour in Vietnam in 1965, I couldn't get a release from the Air Force headquarters until four years later.

Cleared to Return to Southeast Asia

By then, it might as well have been a different country, a different continent. Heck, it might as well have been a different planet. My two tours could not have been less alike. In 1964, we were Air Advisors. The Vietnamese were our allies, the people we were sent there to help. In 1969, the Vietnamese were the enemy, a determined enemy with whom we were locked in a life-and-death struggle. It was our war.

We were fighting the North Vietnamese, but everybody was a target, regardless of whether they were men, women, or children. We were bombing day and night. We believed our cause was just. The North Vietnamese didn't agree.

Most of the missions we supported were on the Ho Chi Minh trail. That was the primary logistical route from North to South in Vietnam. We were determined to cut the trail off as a re-supply route, but we were never able to completely accomplish our mission. The best we could do was slow traffic down.

The North Vietnamese launched their offensives from an area of Southeast Cambodia. Every year, they assembled around the rice paddies in an area of Cambodia called the Parrot's Beak. There, they were able to restore body and soul, stock up on rice and food, and get plenty of rest, since there were no American combat forces in Cambodia. This was an unacceptable situation for the United States.

The Air Force had been kicking around the idea of setting up a full-blown chemical mission in Vietnam for some time, to enhance target identification. Reconnaissance flights, or "recon" flights as they were called, were having difficulty pinpointing targets because of the dense foliage in the jungle. The idea was to use Agent Orange to defoliate. Since the advance team for accepting the chemical mission, which included me, had already received chemical weapons training at Kadena Air Base in Okinawa, Japan, the idea of doing something chemically to eliminate the threat from Cambodia gained traction.

The plan was to insert a small, highly specialized, covert team into an area near the Parrot's Beak in Cambodia, in the winter, to disrupt the growth-cycle of the rice paddies with a non-persistent agent. This would eliminate Cambodia as a food refuge and as a launching point for engaging American forces in Vietnam. Volunteers were recruited and assembled at Tan Son Nhut air base near Saigon. After in-depth consideration of in-country experience, training, and personal interviews, an initial team of 10 was assembled. I was the senior non-commissioned officer. The mission was executed with some difficulties, but no fatalities. While not 100 percent successful, the mission did manage to significantly disrupt hostilities from Cambodia, so much so that other special operations were initiated.

There were many other Air Force-specific special operations that we executed. Whatever the requirement happened to be, it was up to our command structure to get it done. Each special operation had a code name which lasted until the mission was accomplished or discontinued. Once the special ops were terminated, the troops returned to their normal duties and their special experience identifiers were updated. "It can't be done" was not one of the options available to the Air Force (like Tennyson's Light Brigade, "Ours was not to make reply, ours was not to reason why, ours was but to do or die").

Because the Air Force was flying combat sorties around the clock, everyone worked 12 hours on and 12 hours off, seven days a week. We had precious little time off. I remember once, in response to a request for help from Catholic Nuns, we visited an orphanage near Binh Thuy in the Mekong Delta. We visited a couple of times to help with manual labor projects, but the last time we went, the orphanage was gone. I never learned what happened to the kids; hopefully, they made it out all right. It was heartbreaking to see how expendable life was in those places, under those circumstances. It was even more heartbreaking to realize I was part of all that.

But those were the sorts of things we were doing in Vietnam my second time around; and I wasn't comfortable with it. Mostly with the "why" we were doing it.

Our original mission was completely eroded. It was replaced by an "us-against–them" mentality, "them" being the bad guys and "us" being the good guys. I made up my mind fairly early during that deployment that this was it for me. I was going to complete my tour and then no more. I didn't believe I could, in good conscience, support what the mission had morphed into. I decided that, if ordered to return, I would refuse, and I had been mulling over what the consequences to my refusal might be. Given the circumstances, it could be anything from court-martial to a dishonorable discharge and separation from the service with loss of all benefits and allowances, to jail time. I thought about those things very, very carefully because I never took my service lightly. But I couldn't continue supporting a cause that I morally opposed, a cause that was no longer just. I would not return to the conflict.

I guess the timing was in my favor. Around 1971, the whole thing started winding down. America's direct involvement officially stopped in 1973.

I'm not sure when, exactly, the lie about the Gulf of Tonkin became public (that the naval ships were, in fact, not fired upon, as claimed), but when I returned stateside the second time, protests were happening everywhere. It felt weird being the object of so much vitriol from so many people. They were protesting against us. We were being called things like "baby killers." Thinking that we might be responsible for the violent unrest that gripped the country was a bitter pill to swallow. As the protests dragged on and increased in number and intensity, it became apparent that America in general thought we were wrong. The government was wrong; it had lied to us. After 58,000 deaths, it was clear that I had been fooled by my unconscious bias like so many others.

Vietnam Certainly Was Fine without Us

In 1990, as a political appointee in the Administration of President George H. W. Bush, I had the opportunity to return to Saigon, or Ho Chi Minh City as it is now called. I was sent there to close out the American participation in the Orderly Departure Program (ODP) and the Amerasian Program. The ODP permitted qualified Vietnamese to apply for admission to the U.S. refugee program. My assignment with the ODP was to close out refugee processing in Vietnam and ensure an orderly and proper exit of all refugees accepted and cleared for the American refugee program. There were about 3,000 America-bound refugees remaining in Saigon.

Shortly after my arrival, the in-country representative for Northwest Airlines and I toured the refugee camp to gauge the logistical requirements for transporting refugees to Bangkok. North-west Airlines had the contract to fly all refugees and Amerasians there. As we walked through the camp, the residents greeted us warmly. Suddenly, a familiar-looking soul came rushing forward to shake my hand vigorously. I was a bit startled, until I realized it was Tran Van Duc (I told you we would meet him again). He embraced me and began to weep openly. I was caught up in the emotion of the moment and shed tears too. When we were able to speak, he told me that when the country fell, he knew he was persona non grata in Vietnam. His father, mother, five brothers, and one sister were killed during the war. His sole-surviving family member was a brother who had received refugee status in America. So, Tran applied for the U.S. refugee program, but his application for himself and his family, his wife and two daughters was denied. However, he was granted refugee status in Germany. Tran had no idea why I was in the camp or what position I held in the U.S. Government. I told him I was in Saigon to close out the American refugee program. As I did, I could see hope drain from his face. I promised him I would look into his case. He didn't know it, but I fully intended to see what could be done to unite him with his brother in the United States.

After we returned to the Rex hotel where we were staying, I asked the District Director from our office in Bangkok to please join me for dinner. Responsibility for Vietnamese refugee processing came under the cognizance of the Bangkok District Office, and I had promoted the District Director to his current position two years earlier. After I expressed my interest in trying to unify Tran's family, I was assured the case would receive every consideration possible, consistent with refugee law and existing refugee resettlement policies. I thanked the Director, and we spent the next couple of hours catching up.

At 8:00 a.m. the following morning, I received official notice that Tran would be accepted for the U.S. program and was scheduled to fly out in eight days. The Director advised me that Tran had not been told of his status change yet, and he thought I might want to deliver the news personally. I sent my heartfelt thanks to the Director.

After the morning staff meeting, I had a car take me back to the camp. Tran was told he had a visitor. Tran was brought to the NGO Director's office. I could see the surprise on his face when he saw me, and I couldn't hold the suspense for long: I spilled the beans about my conversation with the Director and the happy outcome. Tran fell to his knees and began giving thanks. He then embraced me and wept. I was about to break down, too, so I told him I had to get back to work. We said goodbye and once again promised to stay in touch, but we never did until I met him again by chance a few years ago in Las Vegas, at an IT convention! He recognized me and embraced me fondly. He told me he and his family were American citizens now. His daughters completed law school and were representing his IT firm. He employed around 200 people. He and his wife had another child after they arrived in the United States and were firmly resettled and happy. He thanked me again for my help. I was very touched.

Back in 1990, we managed to close the ODP and tried to clear out as many individuals and families as we could. I made the final determination on all difficult cases, and to this day, I wish we could have taken everybody. But most of those left behind were precluded from the program because of previous criminal convictions that could not be waived. The Amerasian program was quite a mess. We didn't know if the children came from Australian, New Zealand, or American fathers. (Children of African American fathers were easier to recognize.) Many of the applicants claimed that they were raised by one family and then switched to another family as they grew older. There were no documents available, so our adjudicating officers were in a quandary. I had to intervene. I directed that we accept all existing cases at face value and accept applicants claiming multiple family members. Around 1,200 applicants were qualified after our interviews were completed. I suppose it was their lucky day they were on their way to America. May they be well.

While in Ho Chi Minh City, I was able to see a lot of places I'd seen before. It was nice to see that people were surviving; Vietnam was recovering. Life went on. That whole story we'd been told, the domino theory that if Vietnam fell to communism all of South East Asia would also fall... well that didn't happen! The country was thriving.

I grew up believing that America was righteous. That we did the right thing for the right reasons. I still believe that. Yet, people were calling us warmongers. At first, it angered me. But they would say, "Look, count the wars you guys have been in: World War I, World War II, Korea, Vietnam . . . on and on and on, even up to today." Faced with these facts, it's hard to hold on to your bias and not rethink things. It's hard not to say to yourself, "Apparently I don't know our history that well."

Chapter 6

A TIME FOR SOCIAL ACTIONS

In many ways, I was sheltered for most of the Civil Rights era. I was stationed in Europe, basking in the warm glow of being perceived as American by Europeans, while simultaneously hiding from the effect of an unconscious bias which caused me to shun my Mexican ethnic affiliation. The racial strife and problems that started brewing in the military, the issues that brought about the Social Actions program, led to my awakening, especially the race relations programs which allowed me to explore my Mexican identity for the first time with no bias.

And because my own biases were on the wane, I was becoming more and more determined to help those around me see and eliminate theirs.

Institutional Racism Well-ingrained within the Air Force

In that regard, here's a funny story (funny peculiar, not funny ha ha) about the double standards towards Spanish native speakers. It happened when I was stationed in Germany, attending the Heidelberg campus of the University of Maryland at Air Force expense. The U.S. Government was still helping me. In addition to other requirements, the university required successful completion of 20 semester hours of a foreign language in order to qualify for an undergraduate degree, and they only taught German as a foreign language in Heidelberg. But I'd heard that you could fulfill the requirement by taking the final exam of any language course. If you received a passing grade, your exam score became your passing grade for the course. If you failed, you couldn't advance until you actually took the course and passed it. There was a clear and present danger here: you would not be able to graduate until you moved to a location that offered the class you failed, and you had to complete and pass the course. For most Air Force students, this meant at least a three-year delay.

Now, I had never studied Spanish, but it was my first language before it was replaced by English. So, I felt I could pass an entry-level Spanish class examination. I went to the Education Office and I asked if I could challenge Spanish instead of taking the German courses offered there. Of course, the University didn't teach Spanish at its Heidelberg campus, but it was taught in Spain. After a protracted discussion with the Education Officer, it was decided that it could be done. They would ask the campus in Madrid to prepare an examination for me to take. The test would be sent to Germany, I would take it, and then it would be returned to Madrid for grading. I was pleased. We began preparing the application form. The first question the secretary asked me was my name. I told her "Ricardo Inzunza," and she said, "Oh no!" You know that can't be good.

She went on to tell me I couldn't challenge Spanish since, unfortunately, my name indicated I was Hispanic; and, university rules prohibited a student from challenging their native language. I was stunned but being the smart and slightly obnoxious guy that I am, I told the secretary if that was the case, I wanted to challenge English instead. They were probably very confused by me. Their response was that I couldn't challenge English either, since I was an American. I asked her if my name were Smith and the circumstances of my life were the same could I challenge the test. "Yes," she said. I said, "The only language I have ever studied in school is English, so just by changing my name to Inzunza, I am disqualified?" She said, "It does seem odd, doesn't it?" Now, this poor secretary wasn't trying to make me angry, but, unfortunately, she was doing a good job of it. So, I kept pestering her until she referred me to the Education Officer.

The Education Officer said his hands were tied; this was a university rule. The Education Officer wasn't trying to make me angry either, but he was also doing a very good job of it. My complaint was forwarded to the University of Maryland in College Park, Maryland, where it took two years to resolve. I was permitted to test. I seriously believe that Cervantes, the greatest writer in the Spanish language, would have had difficulty passing the exam. But, somehow, I managed to squeak through.

Several years later, while in Ramstein, Germany, the Education Office was looking for someone to teach a spoken Spanish class. When I saw the ad, I went to the Education Office to learn more and apply for the job. They told me that they had thirty students waiting and had no one to teach the non-credit course. I felt I was definitely qualified for the position, if not overqualified. When I expressed my interest, they said that I was the only person who had applied and that I needed to interview with the Education Officer. I felt that it was going to be a slam dunk! The interview was going fine until the Education Officer asked me where I was born. In that moment, I knew I had him. I proudly told him I was born in Holtville, California, But he said, "Oh no!" He went on to inform me that the university required the person teaching the class to be a native speaker. And there we were, once again: he wasn't trying to make me angry, but damn if he wasn't doing a great job of it!

I told him this was absurd. I said, "When I wanted to challenge Spanish, I couldn't because I was a native speaker. But now that I am applying for a job that pays money, suddenly I am no longer a native speaker?" He may have responded something along the lines of "It does sound odd, doesn't it?" as these people were apparently inclined to do, but by that time, I was ready to pull my hair out. I felt like the deck was stacked against me. I told the Education Officer he could keep the job and walked out. To this day, I regret that I didn't make the university see that this was wrong. It was a well-established form of institutional racism that needed to be excised from the system. Sadly, I left it in place, and it would continue to frustrate other Hispanic students.

Superintendent of Social Actions, an Opportunity to Help People

When General Jones asked me to become the Superintendent of Social Actions, and leave Germany for the Pentagon, I hadn't realized I would be the first enlisted action officer on the Air Staff. Because the Air Staff didn't have enlisted Action Officer Billets, one had to be created by converting an 06 (Colonel) billet to an E9 (Chief Master Sergeant) billet to accommodate the new position. Field grade officers, aiming for the rank of general, viewed the loss of a senior field grade billet on the Air Staff as a step backward for them. The chief of staff was taking the Air Force in a new direction, and that ruffled some feathers. As the lowest ranking member of the incoming team, I was an easy target for the disgruntled few.

I don't know if General Jones realized being the first enlisted Action Officer would be tough or if he was just a super-strong Social Actions advocate, but if he happened to be on our corridor, he often found time to stick his head in the door to say hi. Politically speaking, the fact that the Air Force Chief of Staff personally selected me for the new position (and that he would stop by my office to say hello) provided me with immense imputed power. I will always be grateful for that hand-up. I will also be grateful for the General's belief that "A fish rots from the head down." It was this belief that made him insist every flag rank officer in the Air Force was required to physically attend the mandatory race relations training. That insistence really put teeth into the SA program.

My immediate boss was also a member of the new team. General Mann was the first female General in the Directorate of Air Force Personnel. Often when we traveled together, she would muse on her hope of being accepted as an equal in a formerly all-male world. She felt as though the weight of all Air Force women rested on her shoulders. Like me, she was determined to succeed.

I'd never seen myself as representing the enlisted force. Apparently, a lot of enlisted guys at the Pentagon did. At first, my sudden ascendance in stature was a problem for some Air Force personnel who outranked me. However, with a little help from the Chief of Staff, my problems faded quickly.

I was on temporary duty at Randolph AFB. I had finished my inspection and was reviewing my findings and recommendations with the base commander, who was a colonel. He thanked me but respectfully told me that, if I wanted him to take my report seriously, someone with a higher rank than me had to brief him. I was surprised by his response, and I asked him if General Mann, who was heading up our inspection team, had enough rank to brief him.

He said, "of course she does." I thanked him and promised to pass along his words.

At the end of each day, our team assembled to share our findings with General Mann. I related my experience with General Mann and she told me not to worry about it. She would handle it. I didn't know that General Mann briefed General Jones daily on the status of our mission. I also didn't know that General Jones told her not to worry. He would handle it. The next morning, a plane landed at Randolph AFB to pick up the colonel. He was in a class "A" uniform. The colonel had an appointment to meet with the chief of staff, who wanted to give the Colonel an opportunity to air his complaint at the very top of the Air Force chain of command. I don't know what happened at the meeting, but I do know that it rang like a shot through the Pentagon and it filtered down to the rest of the Air Force very quickly. General Jones meant business.

That afternoon, the colonel called me to apologize for our misunderstanding. He asked if I would kindly return to Randolph so we could discuss the report. I did. Soon thereafter, any problems I was having getting people to listen or cooperate with me dissolved.

The Pentagon was viewed, and most likely still is, as the center of the Air Force universe. There is a perception that if you are assigned to the Pentagon, you are an important person. Please notice I said "perception." There were quite a few enlisted personnel assigned to the Pentagon, responsible for providing all manner of administrative support. In other words, they are the backbone of all military departments. So my position as an Action Officer was unique in that regard, and they didn't mind telling me how proud they were of my representing the enlisted people.

The Pentagon itself is nothing short of breathtaking. Working in that place is the experience of a lifetime. It was originally built to consolidate the War Department into one location during WWII. The idea was that it would be turned into a hospital after the war ended. That's why it consists of five concentric rings placed inside one another, interlaced with corridors and surrounding a courtyard.

Me at the Pentagon, circa 1975.

As the Superintendent of Social Actions at the Pentagon in 1972, I, along with others, was responsible for the development, implementation and operation of all Air Force substance abuse programs. We provided counseling, group and individual therapy and drug abuse control training to all Air Force personnel, their families and the civilian workforce. In a way, it was similar to what I was doing back in Ramstein but on a much larger scale.

The job of the Social Actions program was to assist commanders in bringing all the resources of their communities to bear on the social problems they were experiencing. Prior to Social Actions, these problems were dealt with on an ad hoc and piecemeal basis, which proved to be ineffective. Social Actions was required to deal with race relations, gender equality, equal opportunity and substance abuse. Even though drugs were illegal and alcohol was legal, they were both addictive chemicals, so they were treated collectively as substance abuse. If you were coming to work drug-affected, it didn't matter if it was by alcohol or other chemical substance. It was against policy, and the Air Force intended to stop it.

We also operated a drug school at Lackland AFB in San Antonio, Texas, where we trained our officers in the new drug abuse control officer specialty code. Candidates had to complete a six-month intensive drug abuse training course, after which they were required to spend two months as interns at one of the Air Force centralized inpatient rehabilitation facilities. We had such facilities in Landstuhl, Germany; in Chicksands, England; in Ankara, Turkey; and at Clark Air Force Base in the Philippines. These were live-in rehabilitation centers where we sent drug and alcohol affected personnel to complete a 30-day rehabilitation regimen.

The idea behind the rehabilitation program was to be able to say, "Look guys, you were admitted to this facility 30 days ago suffering from delirium tremens. We carried you through withdrawal; we put you through the counseling sessions and got you healthy again. You know how you feel now. Compare that to how you felt 30 days ago. This is your one chance to turn your life around. If you go back to your old habits, you will most likely end up in trouble and be separated from the service." The final step in their rehabilitation was the follow-up support phase. This happened when they returned to duty either through AA (Alcoholics Anonymous) meetings or in group or individual counseling sessions at their duty stations.

The government had a significant investment in these airmen. Many had fifteen or more years of honorable military service, and they held key supervisory positions. Losing them would degrade supervisor responsibility. Unfortunately, at the outset, many were separated. That 30-day program wasn't enough for them.

Race Relations Program, a Different Outcome

In 1971, propelled by the deaths of active military personnel during race riots on military installations, and to counteract a national policy of segregation and inequality, the Department of Defense mandated that every member of the military, including flag rank officers, must undergo forty hours of race relations training. General Jones took this mandate very seriously.

Under his direction, the foundation of the Social Actions leadership-building program included education and training programs in race relations, human relations, equal opportunity and diversity. Special courses and seminars were developed and added to the core Equal Opportunity Advisor Courses, to provide service members in command or leadership positions with an advanced level of equal opportunity and human relations awareness training.

I still remember how General Jones sat through the first race relations class we conducted to set the tone for the program. Of course, there were a lot of airmen snickering about making generals take this training. They disparagingly called it "Watermelon University" but General Jones didn't flinch. Soon it became clear to everyone that the Air Force was taking race relations seriously and no "half-stepping'" would be tolerated.

It was imperative for everyone to understand that all Air Force members, regardless of race, religion or gender, would be encouraged to unlock their full potential by rising to the highest level their ability would support. Further, in pursuit of full equality, the standard would be lowered for no one. You had to carry your weight. So, that was the essence of race relations training. I was the token Hispanic at the Pentagon as well, so I had to double as a Race Relations Officer teaching the block on Hispanic contributions to America's Defense.

Race Relations class, Ramstein, Germany, 1970.

This part of my job had already started in Germany when I was teaching the block at Ramstein. It was the first time I was able to study what Hispanics were, what their history, our history, really was. These things were never taught in school when

I attended. And the more I learned about it, the more absurd it became to me that I had been embarrassed about my heritage and felt the need to distance myself from being Hispanic. What was I running from? These were good people, heroes! By the time I went to the Pentagon, I was actually feeling pretty good about who I was, and being a member of the General Jones team certainly didn't hurt.

If it hadn't been for General Jones, I probably wouldn't have managed to do all the things that I was able to do. For example: a lot of Hispanics, when sent overseas, relied on what we called "care packages" from home to have condiments and food that was familiar and homelike. The commissaries and exchanges had no clue what products might appeal to Hispanic military members and their families. So, the General sent me to meet with the officers in charge of on-base grocery stores, known as Air Force Commissaries, and to the Army and Air Force Exchange Service (AFEX) to talk about getting condiments, music, beauty products, magazines, etc., that would help the Hispanic airmen and their families to feel more a part of the Air Force community. We asked commissary and AFEX officers to stock masa, tortillas, music, magazines and a lot of other items the Hispanic community counts on at home. Not just any products, but brand names that would be familiar, brand names Hispanics knew and trusted and bought at home.

It sounds like a small thing, condiments and tortillas. But they can make a big difference to the morale of people who spend so much time away from home in deployments. Fortunately, commissary and AFEX officers agreed. With our help for brand selection and product quantity, sales of Hispanic products in the AFEX and commissaries increased substantially.

We also started Latin American clubs (open to everyone) in Germany that quickly spread throughout the continent. The idea was to help Hispanics and anyone else to assimilate into the Air Force fabric. The Hispanic community seldom socialized as part of the majority group. They didn't feel comfortable in the Air Force community, so they pretty much kept to themselves. As a consequence, they were not aware of many of the resources available on all Air Force bases. When they came to Latin American club meetings we arranged for librarians, commissary officers, teachers, law enforcement and commanders to actually brief them on what services were available for them. They were delighted. When we brought in the Red Cross to tell them what to do if there was an emergency, they were both pleased and relieved. When we brought in the legal office to explain their legal rights and the service the office provided, they flourished. When we brought in commanders to brief the families on the missions their loved ones were involved in, they were proud and supportive. They asked a lot of questions, and all came out of the meetings a bit smarter than they came in. More importantly, they felt more like real members of the Air Force family.

Because Latin American Club meetings were conducted according to Robert's Rules of Order, I just knew that when these members mustered out of the Air Force they would return (to Del Rio and Harlingen, Texas, or San Diego, California, or wherever they came from), armed with the knowledge that if they wanted to change the system there was a way to do it. There is a democratic process that you can follow. When a meeting was in session, we made them raise their hands to be recognized by the chair before they spoke. Once recognized, they had to rise to speak. Although it wasn't readily apparent, over time, we could see they were becoming more comfortable with the parliamentary process.

I think each of those small things the Air Force did were valuable for everyone involved. They were good for the Air Force, and they were certainly good for the individuals who benefited.

Another responsibility we had as Directors of the Social Actions program was to look at the state of equal opportunity in the Air Force. General Jones made it clear that it was Air Force policy to ensure each member of the Air Force was treated with respect and equality. Yet, in actuality, we knew that wasn't really happening. Minorities and women were getting short changed. We needed a way to determine whether our personnel systems were free of bias. We thought math could help with that.

For example, if the available resource from which we drew our personnel was fifteen percent African American then, if bias was not operating in our personnel system, fifteen percent of all personnel actions, good and bad, should involve African Americans. We looked at promotions, demotions, other adverse actions, discharges, assignments, etc. Unfortunately, our system was riddled with inequality that could only be accounted for by unconscious bias. When we looked at grade structure, minorities and women were overrepresented in the lower enlisted grades (E1 through E6) and disproportionality under-represented in the higher enlisted grades (E7 through E9). The Air Force needed to find a way to eliminate unconscious bias.

In those days, promotions were decided by promotion boards. In the interest of fairness, the Air Force decided to shift to an enlisted promotion system that utilized the "Whole Person Concept." The new system was called the Weighted Airman Promotion System (WAPS). It had the effect of removing human bias from the promotion system. Points were awarded for enlisted performance reports, decorations, previous promotion, physical fitness examinations, specialty knowledge tests, time-in-grade and time-in-service. The points were then totaled into a composite score. The composite score placed everyone in a specialty code striking for the same promotion in rank order. Congress then determined how many individuals in each rank and specialty code could be promoted. If 30 percent of the airmen striking for E4 could be promoted, the list of those eligible was counted until thirty percent were included. All the eligible numbers were then promoted.

After the promotion cycle concluded, everyone received a report card which indicated their score, the score required to be promoted and how their score was assigned. If they were not promoted, the report card indicated areas where improvement was possible. Once the new system was implemented, the clustering created by unconscious bias faded. Minorities were starting to be equally distributed throughout all enlisted ranks. The same type of analysis was applied to the entire personnel system. Minorities and women can now be found equally distributed throughout the Air Force grade structure.

As our analysis highlighted systemic inequalities to Air Staff personnel, the Air Force started to take stock and measure what was happening. One area of special concern was adverse actions. Punishment for facially similar infractions was manifestly more severe for minorities. This was a difficult problem to address, since, under Article 15 of the UCMJ, commanders meted out punishment for infractions in their units as they saw fit. General Jones signed off on a remedy that required all Officer Efficiency Reports to reflect how well commanders supported the Equal

Opportunity Program. In short order, disparities in the punishment meted out to majority and minority airmen for facially similar infractions narrowed.

It was a remarkably interesting time in the Air Force when General Jones was nominated to become Chairman of the Joint Chiefs of Staff. He asked me if I wanted to go with him to the Chairman's office. Again, I didn't know if he was serious. It didn't matter, though, because my twenty years were up and my service was done. I felt it was time for me to make room for somebody else, to do something different. After all, at that point, I still had a family to go back to. But we'll get to that shortly.

During my years at the Pentagon, I was directly involved in many things I was proud of. And yet, there was one incident that I recall with particular relish, although my involvement in it was more indirect. Roy Benavidez, an Army Master Sergeant, was going to be awarded the Medal of Honor. It was about fourteen or fifteen years after the precipitating event (combat actions in Loc Ninh, South Vietnam in 1968), so there was a lot of confusion as to whether or not he was actually going to receive the medal after such a length of time, because there is a time limit for awarding of medals. In the end it was decided that MSGT Benavidez would be given the Medal of Honor, and President Reagan would personally award it to him in the courtyard of the Pentagon.

Now, in the center of the Pentagon there is a courtyard with a stage area where various events are hosted. The venue was set for the President to award the medal there. But then a saluting question came up: whether or not an officer was required to salute an enlisted Medal of Honor recipient. Enlisted personnel must always salute officers, but the reverse is not true, and there is no specific requirement mandating a salute. However, when an enlisted person renders a salute, the officer must return the salute. The saluting question was kicked up to the level of the Secretary of Defense who decided that it was improper for an officer to salute an enlisted person, even if that enlisted person was being awarded a Medal of Honor.

Of course, the whole point was moot, as the courtyard of the Pentagon was a non-saluting area. (It had been designated as such because it was a non-hat area. A proper salute out of doors required that a hat be worn.) But although it made sense rules-wise, it didn't sit well with me. Benavidez was a war hero. We were bestowing him with the highest award we have in the military for valor above and beyond the call of duty. When it comes to the Medal of Honor, they say many are called, but few are chosen. I decided to do something about it.

I had a friend assigned to the military office in the White House, Humberto Saenz. I called him and told him about the decision. I had already briefed him on the question that had been raised about saluting MSGT Benavidez, and how the decision didn't feel right to me. "Let me take it from here," he said. Somehow, he got in to see President Reagan and, stretching the truth a bit, he mentioned that they were thinking of not saluting MSGT Benavidez because he was enlisted. President Reagan immediately reacted to that. "Of course, you salute him; he's a Medal of Honor man," was his response, according to my friend.

The President's wishes were passed down the line. In the end, everyone had to be in uniform (hat on) in order to render a proper salute to MSGT Benavidez during the ceremony. From my time at the Pentagon, this was the incident I consider my little claim to fame: everyone was required to salute a Medal of Honor recipient. Sadly, it shouldn't have come to that. Military people, in or out of uniform, don't have to be ordered. They automatically pay proper respect.

From right: President Ronald Reagan, a protocol officer, MSGT Roy Benavidez, and Secretary of Defense Caspar Weinberger, Medal of Honor awards ceremony, the Pentagon, 1981.

On that note, it was time for me to salute the Air Force and hang up my stripes. It had been a good twenty years. I'm pretty sure that, when he gave me the choice of serving my country or serving time, Judge Shoemaker didn't expect that I would do so well.

Chapter 7

FAMILY MATTERS

After talking so much about my years in the Air Force, you might think that there was nothing else going on in my life. But that's not the case. See, I'd managed to create a family. I just didn't do a bang-up job at maintaining it.

Spending twenty years in the Air Force, on so many different deployments around the world, certainly didn't help me spend quality time with my wife and children.

Military life, back then, was much different. Now, as it should be, families are part of the military institution. They are embraced and enfolded into the military family. A far cry from when I joined the Air Force in 1956 when its mantra was, "If the Air Force wanted you to have a wife, they would have issued you one." What that meant was that we had a job to do and the job came first. Family was definitely not "front and center." The allotment for a married Airman at my pay grade was $178 a month, which even back then wasn't much (it paid the rent but didn't help much with raising twins).

But my struggles as a family man wasn't the Air Force's fault. My own complicated upbringing played an important part in it. Aside from Mrs. Leone, I didn't have great role models on parenting.

It Starts with My Father

My Father, whose house I wasn't allowed to enter as a child with Anita Sanchez, tried to make amends when I was a teenager. He sent me messages, personally and through the family, stating his desire to meet me. Stubbornly, I refused.

Other than his affair with my mother, my father was pretty much a zero in my life. Nonetheless, I turned on him; and I refused his attempts to meet. I knew my upbringing was not ideal or even normal (I'd heard so many negative stories about my mother, both from Mrs. Leone and the State of California.). And yet, I couldn't lay blame for my sub-par behavior on my mother, so I dumped my anger and resentment on my father instead. For me, it was the path of least resistance.

If he was remorseful, I couldn't (or didn't want to) see it. I guess I was playing some sort of stupid game where I was going to "show" him, you know? He didn't want me when I was a kid, and now I didn't want him; I was not going to give him the pleasure. So, I rebuffed his attempts to meet and carried on with my life, keeping my feelings buried deep inside until 1964.

That year, during my first assignment to Southeast Asia, the Red Cross informed me my father had died. By that time, I knew that my father was Ricardo Inzunza (I'd learned that the hard way), although I'd never met him. I was aware he lived in San Diego and that he'd also moved there from the Imperial Valley. I don't know if he was also working in the shipyards or what he was doing, but I'd heard stories of his being an alcoholic. As I understand it, cirrhosis may have been featured in his death.

When we were deployed, mail was seldom forwarded. It was retained at your primary post. Red Cross messages were transmitted electronically, as they were usually time sensitive. But, by the time the Red Cross notification caught up with me, it was already a week or so after the fact.

When the message arrived, we were on a mission at Hiep Hoa, a Special Forces Camp in the Northeast Region of Vietnam, awaiting the cover of darkness to initiate an onward deployment. The Air Force used firebases and Special Forces Camps like Hiep Hoa for countless "special operations," for cover and support. I say this to note the fact that even if I had wanted to attend my father's funeral, there was no possible way for me to exit the combat zone at that moment. It just wasn't going to happen. So there was nothing practical I could do about it even if I could have left. The funeral would have already happened by then.

There was also nothing I could do, in a broader sense, to ever mend our relationship. All my desires, expectations, even dreams, died with him. I would never be able to look him in the eye and ask why things happened the way they did. He beat me at my own stupid game.

And in that game, there were no do-overs.

Mending the Relationship with My Mother

It's ironic, huh? Although as a teenager I'd aimed all my anger towards my father (or rather, towards his absence), throughout the years I had managed to manufacture some anger toward my mother as well. I guess I had had people telling me, "She's not your mother, we're the ones taking care of you," a few too many times. Subconsciously, I bought into the notion, and it affected me.

As kids, my brother Gilbert and I showed a lot of affection towards my mother, affection she never really reciprocated. During the ten years he and I spent in the foster system, my mother came to visit us maybe two or three times. Every time she did, it meant the world to us. (I guess you tend to amplify things when you are a kid, especially a kid devoid of maternal affection.) I remember we'd see her walking up the road toward our foster home, and we'd just run to meet her.

This used to infuriate Mrs. Leone, of course. "I'm your mother," she would tell us, "I'm the one who takes care of you when you are sick, and I am the one who provides for your safety. I am the one who 'mothers' you! Your mother doesn't do anything for you, she just gave birth to you, and then she stopped at the water's edge." Her words didn't really register with me and my brother then, but they slowly started seeping in as I became an adult and enlisted in the Air Force.

By 1964, I hadn't spoken to my mother for about 12 years. The news of my father's death was a wake-up call.

It became quite clear to me that I made a horrible blunder by not agreeing to meet my father when I had the chance. There was nothing I could do about that. But hopefully there was still a chance that I could keep my relationship (or non-relationship) with my mother from suffering the same fate. I had six months left in the country before I was due to rotate out, and there was no way for me to shorten the time of the tour. Suddenly, two major fears consumed me. What if my mother died before I rotated? I wouldn't have a chance to make things right. I know that was a highly unlikely scenario, but I couldn't get it out of my mind. It was pulling me down. The second and less important fear was that my rotation would be "feet first," as they say, I would be the one who didn't make it. I say "less important" because if I died, my problems would be over. The concern for me in that scenario was that my mother would never know how sorry I was for not understanding she had her own cross to bear. Those last few months in the country were quite difficult, and the time just wouldn't pass quickly enough.

Eventually, though, it was my turn for the bag drag (that's what it was called when you were on your way to the airport to rotate out of a combat zone. When you had under 100 days, you had the "two-digit fidgets." Your final word as you boarded the big bird at Tan Son Nhut Air Base was "next."). I completed my tour and was headed for Tan Son Nhut Air Base for lift off, like the commercial says, "Oh what a relief it is."

After a journey back that felt longer than it was, I landed at Travis Air Force base. My wife, along with our children, were in Portland, Oregon, north of Travis. They were expecting my return, but my mother lived in San Diego, south of Travis. I was conflicted. I just knew I had to try to make things right as quickly as possible, so I took a flight to San Diego. I even neglected to notify my wife and children who waited for me, or my mother that I was on my way to see her. This problem was eating me up. It had to be resolved.

As I rode the cab to my mother's house, I was flooded with so many emotions that I thought I would explode. I had rehearsed so many things I wanted to say to my mother that, by the time I knocked on her door, all my words had left me. My mother answered the door, saw me, and greeted me quite casually, like I was returning from a morning run. "Oh, hi," she said. At that moment I was so jammed up that the dam burst and tears flowed in torrents. I think I was dumping a lifetime of bitter frustrations, regrets and dashed dreams on her doorstep. My mother stood silently while the emotions poured out of me. She never hugged me and never uttered a word. Surprisingly, I was okay with that.

I was finally able to understand that I had to accept my mother as she was, not as I wished her to be. She would never behave the way I wanted her to, the way public convention dictated mothers should behave. She couldn't be the mothers I saw on television. That wasn't her. She had to be herself. My behavior must have frustrated and mystified her as much as hers mystified me. So, we talked. I don't think we could ever be 100 percent okay; some of the hurt ran too deep. But whatever number on the conciliation scale we reached, it was far better than the zero I previously held. To me, that was an enormous win.

My brother Gilberto Inzunza and his wife Hazel,
and my mother, Antonia, in the middle.

My children came to know their grandmother once I got out of the way and allowed them to love her on their own terms. Most importantly, I was free to love her without feeling that I was enabling her bad behavior. My mother grew up "Figueroa strong." She may have done many things she regretted, but she never complained or allowed herself to be overcome with sorrow (qualities I admired in others but rejected in her). When I talk to my brothers and sisters today, not one of us harbors any ill feelings toward her. I've come to the conclusion that our mother was dealt a tough hand in life and she played it the best way she knew how. She made difficult choices, certainly. We don't know why or under what circumstances, but at the end of the day, she played her hand and we played ours. Had her choices been different, ours may have been different too. She didn't walk toward us as I would have wished, but she never walked completely away from us either. I am grateful.

Until she passed, six or seven years ago around the age of 95, my mother lived with one of my sisters. We all visited her there. There was never any talk that she was an evil person or that she wasn't a good mother. I guess she had a special charisma about her. Then again, all mothers do, don't they?

I'm tremendously relieved that I was able to mend fences with her before it was too late. But because I never learned how to be a child in a loving family, I had no blueprint for becoming a father myself. And for that, my own family suffered.

A Wedding in Portland Oregon

In 1961 I was on active duty in the Air Force but assigned as an "Air Advisor" to the National Guard in Portland, Oregon. The Oregon Air Guard had been assigned an air defense mission. To execute the mission, they had to be trained and certified on the F102A Delta Dagger. When armed the F-102A's were configured with a mix of conventional and nuclear missiles. The Air Force was there to train and certify them in the safe use and deployment of those weapons. It was during that assignment that I met and married Patricia Fern Duffey (Pat), my first wife.

When the twins, Richard and Guy, were born our "Air Advisor" mission was ending. The Oregon Air Guard was trained and certified as combat ready. There was time to relax. Having boys, as opposed to having daughters, was a big deal in the Air Force then. As tradition would have it, if you had a boy you were supposed to pass out cigars; whereas, if you had a girl, you passed out donuts. As we waited for reassignment orders, three other Air Force wives were expecting too, and all the husbands outranked me. The first to become a dad had a daughter, the second also had a daughter and the third completed the hat trick with a bouncing baby girl. This happened within the span of a month. Then, the lowest-ranking guy had twin boys and got to pass out cigars! I know that attitude sounds weird and old fashioned at best nowadays, but back then it gave me a chance to establish myself. They called me "the maharaja of the maternity ward."

Two weeks after the twins were born; I was deployed in "Operation Jungle Jim" as a Conventional Weapons Air Advisor, to help train the Vietnamese Air Force. This covert deployment suddenly left Patricia alone with two babies to care for. Fortunately, her parents also lived in Portland, Oregon, so she had help with raising the twins for the year that I was gone. We were getting paid so little that she had to go on welfare to make ends meet. That was a common practice in the enlisted ranks then. Nonetheless, she made certain the children were well-cared for and loved. To do so, she had to devise a system which she could control and which permitted her to keep order in the family.

When I returned from my deployment, I expected things to be as they were, with me as king of the mountain. That caused problems. The children had already adjusted to a certain style of parenting when I rode in with my own ideas and expectations of how things should operate on the home front. I guess I had to learn to adapt. However, adapting without understanding is not adapting. It's tolerating. I wish I had learned that lesson when it counted.

My next assignment was in Germany as an advisor to the German Air Force. Initially, I was unaccompanied in order to prepare for the family to follow and join me. Because we were assigned to a German Air Force base, housing was not available. I had to rent an apartment and furnish it. The nearest American Air Base was over a hundred miles away, so our location wasn't supported. (If it had been, the military would have provided furniture.) In this situation, furniture was usually bought from the family that was moving out of the apartment you were trying to rent.

When it was finally time for my wife to join me, she had to embark on quite the adventure with those two boys! They boarded a flight in Portland, Oregon, and flew to Seattle, where she had to change flights. She only had one big bag with everything needed to attend to the children and the darn bag broke. Since she was between flights, all she could do was purchase four little gym bags and fill them up with all their belongings. From Seattle, she took a flight to New York City. In New York, she not only had to change planes but she also changed to a different airport for the transatlantic leg of the trip. From NYC she flew to Paris, where she had to change airports again to catch a flight to Luxembourg. The thought of her making her way across New York and Paris with two strollers, four gym bags, and two overtired babies with no one to help her still makes me flinch. Who said women are the weaker sex? Luxembourg was her final stop. I met her there. When she arrived, I didn't fully appreciate (or understand) the ordeal she had just gone through to reunite our family in Germany. All those flights, strollers and carrying took a toll. By the time she got in the car for the three-hour drive to the Mosel River valley where we were based, she fell asleep. She was out the whole way. The poor woman was completely exhausted.

Now, I can appreciate her commitment to our family.

As I looked back later, it dawned on me that marrying wasn't something for which I was ready. I definitely wasn't mature enough to be a father! I was 23 when we married, and I had no clue what parenting was all about. Patricia was even younger, around 19, but far more mature and goal directed. Nevertheless, it took me 30 years to screw up that relationship, and we were separated the last years of our marriage before we divorced. Since I'm being brutally honest with myself, I think she would have done better if she hadn't married me.

See, I spent a long time self-righteously vilifying my father for having a baby with my mother and running away. To this day, I know nothing about the nature of my parents' relationship: were they in love? Did he "con" her? Did my mother's family break it up? I haven't a clue. I know that my dad had his other family, for which he was a good provider. So, after spending a good part of my adult life picking him apart, his death deprived me of the opportunity to ask him all my questions directly. They will forever remain unasked.

My youngest daughter, Alissandra, was born in 1990 while I was a political appointee.

Back then, President George H. W. Bush was standing for re-election and I knew that co-parenting would cut into my available time to help with the presidential campaign. I immediately reported the situation to Attorney General William Barr. (He was also Attorney General in the administration of President Donald Trump.) As I mentioned earlier, in the Bush Administration, when you accepted a political appointment you tendered your resignation letter (undated) when you signed on in case the President decided to replace you and you didn't want to leave. I reminded AG Barr that the administration already had my resignation, and I could be out of my office in a matter of hours. The AG thanked me for my candor and asked me to sit tight. If the administration needed me to vacate my position, he would personally notify me.

Well, as it turned out, Ross Perot entered the presidential race as an Independent candidate and took 19-percent of the votes, most of them, Republican. In my opinion, his presence on the ballot went a long way toward causing Bush to lose to Bill Clinton. It also caused the political component of my problem to evaporate.

Of course, there was still the practical problem of being a single parent now.

Mrs. Leone (I am aware that I keep mentioning her throughout all my family struggles, but she inculcated this sense of responsibility in me.). She always said, "Las cosas malas se pagan con las buenas." ("The bad things you do are paid for by the good deeds you perform.") Just because you do something wrong, that doesn't mean it's the end. You have an opportunity to redeem yourself with good deeds. She was right, being a lousy parent was not a good deed, but I could try to atone by doing the right things.

When my new daughter was a baby, my life changed. I had to be a parent in a way I hadn't been with my other children. I didn't have to be the first time around. My wife was such a good mother to them I never had to change a diaper or bathe the twins. If they cried during the night, I would simply nudge my wife, who would get up and take care of them. With my daughter, everything was different, especially my attitude.

The relationship with my daughter's mother was not good and we ended up in court. I was awarded visitation rights which meant when I was the custodial parent, I had to bathe my daughter, change her diapers, feed her and placate her when she cried. I never realized how important doing things like changing diapers is, how much bonding takes place between parent and child. As a result, my daughter and I are close. I'm grateful for every changed diaper.

Of course, even if you parent correctly, which I certainly didn't, every child will still be different and still have his or her own personality. After the twins were born, we had another boy, Bret. Bret could have been the poster child for marching to the beat of your own drummer. In ninth grade, he decided to quit school. He refused to return, even when the state and I insisted! We finally sought a solution in court. Thankfully, the judge saw the need for a compromise, so he ordered my son to attend a state sponsored camp in the Oregon Mountains. There, he received classroom training, so he was still able to get school credits. He went there for two years, and by the time he became a teenager, he quit. This time, I didn't protest.

Today, having kids of his own, he realizes he made some poor choices. I really appreciate that, given how much we fought back in the day, he is willing to pick up the phone and call me frequently. But it all goes back to not having a blueprint for parenting. If I had him now, I would approach things so much differently. In those days, most people thought you had to beat sense into children to make them obey or behave. Of course, it didn't work. Sadly, in parenting there are no do-overs either.

Lebanese-American writer Kahlil Gibran, in his book *The Prophet*, wrote, "Your kids don't come from you; they come through you on their own journey. Your job is to help prepare them for that journey." Once I got it into my thick skull that I didn't own my son, that he was a human being and my job was simply to prepare him for life, things became a lot easier for both of us.

Keeping up with the Inzunzas

That mostly sums up the saga of my own family, at least one part of the family tree.

As you may recall, it wasn't until I joined the Air Force that I found out my real name. But when it comes to my family tree and heritage, life hasn't stopped surprising me. With the march of time, I'm learning more and more about my father's side of the family. For instance: I'm not the only Ricardo Inzunza Jr. I also had a half-brother by the same name, including the junior.

I didn't meet my namesake until years later, but, because this world is a strange and funny place, one of my sisters, from my mother's side, met him before me.

At the time, my sister worked in the department of motor vehicles in San Diego, issuing drivers licenses and vehicle registrations. One day, she noticed a person in the line next to her window who she thought looked a lot like me. "As he drew closer in the line, I kept staring at him," she told me, "so he kept staring back, and at some point, he changed lines, and got into mine, and he kept getting closer and closer." When he finally came to her window, she said to him, "You're not going to believe this, but you look just like my brother!" The guy then handed her his driver's license and she realized his name was exactly the same as mine, even the junior part. She told him that not only did he look just like her brother his name was also exactly the same. I guess this guy knew about me because he stormed off. It probably wasn't the way he'd hoped his conversation with my sister would go. (I believe he had something else on his mind entirely. Tough luck.)

That was my first inclination that there were people my age on my father's side of the family.

Years later, when I was close to 40 and consulted for the National Association of Latino Elected and Appointed Officials (NALEO), they hired me to prepare a salute to "Hispanics in America's Defense." In selling the idea for the presentation to NALEO, I postulated that if there was a theme to the participation of Hispanics to America's defense it was, "first in, last to leave." (We'll talk more about this in a later chapter.) So, there I was, writing the script for the presentation, when I received a call from a man named Armando Arias from San Diego who said, "You don't know me but I think I'm married to your sister. She read an article you wrote and believes you're her brother." I thought it was a joke at first, but he insisted. He said, "Her maiden name was Dolores Inzunza." Armando gave me her phone number and asked if I would please give her a call. I thanked him, wrote the number down and it sat on my desk for two or three months. These things are never easy, are they?

My sister Dolores Arias and me.

But one day, I managed to summon up the courage and called her. When she answered the phone I said, "This is Ricardo Inzunza."

Immediately, she started shouting, "Richey, Richey, Richey!" That scared the heck out of me because nobody had called me Richey since I was a kid, but that was my sister, Dolores. She was probably one of those girls who came to play with me while I was waiting for Anita Sanchez outside my father's house.

Later I learned, my father, our father told her of my existence and asked her to never stop looking for me. She didn't, and I'm happy for that. Since I was working on my presentation for NALEO featuring a salute to Hispanic Medal of Honor winners at the Biltmore Hotel in Los Angeles, I invited her and her husband, Armando, to be my guests. The first time I met her was at the event.

From left, my bothers Ricardo, Jr, Feliciano, and Ralph Inzunza,
and my sister Dolores Arias (nee, Inzunza)

When I started meeting the Inzunza side of the family, that feeling that I had been miscast in my own life's story, the feeling that caused me to feel so out of place in my own family, started making sense. It turned out that I was more like this side of the family, my father's side. Many of its members were educators, politicians, judges, mayors. It cleared up a lot of things for me about who I was and where my drive to succeed came from. Ironically, the comment I hear most frequently from my brothers and sisters on my father's side of the family is, "Man, you look just like our dad!"

I may not have had the chance to mend things with my father, but I got to carry on his legacy. Sure, there were bad sides to it (as attested to by my early approach on family and parenting), but I was beginning to realize there were good things I'd inherited from him as well.

In the end, isn't that what every child hopes for?

But that was not the end of discovering members of my extended family I didn't know existed. Some as recently as three years ago.

My sister Norma Servey and me.

From left: My sisters Norma Servey, Delia Inzunza, Dolores Arias,
and Sandra Baca, and me in the middle.

My brother Chuck Fierro. We found each other
just three years ago through Ancestry.com.

Part II

CIVILIAN LIFE, CIVIL LAWS

Chapter 8

"THERE ARE ONLY TWO GOOD BASES"

I often think about the years from 1976 to 1980 because they had such a deep, transformative effect on me, like a new vector, aimed to put me back on track. The years between my Air Force retirement and commencing work for the federal government served as the course correction necessary for my life, for my career, and for my mission in life. It was the impetus needed to propel me to where I needed to be.

Where I needed to be, ironically enough, was exactly where I'd just come from.

When I think back on those times, an old Air Force saying echoes through my mind: "There are only two good bases: the one that you're going to and the one you left." I'm still baffled by the accuracy of these words. See, after a twenty-year hitch in the Air Force, the time had come for me to close the hangar doors, but I wasn't done with my last base. Not by a long shot. On the contrary, through a series of events (both unfortunate and fortunate) that unfolded over the next four years, I found myself drawn back to my old haunts in Washington D.C. and the Pentagon. I was roaming the same halls, although I wasn't the same person anymore.

A lot had changed, in me and around me.

And just like any other transformative process, I had to shed a lot of my old skin first.

The Year Was 1976

After I pulled the plug on my Air Force career, I moved with my family to Portland, Oregon. My then wife's father owned a pest control company there and, due to health-related issues, he was having trouble running it. He offered to sell the company to me, and I accepted. Although I never saw myself in the pest control business, I actually enjoyed running the company for a while. We were, by that time, the largest privately owned pest control company in the Pacific Northwest, but it soon became clear to me that this adventure wasn't meant to be.

No aspect of my life was meant to stay as it was.

While I settled into running the company and assuming more of the day-to-day, management responsibilities, my wife's father had an increasing amount of time to mend. As his health improved so did his work ethic, and he started coming to work more frequently. Only a day or two per week, at first. That was all right, I thought. I sympathized with the man. I understood how difficult it was for him to stay away from his life's work. But as his health improved, so did his reintegration into the management structure, to the point that his frequent presence was confusing to all of us. Legally, I owned the company, but he was the one our staff saw as the brains and boss of the organization and he was, but I was the owner. We had totally different management styles. We were tripping over each other. We both assigned responsibilities and scheduled people. The result was that we ended up double-scheduling and over-scheduling. That is not the way to run a business! Father-in-law or not, I realized it was up to me to find a way to amicably resolve this tricky situation. So, I went to see an attorney, to explore the legal avenues open to me.

"Tricky situation" was, perhaps, understating it. As my attorney was quick to point out, my personal relationship with my father-in-law complicated the business side of things. So, although he felt it was within my legal right (as the company's owner) to have him issue a "cease and desist" letter ordering my father-in-law to stop coming to work, that would only exacerbate my problems at home. By that time, things at home were unsettled. I guess they had been, for a long time, but the tension with my wife's father certainly didn't help restore marital bliss. According to my attorney, the two less quarrelsome options available to me were to amicably convince him to stop coming to work (which I believed would be fruitless) or to try to sell the company back to him.

While the fight with my father-in-law festered and I was considering my less-than-stellar options, I found myself looking for a distraction. I needed something to fight for; a cause that I deemed worthy. It didn't take long for such a cause to present itself.

In hindsight, it should come as no surprise. Immigration was such a core issue for me, so tightly knit to my own identity and early life's struggles, that helping immigrants became my passion. The incarnation of RIA, the company that would, much later on, bring you this book (and, hopefully, help you understand that a second chance for people without an immigration status is not only possible, but also a moral imperative) was realized during those four surreal, turbulent, and formative years from 1976 to 1980.

The Year Was 1977

I'd learned that the former Immigration and Naturalization Service (INS) was incarcerating Cuban children, along with their parents, for extended periods of time (in most cases, more than a year) without providing the children with educational services.

As a behavioral psychology major, I'm a firm believer in something called "The Critical Period Hypothesis." According to this hypothesis, the first few years of our lives are essential for language acquisition. If we learn to speak at a later age than, say, five, the process will be more difficult and ultimately less successful. The same principle applies for every skill we acquire as we grow up. You know how, in the first grade, we learn certain things, and those things become the building blocks for what we will learn in the second grade and so on and so forth? We're always building on the knowledge we've already acquired. But if we, at that critical period of our lives, don't acquire some of these blocks of knowledge, then we are probably going to be facing real difficulties as we grow older. With that thought in mind, perhaps one can start to comprehend the importance I attached to educating these Cuban children whose parents were incarcerated (euphemistically called "administrative detention") for years on end. INS tried to defend its policy by saying it was a law enforcement agency, not a grade school, but I was not persuaded. I believe there is no right way to do the wrong thing, and this was certainly wrong.

Fortunately, I wasn't alone in my belief. The INS had been sued over the question of public education for children who are here without an immigration status. The question was settled once and for all. In its decision, the Supreme Court struck down a Texas statute denying funding for education to children of non-immigrated residents, as well as a municipal school district's attempt to charge an annual 1,000-dollar tuition fee for each non-immigrated student. The court's decision left INS with two options: either provide education services to children incarcerated for periods longer than sixty days or release them so they may be enrolled in public schools. But perhaps I should backtrack a bit.

Thinking that someone had to be a voice for these voiceless children, I started a group called CRIA, "Children with Rights in America." The word "cria" is a Spanish word that refers to "a brood of chicks" and can also be used to refer to babies and youth. We thought it made for a fitting acronym. There were three of us in that group, working from basements and operating on public donations. All of us were motivated and passionate about helping the Cuban children and many others. With the CRIA group, we fought for full education rights for children in the country without an immigration status. From 1977 to1979, we lobbied Washington to pass legislation which would mandate enforcement of the right contained in the U.S. Constitution which required that any child residing in America, without regard to immigration status, was entitled to a free public education. We knew we were right.

But we weren't getting anywhere.

Specifically, the Department of Education was opposed to providing education services to Cuban children in administrative detention and generally to any children here without an immigration status who were not in detention. According to them, school budgets are determined by people who pay property tax. They argued that these were children of people who lived here without an immigration status, thus not paying property tax. Our rejoinder to the allegation that they don't pay property taxes was that yeah, they do. They just don't own the property; they pay rent. The rent, if the property owner is smart, covers all property expenses, including property tax. So even though they don't own the property, they are, in a way "buying it" for the owner. Now, these non-immigrated residents may not pay income tax, but that's because without a social security account number they can't legally file a tax return (even though the employer withholds the employee's wages). This means these workers derive no benefits from their withheld wages.

All this happened during the Carter administration. Jimmy Carter, I have to say, was an inspiration to me. He was, and still is to this day (as he also happens to be the oldest living former President of the United States), such a compassionate, caring, and decent human being. Under his administration, he strived for a government of the United States that was "competent and com- passionate," responsive to the people and their expectations. In retrospect, Jimmy Carter was probably too good a guy to become the President. As history has shown us, one needs to be a man (or woman) for all seasons to be a good POTUS. The ability to be an autocratic leader when you need to get tough, or a democratic leader when the situation calls for it, are traits indispensable to becoming an effective President. It was Theodore Roosevelt who said, "Speak softly and carry a big stick." This proverbial saying advised the tactic of caution and non-aggression, backed up by the ability to carry out forceful action if required. Jimmy Carter wasn't like that at all.

President Carter was willing to listen to everybody and any- body who had an idea to share with him. For that reason, if he didn't go along with something his executive staff suggested, they would often try to repackage the idea and present it to him again, as he was known for changing his mind. Unfortunately, this mind set unnecessarily delayed some executive actions. (The stark con- trast to President Reagan's unwavering personality comes to mind. If President Reagan said "no" to something, he wouldn't change his mind, not without a whole lot of badgering from everybody else in the world.) Nonetheless, Carter for me was an inspiration;

and, just like me, he came out of the woodwork. Nobody had even heard of him, a peanut farmer from Plains, Georgia, when he was campaigning. I remember people used to say, "Jimmy Who?" But his timing was right, his message was right, and the competition lined up the right way. And so, Jimmy Carter, an unknown no more, won the presidency.

All this to say, President Carter's kind personality cultivated a feeling that we should fight for what is decent and right, for treating our fellow human beings with dignity. It was during the Carter presidency that the Mexican American Legal Defense and Education Fund (MALDEF) picked up the children's case and sued the state of Texas for denying education to non-immigrated children. MALDEF was a bigger organization than CRIA and they were backed by the money and lawyers we didn't have at the time. Consequently, they were able to take the matter to the Supreme Court; and, in 1982, they prevailed. The Supreme Court decided the Constitution was clear: all persons residing in the United States were entitled to a free public education. Since the Constitution made no mention of immigration status, the Supreme Court decided that, under the plain meaning of the Constitution, children are persons, and therefore, entitled to a free, public education (even if their parents are incarcerated).

To this day, I don't know what happened to the Cuban children. Were they released? Deported? Allowed to stay in the country? I just know that CRIA, with our limited resources, did our best to help them. And with MALDEF getting involved and winning this battle, I was able to tell myself that we were on the right side of history. Ours was a just cause.

Helping those children was an immigration matter. From my days on the border, I knew I had a penchant for wanting to help immigrants (migrants, refugees, asylum seekers, parolees, whatever you want to call them), and now I discovered that this was where my true passion, my true calling, resided.

I was beginning to suspect I would definitely not find these things in the pest control business.

The Year Was 1978

While still embroiled in the father-in-law company drama (family dramas, much like Greek tragedies, tend to take time to unfold), I joined a political action committee. Its name was, "Americans for Change, Ronald Reagan for President 1980." See, regardless of being inspired by Jimmy Carter on a personal level, on a political level I leaned toward the Republican Party.

Being Republican and a Hispanic was somewhat of an oddity, or it certainly was back in 1980 (and I'm sad to say it's becoming so again). I grew up in a Catholic and Democrat environment, but after I enlisted in the Air Force, I started becoming more politically conservative. I actually found out that my mom and I were very much alike when it came to our political views. We both jumped into the Republican Party about the same time. Back then, it wouldn't be an exaggeration to say that we were the only two Hispanic Republicans that I knew! Ever since Franklin Roosevelt's "New Deal," Hispanics have been Democrats. Bit of Hispanic trivia here: most Hispanics of that time couldn't pronounce Roosevelt's name. They called him "Presidente Rosbel." So, you may meet some older Hispanic guys today whose first or middle name is Rosbel, or they may even call themselves Ross. If you ask them where they got that name, they will respond, "They named me after the President." Rosbel was as close as we Hispanics could get to saying "Roosevelt." I think that's very interesting.

Anyway, that political action committee (PAC) was a way for me to embrace my newly found civilian liberties. When you serve in the Air Force (in any military service, really), you have abridged civil liberties—you can't participate in campaigns, and you can't advocate for a political candidate. All these avenues are closed to you. You can't attend marches or demonstrations in uniform. If you do it in civilian clothes you might get away with it, but I wasn't inclined to do that. Once I was retired from the Air Force and just a civilian living in Portland, Oregon, I found myself veering towards politics. I joined that political action committee. I even became finance chair.

Our job was to raise money for the Republican Party of Oregon, and the Party would subsequently be making contributions to the Reagan campaign. The Republican Party back then was an attractive party to me, their values lining up very much with mine. I have yet to meet any organization, be it a political party, sports team, or religious institution that's going to give you 100 percent of what you want or align with everything you believe in. But the Republican Party aligned with my values in great measure. Back then, it was the party of the "big tent." There was room for everyone there, and I was proud to be a Republican.

Once again, I found myself being part of a group that was small and did not have a lot of influence. But we did our best, and we did well. Ronald Reagan won the 1980 presidency with his economic recovery message: America was in a malaise, in a decline, and it was time for economic recovery. He was going to champion that cause and he did. Our PAC certainly didn't have a big role to play in the election, but I was elated to see Reagan win.

It strengthened both my interest in politics and my conviction that I should be more actively involved in the causes I believed to be worthwhile.

The Year Was 1979

My transformation was almost complete. My work at the pest control company only brought problems and discord, both with my father-in-law and the already strained relationship with my wife. The feeling that I belonged somewhere else, somewhere I would be able to focus on what was really important to me as a person, continued agitating inside me. However, there was still another chess piece that had to be moved on the board for my whole game to change.

And that piece, almost led to my untimely checkmate.

When my wife was pregnant for the first time, back when I was still in the Air Force, she delivered twin boys (making me, as you may recall, the "maharaja of the maternity ward"). One of our boys was born with a ventricular septal defect (VSD), which is a hole between the heart's lower chambers. Every time his heart contracted, it allowed blood to pass from the left to the right chamber. The oxygen-rich blood was then pumped back to the lungs instead of out to the body, causing the heart to work harder. Small ventricular septal defects sometimes close on their own. Larger ones require surgery. My son was lucky: his VSD never closed, but he didn't require heart surgery. Our next child had a bigger whole in his heart. To our great sadness, he died from that when he was two months old. As you can imagine, I didn't know my family's medical history or heritage. Even so, I had never heard of heart conditions running in our family, at least not on my mother's side.

I postponed having my heart checked for a long time, perhaps afraid of what the outcome would be. I finally went to the Oregon Health and Science University, a teaching hospital and probably the best one in Oregon. There, I was diagnosed with something called IHSS, "idiopathic hypertrophic sub-aortic stenosis." It's a long-winded way of saying that the septum of the heart is thickening and will keep getting thicker, to the point that it will cut off the blood supply to the rest of the body, resulting in death. I had been told I had it before, but when a second opinion officially confirmed the diagnosis, I was just thirty-nine years old; too young, to be facing such bleak prospects. On the other hand, I was perfectly poised for having a mid-life crisis one decade earlier than usual.

Because IHSS is a hereditary disease, I had to bring my whole family in for testing. The verdict was that I had it as well as my son, the one with the hole in his heart. I then found myself in the surreal position of having to ask the doctors, "How much time do I have left?" They didn't know. It was their first time to diagnose this issue. They measured my septum and asked me to come back in a year to see how fast it was closing up so that they could make more definite predictions . . . and I could plan my affairs.

A year later, however, I was already in Washington, D.C., and there was a clinic in Maryland that specialized in the condition. By that time, they had developed a dual echocardiography machine that took pictures of both sides of your heart at the same time. I don't know how that helped the process exactly regarding my situation, but the doctors said the new machine could produce a much better view of my heart and, thereby, permit a more comprehensive diagnosis. The year came and went, and another year followed. My anxiety was building. So, I finally went to see the doctors in Maryland. They wrote to the Oregon Health and Science University for my medical records. At first glance, the doctors were inclined to concur with the IHSS diagnosis. But they assembled a panel of six heart surgeons to investigate further. They took pictures of my heart and concluded that it had an abnormally large septum. Apparently, that's all it was. It wasn't going to inhibit me in any way. They told me I should stop worrying and asking questions about IHSS. I should just live my life!

My initial reaction, believe it or not, was anger.

I'd spent so much time trying to accept my situation, to accept that there was an end and that I might soon know when that end would come knocking on my door. Then, suddenly, I had all the time in the world. Of course, the anger quickly gave way to a flood of relief.

However, in 1979 in Portland, Oregon, I had no way of knowing everything would turn out fine. And the health scare, combined with my family falling apart, made me decide to make the "Hobson's choice" that the attorney pointed out to me. Either I accepted things as they were or sell the company back to my father-in-law. So, I approached him, and, after congratulating him for feeling better, I asked him if he wanted to buy the company back. Perhaps it shouldn't come as a shock that he, indeed, wanted exactly that. In hindsight, that may not have been my smartest move, but we signed an agreement. He bought the company back from me, and I suddenly had one less thing tying me to Portland.

As my last assignment with the Air Force was in the Pentagon, I had fond memories of Washington, D.C. I also had a sense that, if my time in this world was limited, it was probably the place I could make the most of it. In Washington, I could, hopefully, affect more change and fight for the right causes.

So, I decided to leave Portland (and my wife and family) and move back to Washington, D.C. There are only two good bases, after all. Isn't that how the saying goes?

The Year Was 1980

I came to the nation's capital with an attitude, feeling like a hot commodity, like everyone would be looking to snap me right up. But when I got there, everyone told me it was the worst time to look for work. Apparently, President Reagan was slashing government job's and nobody was hiring. In my arrogance, I would reply something along the lines of, "That's exactly why I'm here!" or "When it's too tough for everybody else, it's just right for me!" or "These are the conditions I've been looking for, so I will prevail."

After nine months of looking for work in vain, I had a lot more humility under my belt.

That's not to say my stay had been completely fruitless. I had been offered jobs in the federal service, what they call general service (GS) jobs, but I aimed higher. You see, in government employment, there are three primary pay grades. The first is general service jobs (GS). They have different GS grades which amount to a different salary scale; ranging from one to 15, with most people hiring in GS grades 3, 4 or 5. If you have a college degree, you might start off at grade 6 or 7. Twenty or 30 years later, you may have climbed up the financial ladder to GS grade 14 or 15, depending on where you're assigned. Because it's the seat of the nation's government, Washington, D.C., normally has higher-graded jobs. So, a GS grade 15 in Washington DC might only be a GS grade 13 in Omaha, Nebraska. The responsibility is the same, but the pay grade changes since the cost of living is significantly higher in the capital. The jobs I'd been offered were at grade GS 13 and 14 but I wanted a job in the Senior Executive Service (SES).

The SES is the senior manager level. It goes from 1 to 6 (SES 1 being the lowest, SES 6 being the highest). Above SES are the PAS appointments, Presidential Appointment Senate Confirmation, which includes Cabinet members, undersecretaries and heads of Special Agencies. The jobs I was hoping for, both in terms of salary and responsibility, were at the SES level.

So, I kept the job hunt going.

Every morning I would wake up, put on a suit, and walk the halls of the Pentagon. I would visit the Department of Energy, the Department of Labor, all the departments, really. I also applied to the World Health Organization, the World Bank, the African Development Bank and the Latin American Development Bank. I was leaving no stone unturned, handing out my resumes, actually standard form 171, which is a government application used in lieu of a resume. It requires you to list every job you've ever had. I think my SF 171 was probably forty pages long, and I'm sure not a lot of people had the time to read the whole thing.

But the overall sense I got was that there was, indeed, a wave of cutting back on government jobs. Reagan had the dubious distinction of being the only President who managed to cut the growth of government. You have to understand, the U.S. Government is a big, sprawling monster of an organization; it keeps growing, expanding, and consuming. Nobody has figured out a way to get around it yet. President Reagan couldn't reverse the process, but he did slow the growth for a while.

At the end of each day, I would go to a bar called "Bronco Billy's Good Times Saloon." It was the only country and western bar in Washington. Marines and military guys would frequent the place because of the country music it played. Bronco Billy's also served free snacks from five to six in the afternoon and you could buy a beer and have a free supper of barbecue or "Buffalo Wings" and assorted snacks. I would go to eat there every single day. I might have mentioned that already, but living in the capital was expensive, and not having a job didn't exactly help one's budget. Still, I kept at it. It took me 9 months to land a job.

I still remember the day when it finally happened. I went straight to Bronco Billy's and shared my good news with a Canadian guy, a math teacher who was also a regular. "Oh, you mean you got promoted?" he asked. I explained that I had just been hired, but he didn't understand what I was trying to tell him. He thought that I was, perhaps, changing jobs. When I explained that I had been job hunting for so many months, he was stunned! Like most of the patrons of Bronco Billy's, he thought I was simply getting there straight from work every day. I guess that would have been the more logical thing to conclude. But the fact that I had been social all this time really helped me network and finally land a great job.

Dress for the life you want, isn't that what they say? I was not only dressing, but also behaving, as if I was already living it.

It wasn't always easy. During the first few months it felt normal to face difficulties, of course. After all, nobody knew me in Washington. There was no reason to really look at me in any different light than all the others who were applying for a job. But as the months went by, I really started doubting myself. Could I make this happen before I ran out of bravado, money, or time? The worry clock over my perceived health issue kept ticking in the back of my mind even as I tried to ignore it.

But finally, it happened. I was hired into the senior executive service at SES 6 level as a political appointment (even higher than what I was aiming for). They say it's a matter of who you know. I didn't know anybody. I sort of stumbled onto this particular job. Nowadays, I think it was just meant to be. I met some people one night and they said that I should go interview at their department because they were looking for a director. I interviewed and I was hired on the spot with the proviso that they had to check my political credentials. As this was a political appointment under the Reagan administration, they had to make sure I was a Reagan Republican and that I had helped in the Reagan campaign somehow. Well, no problems there.

One phone call to the Chairman of the Oregon Republican Party at the state of Oregon confirmed everything they needed to know about me. That small group I had joined may not have worked wonders to get President Reagan elected, but it sure worked wonders towards making sure I was eligible for my first government job. Isn't it funny how life works sometimes?

Speaking of funny (funny ha ha, not funny peculiar) after being in that job for two months, I received a rejection letter notice from a job I had applied for in the department I was now in charge of. I really felt like going down to personnel looking for the person who signed the rejection letter that said I was not "qualified" for the position. But better judgment prevailed. I had applied for about 50 jobs at the Pentagon, so by the time one of my former applications had worked its way through the system, I was already the Director of Military Equal Opportunity.

Landing this job was quite an accomplishment for me in my new civilian career! As the Director of Military Equal Opportunity for the Department of Defense, I was responsible for all matters pertaining to equality of gender, race relations, and equal opportunity for all armed forces of the United States, including the nation's Reserve and National Guard units. Sounds lofty, doesn't it? The interesting thing was, at my last posting with the Air Force at the Pentagon, our chain of command to the Department of Defense included reporting our activities to the Director of Military Equal Opportunity. Now, I was that guy I used to report to.

This meant that some of the guys I served with who were still in the military at the Pentagon, now worked for me. All matters related to social actions, drug and alcohol abuse control, and equal opportunity, in all of the military departments, fell under my purview.

I really felt that I was the best guy for this job. I understood it, had empathy for the issues and knew my way around the system. That being said, I knew next to nothing about politics and how to navigate the shark-infested waters of Washington, D.C.

As these four surreal years of my life were coming to an end and a new chapter filled with fresh challenges was beginning, I was smart enough to understand I needed help. Not only to survive, but to thrive in my new post.

Chapter 9

A FORCE OF NATURE
AND EQUALITY

If my nine months of job hunting in Washington, D.C. taught me anything, it was that being offered a job in the government is not easy.

Along the way, I developed a better understanding (and sympathy) for the people who, unlike me, start out looking for specific jobs. These people draft letters of support and mount strong lobbying efforts to get White House personnel to bless them. White House personnel scrub applications down, conduct initial and follow-on interviews, and oversee FBI background checks. When they determine all is in order and feel comfortable that nothing in your past will embarrass the administration or the President, they send a selection list to the President for approval. Of course, the President can add any name to the list and select that person, although that individual must still be vetted by White House Personnel. (The White House Personnel is there to protect the President and the administration from embarrassment. At least, that's the concept.) Now, the White House Personnel also has something called a "must hire list" which can be strongly influenced by the Party's elite. They can basically tell White House personnel who to place on that list. For this reason, your lobbying may well be for nothing.

Thankfully, during those nine months that I was looking for work, as well as during the eight following years that I served in the Reagan administration (from 1980 to 1988), I never had to lobby for a job. At my (many) interviews, some positions that might have fit well with my skill set were neither explored nor offered.

I knew the job well. I knew many of the folks who were going to be working for me, as I had previously worked for them before retiring from the Air Force. I was familiar with and interested in the issues. So, I felt confident about that job.

My next job posting as Director of Consumer Affairs for the Department of Energy, was a hand-picked job. Some issues were flapping in the breeze that involved transportation and storage of nuclear munitions, and my previous background with them made the Secretary of Energy comfortable that I would be able to speak intelligently about those issues. I want to believe I did.

I also did a stint as the Deputy Director of Asylum Policy and Review, reporting directly to the Attorney General. I credit my understanding of immigration on such a deep, personal level (as well as my familiarity with equal opportunity processes and the mindset that comes from it) for getting that short-lived, but important, job posting.

The only government appointment I lobbied strongly to get came later on.

It was my post in the George H. W. Bush administration as the Deputy Commissioner of the former Immigration and Naturalization Service. Having grown up on the border and having lived the immigrant life actually and vicariously, I felt my mindset was the right one for the job. I also believed the agency could use some improvements when it came to equal opportunity. I spent quite a bit of time before my White House interview learning about technical immigration issues. I felt I knew more about the issues at stake than anyone else who could be appointed. The guy who was handling the Department of Justice portfolio for the White House Transition Team, which included INS, was a friend of mine from Houston, Texas. While acknowledging that I would be a good fit, my friend also warned me that there were many Republican Party heavy hitters lobbying him for the same job. "Line your ducks up," he told me. I made sure that I took his advice.

I put on a full court press to get on that short list. I had previously met the President-Elect on personal immigration issues when he was Vice-President (George H. W. Bush served as Vice-President during both Reagan's terms), so I believed he would remember me if we could meet. I had consulted for an immigration bondsman in Dallas, Texas, whom I knew to be close to George H. W. Bush, so I spoke to him. He agreed to set up a dinner for me to glaze and amaze the President-Elect. I guess I must have done something right to convince the senior Bush that I was, indeed, the best candidate for the job because, even though the Party heavy- hitters pushed the President hard for their own candidates, I was the one selected in the end.

And that, as they say, is a story for another time.

For now, I will just say this: if being offered a job in the government is not easy, being offered the right job is next to impossible. You know the kind of job I mean, not merely the right fit for your skills and ambition, but also one that aligns with the values and causes that are close to your heart. Throughout my 11 years as an employee of Uncle Sam, I was blessed with the latter not once, but twice.

Still, I would not have lasted a month if it hadn't for a remarkable woman, my secretary Joan "Mac" McKenzie. I can't talk about any of my jobs without talking about her first. Hiring Mac was one of the best things I did when I started working for the government.

Joan McKenzie, a Force of Nature

The posting of the Director of Military Equal Opportunity at the Department of Defense required me to have a secretary, so I got one. Her name was Joan McKenzie, but I called her Mac. She was my secretary for 11 years, and a force of nature.

Mac was everything you'd want in an assistant and more. She was like my external memory disk. She knew which calls needed to be returned and which didn't, what were priority items and what weren't. I knew next to nothing about the intricate, political power games played within Washington, DC, when I started. I could have easily blundered if it had not been for Mac saving my hide on a daily basis. People would call my office, and I would have no idea who they were, so I would have to ask her, "Mac, who is this person?" Often, she'd insist I'd talked to him or her before. When I swore that I hadn't, that I would have remembered, like a magician, she'd produce a letter I had written to the person we were debating. That usually jogged my memory.

Year in, year out, Mac would make sure I didn't slip up in situations like that. She had my back even when I didn't know it.

Whenever I had a meeting, she sat down next to me and took notes in shorthand on what was discussed in the meeting, things people said they were going to do for me, things I had promised to do for them. Then, she would type up her notes and put them in the top right drawer of my desk. Every time someone came in to see me, I'd open that drawer. If I noticed there was some task that person was supposed to do for me, I would casually work it into the conversation usually as an afterthought right before they left. I would say something along the lines of "Oh, by the way, how is that report going?" Because of this, I enjoyed a reputation of having an astonishing memory, which of course wasn't true.

I didn't need to have a good memory. I had Mac.

As the years went by and my job postings became increasingly more demanding, Joan McKenzie wouldn't even let the phone ring in my office. She put a literal and metaphorical wall in front of her office and mine, and she controlled all the traffic. People couldn't just stroll by to see me; they had to go through her first. Before she allowed them in, she would come storming into my office to make sure that my desk was arranged to perfection.

The things I needed to sign were always neatly stacked up. Next to them, were all the documents I needed to review. If by any chance, when done with these two stacks, I had any time left in the day, she arranged yet a third stack of documents for me to look at. Joan McKenzie kept me on my toes. She always arrived at the office in the morning before I did, and she would still be there when I left in the evening, despite the fact that sometimes I didn't leave until 8:00 or 9:00 p.m.

To this day, I don't know how she did it.

I owe a lot to Joan McKenzie. "Let me handle this," she would say. She did this in so many different instances, for so many different little things. And she knew me well. She knew, for example, that I don't like typos in documents or letters I have to sign. She had a master's degree in English, I think, so she proofread every document that came into my office and required my signature. If it wasn't 100 percent correct, she would send it right back. This gave her a lot of imputed power, which she didn't shy away from using. All she had to do was say, "The Deputy won't like this" (although I'd never laid eyes on said thing), and it went back until it was right. Only when she was happy with it, would she bless the document and allow it to be signed by me.

That's not all she did for me though. I can recall one occasion where, if it hadn't been for Joan McKenzie, I would have probably gotten fired.

In 1987, I was invited to Taiwan to talk about deportation of individuals who fled that country to avoid criminal prosecution. The invitation came from the government of Taiwan, although we didn't have diplomatic relations with them. President Nixon's trip to China in 1972 opened up our diplomatic relationships with the People's Republic of China after years of isolation, and President Carter declared afterwards that we would no longer recognize Taiwan as "Republic of China" (as the country's official name remains to this day). We had moved the U.S. Embassy from Taiwan to Beijing, China. However, we created, the American Institute in Taiwan (AIT), as a place to issue visas and handle all diplomatic relations between our two countries.

It was AIT that invited me. Since I was on my way to China anyway on official business, Joan McKenzie booked my trip details as she always did.

I arrived in Hong Kong, where I was scheduled to confer with the Director of Immigration (Hong Kong was still a British protectorate then). I entered Hong Kong on my diplomatic passport, but since my trip to Taiwan was a sidebar, I left Hong Kong for Taipei on my personal passport. In Taiwan, I stayed at a modest hotel for three days before rejoining my team back in Hong Kong and continuing my trip on my diplomatic passport as the head of mission. When I was in Taiwan, I received several calls from the people of AIT who probably wanted to give me advice and offer some do's and don'ts (as we didn't have diplomatic relations with

Taiwan), but I didn't heed any of them. Eventually, I returned to the United States after what I perceived to be an uneventful trip.

Two or three weeks later Mac received a call from the State Department's office of Diplomatic Security. They wanted to come and see me. I had no idea why.

I told Joan as much, but of course we scheduled their visit. When they arrived at my office, I was informed they were investigators and they were looking into the circumstances of my trip to Taiwan. Apparently, on my trip to Asia, I had entered certain government buildings without permission. I was dumbfounded! I didn't have a clue what they were talking about. But they flashed their badges and produced identification, so I knew this was official business. Despite my surprise, I tried to cooperate as best I could. I explained to the investigators that any buildings I entered during my trip were, literally, all Chinese to me. They had Chinese writing on them, so I couldn't have known where I had entered as I don't speak the language. The investigators said that AIT had reason to believe the government of Taiwan paid for my travel and lodging in Taipei. Further, they believed I met with certain dignitaries without permission. I told them I didn't know what they were talking about. That's all the information I could convey to them at that point. Unsure it was enough, I was worried.

As soon as they left though, Joan McKenzie came into my office. And as always, she came well prepared. She was carrying a ton of papers and documents that could help shed light on the situation. She had my diplomatic passport, with a chop on the page where I'd entered Hong Kong (they don't do that so much anymore because everything is done online, but in those days they used to chop or stamp your passport to mark the places you'd been to). She also had my personal passport with exit and entry chops from Hong Kong and Taiwan, a receipt for the charge on my credit card for a round trip flight from Hong Kong to Taipei, a receipt for a charge on my credit card for the hotel where I stayed, and, perhaps most importantly, a record of her call to the State Department informing them of my trip to Taiwan. Mac reported to the State Department whom I was going to meet and asked if I needed special instructions or clearances. They had said no. Mac being Mac, also called them when I returned, to inform them of my progress.

Long story short, the State Department completed a 300-page investigation, only to conclude that we'd done everything within our power to follow the law and existing policies. (The fact that those policies needed to be improved was the State Department's issue, not mine.) I have a feeling the investigation might have yielded different results if it hadn't been for Joan McKenzie being so experienced and meticulous at keeping records, receipts, and triple-checking everything.

Of course, like any human being, Mac had her flaws. I say this lovingly, but the woman could be a bully. She had problems with ceding control and delegating, and that became crystal clear when, at some point, she needed an assistant of her own.

After interviewing a young woman for the position, Mac brought her in for my approval. They seemed to be getting along fine, but when the time came to write an efficiency report for her assistant, Mac rated her job performance marginal. As I was the reviewing officer and had to add my remarks after hers, I was surprised to see that this young woman was barely cutting it. When I asked Mac about it, she gave me this story about all the things her young assistant was apparently not doing right. "Well," I asked, "have you talked to her about it? Have you given her a chance to understand what she's doing wrong and how she can improve?"

Perhaps it should have come as no surprise to me that Mac hadn't. She probably expected that young woman to just figure everything out on her own and become as good as Mac was, right off the bat. When I told her she needed to provide clear feedback, Mac huffed and puffed and left my office. I didn't sign the darn thing for three or four days, until it was close to being due. Mac, who hated delays, had to eventually talk to her assistant and air her grievances. They hugged, kissed, and were fine working together after that. The woman even went on to get promoted later and moved to a different office. (I think she is now in charge of Asylum, Refugee, and Parole for the government.)

It goes to show how important giving clear directions to people is, but also how important it is to award them with second chances.

Mac and I never discussed that incident again. Knowing her, she didn't want to admit she had been wrong about something. Stubborn and proud. She was also brave, trustworthy, loyal and true. She stuck with me through all my different postings. When I left the Pentagon, she came over to Immigration with me. She even went with me to Gitmo (the Guantanamo Bay Naval Base) when I was in charge of the Haitian refugee processing there, to bring her superb sense of order to that whole chaotic process.

When I first met Joan McKenzie, she was a GS5 secretary. By the time I left the government, she had progressed to a level GS14. I like to think that she grew and evolved with me.

I certainly did with her. Let me tell you more about it.

Government Postings and Strong Women

And I don't just mean Mac.

As the Director of Military Equal Opportunity, I was responsible for the "Women in the Army" (WITA) study: a comprehensive review and analysis of gender equality in the Army. This analysis really started the ball rolling on meaningful and durable change in how women were treated in the military. It certainly opened my eyes to problems I wasn't aware of, problems that, thankfully, my time in the Air Force prepared me to deal with appropriately.

As I was approaching these issues from my military background, it was interesting to see the policy differences between equal opportunity in the military as opposed to the civilian side, which is called equal employment opportunity. Equal employment opportunity is mandated by law. It's against the law to discriminate against employees based on their gender, physical features, health condition, etc. Well, in the military, it's not. They can reject you if you're too tall, too short, or too heavy; if you have a handicap, are the "wrong" sex or sexual orientation and if you have an illness. They don't even have to argue about it. On the other hand, the Department of Defense's (DOD's) official policy says that "every person in uniform will be allowed to rise to the highest level their ability will support."

Translation: they're not going to lower the bar for you or let you go under the bar. You will have to clear it, and they will do everything in their power to help you. But if you can't meet the requirements, then you can't get in or stay in.

Looking at the military today, I find it interesting how far superior it has become to anything in the civilian community in matters of equal opportunities. I mean, they're even keeping people who were maimed in combat deployments. People who lost their legs and are walking around with prosthetic limbs are still on active duty. It really is fascinating! The military is also more inclusive towards family members now. It's finally occurred to them that if a soldier's family is not safe, comfortable, and secure, it will impact the individual's performance of duty. They are probably not going to have a good soldier on their hands. They have come such a long way since we were told that "if Uncle Sam wanted you to have a wife, he would have issued you one."

Back in my day, being a single parent in the military was a problem. Now they have 24-hour nursery services on all military installations that feature shift workers and single parents. Back in my day, if you got pregnant and were not married, they discharged you. This policy only applied to women. Men who were single fathers, were allowed to remain in the service, provided they could prove their child would be attended to in the event of a deployment. Now that this policy has been opened to women as well there are many single mothers in the military that are on shift work. Up until the current administration, the military had also evolved spectacularly in terms of sexual orientation policies. Sure, the official policy was that sexual orientation could disqualify you from service, but everyone unofficially implemented a "don't ask, don't tell" approach. "We're not going to ask and you don't have to tell us," they would say. And that's how gay individuals have been able to exist and serve in the military for all this time (and only very recently be openly "out"). Under the current administration, however, I see this changing back to a less tolerant approach. I believe this is an unsettled matter.

But I want to focus on the positive. The military today is head and shoulders above any other U.S. agency or entity in terms of equal opportunity. They are the most inclusive in terms of anything related to personnel, from promotions and demotions to adverse actions.

The WITA study was an ambitious undertaking. Today it is simply a reality. Women are fully integrated in the military. You can see them in combat, piloting planes, and holding general and admiral positions. They exist in all branches of the service, and rightly so. The same goes for African Americans, Asians and Hispanics.

Military jobs are good jobs. Many people on the lower end of the socio-economic ladder get into the military, as it gives them a chance to develop as human beings and individuals, to be part of something that makes them proud. They learn job skills (because the military has the best training in the world) and acquire job experience. When they leave the service, even if they don't elect to stay the full 20 years, but go three or four years after, they still have a resume and job experience. And they are more mature. Many are able to hone their leadership skills, so they leave the service very marketable.

In addition, the military plays an important role in our economy. It doesn't get a lot of credit for that, but its economic impact on our country is significant. It certainly played an important role in my life.

I couldn't have done the things I did if I hadn't been forced to join the military. I was, at that point in my life, hanging out with "bottom feeders" who were pulling me down, and I didn't even know it. It felt normal. Change was not something that would come easily. These groups don't like deviation. They like things to stay as they are. Sadly, they believe that's the way it's supposed to be. Most of the guys I hung out with before I joined the military either landed in jail or were killed somehow. Not many of them made it to fifty. But once I got into the military, it was okay for me to change and not be that guy anymore. The military does a fine job of taking individuals from all walks of life, breaking them down and building them back up as military personnel, as something much larger than themselves.

As a former military man, it was interesting to observe the civilian side of the Department of Defense and the Equal Employment Opportunity program. Things on the civilian side move at a different pace. If you file a complaint about discrimination, for instance, it's probably going to take at least three years to be heard. And then, if they think it has merit, it will go into the court system where another three years may pass before you finally get a resolution.

I know that system well. Bizarrely enough, when I was the Director of Equal Opportunity, I was sued by a Marine Corps Major who thought I had a bias against her.

This Major came to me to lodge a complaint against an Army Lt. Colonel who was making unwanted sexual advances towards her. It was the first time I was handling a complaint of that nature, so I listened to the grievance carefully. After hearing the Major out, I asked if I could conduct an informal investigation. After receiving permission to do so, I went to speak to the Lt. Colonel. He freely admitted to saying the things he was accused of. In his defense, he told me he only said them because a co-worker, an Air Force Captain, said the same thing to her and she didn't object. I told him the complaint was against him. I then gave him a cease-and-desist order. I briefed the Major on the finding and I told her I would check with General Counsel to determine our next move. She said that was fine as long as the advances stopped. I then mentioned to her that the Lt. Colonel indicated he made his advances because an Air force Captain made the same advances and she had not objected. According to the Major, the reason she didn't object was because she was flattered by the Captain's attention. Apparently, that was the reason she hadn't complained about his behavior.

Things were becoming too murky for my liking, so I went to both the legal and personnel departments to discuss the incident and receive guidance.

Both departments concurred that the problem we had was larger than it appeared. By the looks of it, all three officers were engaging in flirting behavior instead of focusing on their jobs. This is contrary to DOD policy, so I called all three in and presented them with my remedy: I advised them to stop the flirting behavior immediately because it was contrary to DOD policy. Since the three of them engaged in this inappropriate behavior, I informed the Lt. Colonel he would receive a letter of reprimand. If, after 90 days, there were no further reports of policy violations, the letter would be pulled from his promotion file without prejudice. I informed the Major and the Captain that they would each receive a letter of reprimand with a similar 30-day removal period. Well, the Major did not like this at all. She stormed out of my office and went to the National Association for Women, who took up her case. They sued the Department of Defense, me, and the President of the United States in his capacity as Commander in Chief.

This was a long, trying ordeal for me. It took two years for the case to clear the court and when it finally did, the judges decided in my favor. I had taken all the proper precautions and had acted in accordance with DOD policy. My decisions were correct. Eventually, the Major retired from the Marine Corps because she felt it was a place where she did not want to work anymore. The two men moved on to other assignments, and I lost track of them.

It saddens me that the Major couldn't believe I acted in her best interest and in the Department of Defense. I actually liked her. She was a good officer and a good writer, and I enjoyed reading what she wrote in regard to the case. But she believed, in her heart, that I was against her (although I served her with the least amount of punishment that was permissible based on DOD policies). I was just trying to do the right thing.

Thankfully, I was able to act in the best interest of many other female soldiers and officers during my time as the Director of Equal Opportunity. You can't win them all, but you can win enough to make a dent, perhaps.

Integrating Women into Combat Units Was Quite a Challenge

The challenge was mostly for the guys, who didn't believe women belonged in combat. I suppose they believed women couldn't carry their weight.

Among my responsibilities was the handling of appeals for individuals from all military branches who were being separated from the service because they couldn't accept or understand the need for change. I was the final arbiter on their separations. After reviewing their files, I offered recommendations to the Secretary of Defense about whether they should, indeed, be separated from the service or not. The first case I considered was about an Army Private Second class who was being discharged for disobeying a lawful order. It involved a female Army soldier who successfully completed basic training and technical school but got in trouble during a war game exercise they were practicing on her base.

This particular war game simulated, among other things, a chemical attack. Soldiers were bivouacked and were instructed to remain covered until all clear was sounded. But it so happened that the war game took place during this soldier's menstrual cycle. The woman, who was used to a certain level of hygiene, told her Supervisor that she had to step away from the simulated battlefield for a minute to take care of a personal matter. He responded that she couldn't because they were "under a chemical attack" and this was "war." The woman apologized again and explained what she needed to attend to but was warned that it would get her in trouble if she left the area. At this point, she felt that she was already in trouble, so she went ahead and took care of her business before returning to the war game.

Her sergeant referred her to the commander who pressed Article 15 charges against her.

In the military, the most frequent type of discipline is what is called an "Article 15" or "non-judicial punishment." Soldiers can either accept this or opt for a court-martial instead. The woman felt she was being wronged, so she elected the court-martial. She was found guilty and slated for discharge from the Army. She appealed the verdict.

I remember looking at her case and thinking, wait a minute! We've got a big investment in this soldier. There is a training slot that she's scheduled to fill five years down the road. Are we really going to dismiss this soldier from the service for an issue almost all military women will face monthly? This didn't make any sense to me.

My recommendation was that the soldier should not be separated. Removal from service would be the harbinger of bad things to follow. Fortunately, the Office of the Secretary of Defense agreed with my recommendation. Not only was she not discharged, but the court-martial conviction was vacated.

Setting aside any anti-female bias, integrating women in combat positions carried with it all sorts of practical problems which had to be solved. We were only just realizing how many issues there were. For example, then women didn't have their own uniforms.

They had to wear the men's uniforms. So, the military just ordered smaller sizes. But those uniforms didn't fit right. Same thing with the boots, they were not women's boots. They were simply smaller sizes of men's boots. Women were developing blisters from ill-fitting boots and rashes from ill-fitting uniforms. When they went on sick call they were accused of "goldbricking." It was a classic case of blaming the victim.

Another issue was integrating men and women into the same basic training units where the men, most of them anyway, were physically stronger than the women. If you put soldiers, of both genders, on a five-mile march or a five-mile run and the guys are in the front, many of the women will fall behind. If you put the women in the front, many of the guys wouldn't work up a sweat. In the end, it was decided to refrain from putting them in the same units for physical training. Men and women received physical training separately, which meant everyone could be pushed to their maximum capability.

We then reintegrated them for the academic portion of the training. Of course, in the academic segment, the women did as well, if not better, than the men. It was clear to me that when both teams were allowed to compete on their own level, they both did very well. It's interesting to see that only recently men and women have started going through basic training together. I think the Marines were the last corps to integrate basic training, this year.

We weren't ready for that as a society when I was the Director of Military Equal Opportunity. But I believe that what we did back then paved the way for the military of today.

Chapter 10

EQUAL NOT IDENTICAL
OPPORTUNITY

My posting as Director of Military Equal Opportunity for the Department of Defense was supposed to be about leveling the playing field for everyone serving in the Armed Forces, but it also turned out to be a journey of self-discovery.

My job was to provide a discrimination-free environment for all active duty, reserve, and National Guard units in the United States. That's a pretty big responsibility. Without counting family members, this was about five million people. I was also responsible for developing and implementing all training conducted by the DOD Race Relations Institute (DRRI) at Patrick AFB, Florida. All military Equal Opportunity (EO) Officers were required to attend and satisfactorily complete the DRRI's Equal Opportunity course of study.

When I signed on to the job, I was briefed by the Institute on the status of all components of our EO program. It didn't take me long to note that the Hispanic training module was sparsely researched and grossly lacking in content. I was assured that this was not an oversight; information on Hispanic military contributions was simply not available. Drawing on my Social Actions experience,

I doubted the accuracy of what I was being told, so I established a working group in the Pentagon to research the matter.

Development of the Hispanic Module,
a New Beginning

From the outset, I was receiving a negative vibe from the working group. The members of the research team thought they were on a "snipe hunt." "For some reason," they told me, "the contributions were not documented." I held their toes to the fire and, low and behold, the information was all there; pictures, news articles and military records, all neatly stored in the Navy Media Content Operation Center on Bolling Air Force Base in Washington, D.C., and at the Defense Visual Information Center on March AFB in California. It was a treasure trove of information. The staff, now motivated, briefed me weekly on the status of their research, and after each status report, I could feel the pride growing inside of me. Honestly, for the first time in my life it felt OK to be me. In fact, it felt pretty damn good to have a Mexican cultural legacy.

As I was learning about the contributions of the military side of my Mexican heritage, growing pride started displacing the self-loathing that had existed in me for far too long. The more I learned about the bravery, sacrifice, and the full measure of devotion Hispanic soldiers unflinchingly gave to the nation, the more my pride and admiration grew. I was eager to share our story. I wanted the world to know what Hispanics contributed to America's defense, growth, and well-being. Our race relations training module was widely acclaimed, but in my heart, I knew where the real transformation took place. In an oblique way, the EO directorship started me on my journey of self-reflection.

One of my office's responsibilities was completing DOD preparations for the military side of Hispanic Heritage Month. Americans observe National Hispanic Heritage Month every year from September 15 to October 15. Preparing for the event is a big deal within DOD. Celebrating the histories, cultures, and contributions of Americans whose ancestors immigrated from Spain, Mexico, the Caribbean, and Central and South America requires a huge team effort. The observance started in 1968 as Hispanic Heritage Week, when President Lyndon Johnson signed the first proclamation. It was expanded by President Ronald Reagan in 1988 to cover a 30-day period. The day of September 15 is significant because it's the anniversary of independence for Costa Rica, El Salvador, Guatemala, Honduras, and Nicaragua. (Mexico and Chile celebrate their independence days on September 16 and September18, respectively.)

Previous to my arrival, preparation for the event included reprinting a 16-page DOD booklet titled "Viva," which glossed over Hispanic military accomplishments. Needless to say, the message it sent didn't reflect well on DOD. Based on the experience gained from developing the race relations module, I knew the "Viva" pamphlet could be significantly improved. There was a problem though. I didn't have a budget for researching and printing an updated and expanded booklet! I guess there wasn't an appetite for spending money on an effort as mundane as Hispanic Heritage Month within DOD, but I believed President Reagan would help. So, I took my case to the Office of Public Liaison in the White House and, in short order, I received a memo from the office of the Secretary of Defense suggesting that it would be fitting and proper to update "Viva." We set to the task immediately.

The finished product was a 137-page, comprehensive history of Hispanic participation in America's defense. With encouragement from the White House, Budweiser paid for the research, upgrade, and worldwide distribution of the new booklet. I was quite proud of the effort. It was quite a feat for a guy who didn't like the sound of his own name once upon a time.

Cover of pamphlet, 1983.

The thing I'd started realizing since my days with the Air Force Social Actions program was that whenever America has called, Hispanics have answered. As the story of Hispanic presence in America's defense began to unfold, I detected a theme to our participation. It's "first in, last to leave." Take Vietnam as an example. There are so many stories to tell about Hispanics in that war!

During the August 1964 Gulf of Tonkin raid, sixty-four aircraft were launched from the USS Maddox and USS Turner Joy.

Two aircraft were lost. One A4 Navy pilot was killed and one A4 pilot, Lt. Everett Alvarez Jr., was shot down and captured. He became the first Vietnam prisoner of war; and he spent eight-and-a-half half years in captivity! That is the longest confirmed time as a POW in our nation's history.

In November 1963, SFC Issac Camacho was assigned to U.S. Special Forces personnel at Fire Base Hiep Hoa in Long An Province when they were attacked by a reinforced battalion of Viet Cong. The attack occurred at night, and the defenders were caught off guard. Although Camacho fought bravely, the Viet Cong overwhelmed the camp and he was taken prisoner. SFC Camacho was a POW for 20 months. On July 9, 1965, he managed to escape from his captors and make his way to freedom by crossing miles of Communist infested territory, the first American to escape from the Viet Cong. SFC Camacho was awarded Silver and Bronze star medals (with "V device," which meant "for acts of valor and heroism") and received a battlefield commission to the rank of Captain.

On April 23, 1975, Master Sergeant Juan J. Valdez was the Noncommissioned Officer in charge of the Marine Security Guard at the U.S. Embassy in Saigon when Viet Cong forces began to shell Bien Hoa Air Base. By April 29, the air base was attacked by ground troops, and Saigon was isolated. The embassy had to be evacuated by helicopter. The Marine Guards provided security for evacuation of embassy staff while they were lifted from the rooftop into the helicopter. Only when the staff had been safely evacuated, did the marine guards follow. Master Sergeant Valdez was the last person to be safely lifted onto the helicopter, ending a 15-year saga in which Hispanics were among the first to enter Vietnam and the last to leave. A truly remarkable and honorable record.

But wait, that's not all. In 1981, Master Sergeant Roy Benavidez was awarded the Medal of Honor by President Reagan in the courtyard of the Pentagon for his deeds in Vietnam. His citation read, "For conspicuous gallantry and bravery in action at the risk of his life above and beyond the call of duty." Benavidez spent almost a year in hospitals recovering from his injuries. He had seven major gunshot wounds, 28 shrapnel holes (from his scalp to his legs) and both arms had been slashed by a bayonet. His right lung was destroyed. In spite of his numerous wounds, Sergeant Benavidez continued to help his wounded comrades. He was clubbed from behind by an enemy soldier who tried to bayonet him. In the ensuing hand-to-hand combat, Benavidez wrested the rifle from the Viet Cong soldier and killed him along with two of his Viet Cong compatriots. In 1981, eighteen years after the event, Master Sergeant Benavidez became the last American citizen to receive the Medal of Honor for action in Vietnam. He became quite a star in the Hispanic community. Several schools in Texas were named after him.

It doesn't end there though. In 2000, President Bill Clinton awarded the Medal of Honor to a Mexican-born immigrant, Army Major Alfred Rascon, for his actions as a medic near Long Khánh Province during the Vietnam War. I met Al Rascon, who was born in Chihuahua, Mexico, when I was INS Deputy Commissioner and we were exchanging Viet Nam war stories. Mr. Rascon was an INS employee. He had not yet been awarded the Medal of Honor. When asked about his courage on the battlefield fighting for America even though he had yet to become a citizen, Major Rascon replied, "I was always an American in my heart."

Hispanics, as an ethnic group, have distinguished themselves in all of America's wars. More than 60 men of Hispanic heritage have been awarded the Medal of Honor, more than any other ethnic group. Of these 60 medals, two were presented to members of the United States Navy, 13 to members of the United States Marine Corps, and 46 to members of the United States Army. More than 20 percent of the recipients of the Congressional Medal of Honor in U.S. wars have been immigrants. Many were presented posthumously.

During my time as Director of Military Equal Opportunity, I learned that seven Hispanic Medal of Honor winners were still alive and living in the United States. They had never met one another or come in contact with the Hispanic community. I was astonished. I contacted the President of the National Association of Latino Elected and Appointed Officials (NALEO), the leadership organization of the nation's more than six thousand Latino-elected and appointed public officials. They were making plans to host their national convention, so I briefed NALEO's president on what I considered an oversight of epic proportions. He agreed with me and asked if my office would help them host a special "Salute to Hispanic Medal of Honor Recipients" during one of the nights of their national conference. Without hesitation, I agreed.

So, in 1981, NALEO hosted a reception at the Biltmore Hotel in Hollywood, California, where, for the first time, the Hispanic Medal of Honor Recipients were assembled in one location. The dais had three rows of seats, but the top row was reserved exclusively for the honored guests. Prior to the "Salute," the Medal of Honor Recipients were hosted at a meet-and-greet reception with many of the Hispanic luminaries who attended the conference. The Honorable Caspar Weinberger, Secretary of Defense, was the featured speaker. He sat in the second row of the dais. Additionally, a whole host of Hispanic Flag Rank Officers and Hispanic celebrities were in attendance to pay their respect to these Hispanic patriots. The Biltmore's main conference room was filled to capacity by more than a thousand guests. There were many fine and uplifting speeches, but, for me, the highlight of the event came when the Medal of Honor Recipients were individually recognized.

The tribute began with the showing of a 15-minute film prepared by the Budweiser Brewing Company, titled "Heroes." It showcased the contributions of Hispanics to America's defense, as only film can do, with a tightly written script and breathtaking cinematography. When the film ended and the ballroom lights came on again, the guests were on their feet applauding and showing their appreciation for the film. Suddenly, the lights slowly dimmed. When the ballroom was completely dark and the crowd sitting in silence, wondering what was going on, a single spotlight shone on a lectern on the right side of the dais where a Marine Colonel, resplendent in his best mess dress, stood at attention. After a moment he stepped to the lectern and, booming in his best military voice, he announced, "By order of the President of the United States."

When he started speaking, another spotlight illuminated Silvestre Herrera who was seated on the left side of the top row of the dais. He rose and stood at attention, proudly wearing the Medal of Honor. The Colonel continued reading the citation, "Private Herrera again moved forward, disregarding the danger of exploding mines, to attack the enemy position. He stepped on a mine and had both feet severed, but despite intense pain and unchecked loss of blood, he pinned the enemy down with accurate rifle fire while a friendly squad captured the machine gun." When the Colonel completed reading the citation, he stepped back from the lectern and continued at respectful attention. In a moment, he returned to the lectern and repeated, "By order of the President of the United States."

A second spotlight shone on Warrant Officer Louis Rocco, who rose and stood at attention. The Colonel continued reading, "As the helicopter approached the landing zone, it became the target of intense enemy automatic weapons fire. Disregarding his safety, W/O Rocco identified and placed accurate suppressive fire on the enemy position as the aircraft descended toward the landing zone. Sustaining major damage from intense enemy fire, the aircraft was forced to crash land, causing W/O Rocco to sustain a fractured wrist and hip and a badly bruised back. Ignoring his injuries, W/O Rocco extracted the survivors from the burning wreckage, sustaining burns to his own body. Despite withering enemy ground fire, W/O Rocco carried each unconscious survivor across approximately twenty meters of open terrain to safety. On each trip, his severely burned hands and broken wrist caused excruciating pain, but he continued his rescue efforts. The lives of the unconscious crash survivors were more important than his personal discomfort. Once in a secure area, W/O Rocco began to administer first aid to his wounded comrades until his wounds and burns caused him to collapse and lose consciousness."

And so, it went, until all seven recipients were standing. As soon as the reading of the last citation was completed, but before the audience could respond, the ballroom again went to black. The audience was confused, but in a moment another spotlight came on from the opposite side of the ballroom, where a lone bugler stood at attention, poised. The Colonel's voice sliced through the darkness, "Ladies and gentlemen please remain standing while we offer a last call salute to our brothers and sisters who have fallen in combat." As soon as the Colonel finished speaking, the bugler began to blow "Taps." When he finished, he remained standing at attention until his spotlight extinguished. As the house lights came on, I promise you, there was not a dry eye in the house, mine included. It was truly a moving event, especially for me. In that moment and in every moment since, through my tears, I was extraordinarily proud to be Mexican. The Colonel then announced, "Ladies and gentlemen, your Hispanic Medal of Honor winners! Please come up and say hello." The place broke out in an applause I thought would never end.

Hispanic Medal of Honor recipients, Washington DC.

Roy Benavidez, the MSGT who I'd helped make sure would be saluted when I was still serving on the Air Staff at the Pentagon, was one of these seven Medal of Honor Recipients that night. I believe that the Hispanic community genuinely appreciated our shining a bright light on the contributions that people from their culture, our culture, my culture, had made.

On a personal level, that night was important for me, too. And not just because I was able to meet my sister for the first time (as I've mentioned before). I spent my life denying who I was because I didn't know anything good about Mexicans, who Hispanics were, and what, if anything, they had done to make anyone proud. I just knew that being Mexican wasn't something the people I knew aspired to be. That night became for me a tangible example of all the uplifting things associated with the Hispanic culture that I had never allowed myself to see.

The ripple effects of the event were many, including the creation of a postage stamp by the U.S. Postal Service. It was called, "The Hispanics and America's Defense."

I was proud to be able to do this for the Hispanic community!

The other day, in the news, I stumbled across an article about a Hispanic man who was deported. His parents brought him into the country when he was three years old. He lived in the United States his entire life and was an Army Veteran who served two tours in Afghanistan. As a result of his combat tours, he developed Post-traumatic Stress Disorder (PTSD). This case is a tragic example of what can happen when national immigration policies are based more on hate than on logic and when immigration officials don't feel accountable to anyone.

I believe veterans of the United States Armed Forces, even those without an immigration status, have earned the right to reside in the United States, especially if they have served in combat. But the situation is so ironic right now. These veterans, when they die, have the legal right to be buried here in a military cemetery "with full military honors." But, without an immigration status, as long as they are alive, they can't enter the United States (not even for medical care at a Veterans Hospital, which they are entitled to). We still have much work to do.

I feel there are valuable lessons to be learned here, about the good things that can happen in immigration when you implement policies of inclusion rather than making it your life's work to promulgate policies of exclusion.

A Policy of Non-Discrimination

Speaking of inclusion instead of exclusion, before accepting the posting as EO Military Director, I was acutely aware that problems between the races had vexed the military for a long time.

In 1968 the Department of the Army's official report on "Racism in the Military" bragged that racism had been defeated in the armed forces. The Pentagon actually thought it had eliminated racism from its ranks. Then troops began rioting. The explosion of racial violence at Camp Lejeune, Cam Ranh Bay, Travis Air Force Base, and aboard the Kitty Hawk and many other military installations around the world, left many casualties and fatalities. Dozens were charged with crimes, including homicide.

The racial tension and violence that convulsed the nation during the summer of 1967 erupted in Vietnam as well. In large part, this was because of the inability or refusal of military leaders to address adequately complaints of racial discrimination. But there was a potent domestic factor at work as well. The assassination of Dr. Martin Luther King Jr. in April 1968 was the catalyst for rioting in more than sixty American cities. It challenged the belief that racism and discrimination could be ended through personal relationships and peaceful protest, both at home and in Vietnam. It wasn't that simple though.

True, minority and white soldiers formed close bonds of friendship in Vietnam, especially on the front lines. However, the claim that the military had eliminated "race as a factor in human existence" was far too rosy. It reflected the belief of many that racial discrimination was a personal issue between whites and minorities, and not a function of institutional racism. It still is.

In fact, throughout the Vietnam War, minority soldiers were disproportionately assigned menial duties, denied promotion to the rank they deserved and were unfairly targeted for punishment and excessively punished. A 1972 Defense Department study found that even though minorities made up only 11 percent of the total troops in Vietnam, they received 26 percent of non-judicial punishments and 35 percent of court-martials in Vietnam. Not surprisingly, given these numbers, minorities were over-represented in military prisons. In December 1969, they represented 58 percent of prisoners at the infamous Long Binh stockade, near Saigon. Minorities accounted for 25 percent of all combat deaths in Vietnam.

When I assumed the mantle of Director of Military Equal Opportunity, DOD had made significant strides in improving race relations within military departments. Things were better, but they were far from where they needed to be. It was my hope that I would be able to continue and improve the EO program's record of success.

During one of my briefings, I noted with some concern that, although DOD was collecting relevant statistical data on all minority groups, it did not correctly interpret them. This worried me because DOD embraces a policy of non-discrimination consistent with law, at least officially. But in reality, as I've mentioned before, DOD can legally discriminate against you if you are too tall, too short, weigh too much, weigh too little, have a handicap, or are physically unfit, etc. Yet, within the scope of its policy, DOD promises to provide an environment free of bias where every military member can rise to the highest level their ability will support. This policy applies to all active duty, and inactive reserve units, National Guard, and Coast Guard activities. It was my job to hold this policy up, so that everyone in DOD could see it and then, to make certain the Department adhered to it.

Back then, the concept of equal opportunity was still misunderstood and covertly (and overtly) resisted by many. There was a widespread belief that equal opportunity meant that minorities were favored over whites. To overcome the skepticism, DOD needed a way to measure bias. It settled on science.

If bias was operating in any of the military personnel systems, it could be measured mathematically. Bias could be working in favor or against any particular group. For example, if the available resource from which the military draws its members is 62 percent White, 19 percent African American, 12 percent Hispanic, four percent Asian and two percent Native American (made up percentages), and there is no bias operating in the personnel system, then these percentages should be appropriately reflected throughout the personnel system. If that isn't the case, you need to be able to account for it. If you can't account for it, you need an Equal Opportunity plan for fixing it. When I arrived on the scene, the EO program had been on the books for quite some time. The results were not something to write home about.

This is where the matter became problematic.

As I mentioned, DOD was capturing statistical data on all minority groups, but when it came to women and Hispanics, it was not proficient in interpreting the data. For example, the data was telling us that Hispanics were underrepresented in the officer corps and over-represented in certain enlisted ranks. The clustering was primarily in the lower-enlisted ranks. In the 1980s, 96 percent of Hispanics in the military were of Mexican American Heritage, while four percent were from a variety of other Spanish-speaking countries. Yet, if you asked Mexican American military members about the ethnic affiliation of any Hispanic officer, they uniformly assumed the officer was of Puerto Rican or Cuban descent. This perplexed me. From my time as the superintendent of Air Force Social Actions Program, I knew most officers enter the military with college degrees in hand or via ROTC (Reserve Officer Training Corps) programs.

The conventional wisdom in the EO community was if you want more Hispanic officers you need to open ROTC units where Hispanic's attend college or recruit where it is likely that Hispanics will be graduating. DOD instituted such programs. In Puerto Rico there were two universities, each with a ROTC unit, where 99 percent of the graduates were Hispanic. Other ROTC units were operating in Florida, New York, and New Jersey, where the population of Cuban students was substantial. But ROTC units were conspicuously absent from universities with large populations of Mexican Americans.

As my staff analyzed the data on military minorities DOD had been collecting for years, we quickly discovered that the perception of the Mexican American enlisted troops was indeed correct. Hispanic officers represented four percent of all DOD officers. Within the Hispanic officer group, however, fewer than 11 percent were of Mexican descent; the other 90 percent or so of Hispanic officer's corps were non-Mexican. Not only were Hispanics generally under-represented in military officer ranks, but within the Hispanic ethnic group, Mexican Americans as officers were almost completely absent. Once we briefed Recruiting Command Leaders about the problem, ROTC units started springing up in colleges and universities with high concentrations of Mexican American students. Today, the numbers are still not in order, but they have significantly improved. The imbalance resulted from an archaic personnel structure that systematically took the path of least resistance. A path which—surprise, surprise—ended up discriminating against minorities.

Nowadays, as the country has become more racially and ethnically diverse, so has the U.S. military. Racial and ethnic minority groups composed 40 percent of Defense Department active-duty military personnel in 2015. That's a huge increase from 25 percent in 1990. In 2015, 44 percent of all Americans (ages 18 to 44) were racial or ethnic minorities. The share of the active-duty force that is Hispanic has risen rapidly in recent decades. In 2015, 12 percent of all active-duty personnel were Hispanic, three times the share in 1980. It makes me happy to see that.

One component of DOD's Equal Opportunity fix was to try to make the armed forces friendlier and more home-like to active-duty personnel and their families. Part of the fix included stocking racial and ethnic hair and skin-care products, make-up, music, magazines, clothing lines and ethnic food products on Post Exchange and Commissary shelves. DOD also mandated race relations training for all armed forces members. Their family members were encouraged to sit in on this important training. Moreover, DOD began pressuring senior career officers to fall in line with the new thinking or get out of the military.

The one thing you have to know about the Armed Forces: they can't change the way you think, but they certainly can change the way you act. If you want to remain a member of the armed forces and get ahead, supporting Equal Opportunity better become a priority for you. In the end, I believe DOD is doing a good job of improving race relations, although white nationalism in the military is still a problem. Conditions in the armed forces today are immensely better and more egalitarian than they were during the Vietnam War. You have a lot more people of color and women in senior leadership positions, and that's going to change the culture of the military.

Integrating women into non-traditional career areas has always been a challenge. And not because of them. Women have always been quite capable and eager to shine. Men are the problem. Here is a simple example with far-reaching consequences. In this example, DOD failed to train men on the standard dress requirements for the different female uniforms. In the eyes of some male supervisors, the longer the women's hair and the shorter their skirts, the better, when they were in uniform. Of course, they were out of uniform. Unless a female supervisor was available, few males knew what the dress codes were for women, including hair, make-up, nails, stockings, and jewelry standards. Heck, we didn't even know what the uniform of the day was for women.

I put a Navy Captain and an Army Colonel from my staff, who were both females, in charge of the gender integration portion of the Military Equal Opportunity Program. Their responsibility was to ensure everyone in the armed forces knew the dress standards for women and how to enforce them. These officers were tough but firm. They helped us solve a lot of the problems we were facing.

The attitude of some of the military male members, who were eager to see females fail, perpetuated inequality problems. Their stance was one of passive resistance. People don't like change, and the military was changing in front of their very eyes. I suppose they thought we were going to hell in a handbasket, so they found little ways to try and stop us, or at least slow us down.

In the end, they couldn't stop progress, not for long. We were on the right side of history.

Chapter 11

SOUTH OF THE BORDER, NORTH OF 40 PERCENT

After the Pentagon, my next post was in the Department of Energy (DOE).

As Director of Consumer Affairs for DOE, a Senior Executive Service posting, I was responsible for telling the story of the Department of Energy to the American public; to talk about things DOE was responsible for doing and things they were not supposed to do.

You may not know this, but all the nuclear weapons that the Nation has are under the care and custody of the Department of Energy. They are stored, transported, and controlled through various nuclear regulatory agencies, of course, but they all report to the Department of Energy. And that part was the one I talked about the most. It tied back to so many of my assignments in the Air Force across Europe, as well as my first foray into Southeast Asia. I had worked in several assignments configuring or teaching people how to handle nuclear weapons, so my expertise came in handy.

I was well aware, of course, that I was a civilian now. I understood that. The military was a different world where we had to cleave to one another. We always worked as units, always took responsibility for each other. As a civilian (and this I experienced in my postings in two different departments), you're a one man show. You work for the President of the United States, you serve at his will, and you report up. You don't report down.

Thankfully, the staff that worked for me at the Department of Energy were all career people. They knew their jobs; they didn't need me to do their work. My job was to make sure that the word of the President of the United States was reflected in our work. If he, for example, said we were going to create more energy, then we had to espouse that point of view. I was charged with expressing and defending the Administration's message in all matters.

Additionally, if the President was going somewhere and was slated to talk about energy, his speech writers would notify me that they required an input for his talking points or speech. Normally, presidential support requests had short response times, generally a matter of hours. For those types of requests, the entire agency responded. I would hand-carry my write-up to the office of the Secretary of Energy after I had walked it through the offices of the people who needed to review the document before it could be presented to the Secretary. I waited for the document to be cleared in each office. Once the Secretary of Energy blessed it, he would send it over to the White House, where it would be given to the speech writer. Now, the information might or might not be in the President's speech, or it might appear in such an altered form that you would not recognize it as your input. So, you couldn't have any pride of authorship. That's the way the system worked, and I was part of it.

I worked in the Department of Energy for about eighteen or nineteen months. Most of my-day-to day involved public speaking about the Department and about some of the projects being worked on. Of course, I was always available for assignments from the DOE Secretary that were classified. I recall one project I spoke about that generated a great deal of interest: a porcelain engine. Porcelain reduced friction, which reduced heat, and less heat reduced wear and tear on the engine. I talked about that porcelain engine a lot during my time! But then I left my position and I never heard about that project again.

Every now and then, I like to imagine a future where engines are made of porcelain. I think it would be interesting if it ever came to be!

Government Posting with Department of Justice (DOJ)

At the DOJ, I served as the Deputy Director of the Asylum Policy and Review Unit. In those days, America had its nose under a lot of tents in Central and South America, El Salvador, Guatemala, Nicaragua, Honduras, Chile and there was a lot of political strife in those countries. For some reason, we have this tendency as a country to support the wrong causes (I dare say we're the champions in that regard). No matter how good our original intentions were, in most of those countries we were on the wrong side of justice. And that caused a lot of spontaneous migration flows to the United States. Most of the families in flight were from El Salvador, Guatemala, and Honduras. Today we refer to those countries, collectively, as Northern Triangle countries.

So back in the day, civil wars, domestic violence, greed, and corruption caused mass migrations of people looking for a better and safer way of life. Most came to the United States hoping to win a grant of asylum protection. The Immigration and Nationality Act authorizes the Attorney General to grant asylum if an individual is unable or unwilling to return to his/her country of origin because he/she has suffered past persecution or has a well-founded fear of future persecution because of race, religion, nationality, membership in a particular social group, or political views.

Perhaps here would be a good place to explain the difference between asylum and refugee status. It's practically the same benefit, but with one crucial difference: to apply for asylum you must be inside the United States; whereas, to apply for refugee status, you must be outside of the country. And so, those people who were fleeing the Northern Triangle by the thousands were bound for the United States to seek a grant of asylum. Once they crossed the border they sought out the nearest border patrol agents, turned themselves in, and made an asylum request. That was the only legal option available to them. Their entry without inspection normally would have been a civil infraction but applying for asylum made it legal.

So, a situation had arisen where asylum-seekers were arriving by the thousands, and we didn't have anyone trained to provide asylum interviews. We just took immigration officers and told them, "Look, you're going to interview these people today from Honduras and from El Salvador." But the immigration officers knew nothing about the conditions in the countries from which the refugees were fleeing. They knew nothing about conducting asylum interviews, they knew nothing about testing stories for internal and external consistencies, and they knew nothing about how to write interview reports that would hold up under empirical scrutiny. They just weren't trained. Still, they were the ones denying asylum. It was a charade.

When Attorney General Edwin Meese asked me to join the Asylum Policy and Review unit, it was new. There was a great deal of discontentment in the United States about asylum. Even though America knew asylees were coming from war-torn countries, very few were winning grants of asylum. The Department of Justice was buried in a mountain of complaints questioning the quality and legality of asylum interviews. Attorney General Meese tried to defend the process, but he lost several major lawsuits, which caused him to set up the new unit. His back was to the wall, so he promised to not deport another asylum seeker until this new unit had thoroughly reviewed each case. Enter my job: the staff had to review each asylum case scheduled for deportation on behalf of the Attorney General and I had to certify that, in fact, the applicant had received a fair and legal interview and didn't qualify for a grant of asylum.

The sad truth of the matter was 90 percent of the cases we reviewed hadn't received a fair shot. Some received adequate interviews, but for most that fact was not discernible from a review of the record.

I was required to report these facts to the Attorney General, and I did. He asked me to take a look at what could be done to improve these applications. My immediate response was that we needed interviewers on board who knew what they were doing. I didn't know what I was doing when I started either. I picked it up as I went along. But because I was conducting case reviews day and night, I was becoming quite proficient.

Some of these applications were quite difficult to process. People had trouble revisiting times that were traumatic for them, times when they dealt with all manner of troubles, from deaths in the family to hunger, beatings, rapes, and arrests. You had to be somewhat sensitive and empathetic. So, in my report I recommended the creation of an Asylum Corps. I didn't hear much about it until I became INS Deputy Commissioner. I came to that job knowing an Asylum Corps was needed, so I created it.

We immediately moved to create a training facility in Artesia, New Mexico, where we started graduating classes of immigration officers specialized in asylum and refugee processing, refugee law, interview techniques, and country conditions. Seventy percent of the newly formed asylum corps were attorneys, so we had a good cadre of people who at least understood law. Enrollment wasn't restricted to attorneys; however, all applicants had to graduate from Artesia.

We also created a Resource Information Center in Washington, D.C. The Center was responsible for staying current on all countries that had refugee flows. Any Asylum Officer scheduled to interview refugees or asylees from anywhere in the world, could receive current country condition reports. That way, interviewing officers could put the interview into context. The Asylum staff told me the name for the Resource Information Center was selected so that the acronym could be RIC. It was referred to as the RIC. I was humbled.

My posting wasn't a permanent one. Once the complaints declined to a normal level, there was no need for the Attorney General to have a Deputy Director of Asylum Policy and Review unit. So, that job quickly disappeared. But before it did, it gave me quite a few stories.

One of these stories concerns a certain Indian mystic/guru named Bhagwan Shree Rajneesh (born Chandra Mohan Jain) who, in 1981, purchased a 65,000-acre ranch in Eastern Oregon, about eighteen miles Southeast of Antelope, and turned it into an Ashram or his religion's world headquarters. Once there, he accumulated a big following. People were donating a lot of money to him. The Bhagwan renamed his ranch "Rajneeshpuram," and he incorporated it as a city. This brought a boom of thousands of his followers to the area. His people were coming and going from that place in droves, which the 47 residents of Antelope and authorities didn't appreciate very much. At that point, the guru had something like 20 or 30 Rolls Royce's. I guess he irritated people.

There were many charges raised against him and his community. One that focused the Department of Justice's attention was that Bhagwan's commune was harboring persons in contravention of immigration law and persons who had drugs and weapons. So, the Department obtained a search warrant to find out exactly what was going on.

Normally, prior to operations of this type, the Department of Justice conducts closed-door meetings to assign areas of responsibility and specific duties for various aspects of the operation. For example, one responsibility was to be certain the commune was properly sealed off by controlling traffic flows on all roads in and out of the operational area. The Sheriff's office of Wasco County was contacted. In this particular case, as they suspected weapons were in the commune, they wanted the folks from Alcohol, Tobacco, and Firearms to secure the area before anyone else entered. When the area was physically secured, our immigration folks would enter to determine if immigration laws had been violated and to detain individuals, as necessary.

So, there we were, having our meeting and determining agency responsibilities for the operation. I was representing the Immigration Service. There's always a senior officer in charge of these events, and ours was in the process of briefing us. We were setting timetables, what people were going to do at what time, etc., when one of the attorneys in the room asked, almost jokingly, "Did anybody ask him if he'll surrender?" The senior officer quickly replied that yes, of course the guy had been asked to surrender. Then he paused and added, "We did ask him, didn't we?" The room went silent. The only thing we heard was our senior officer muttering, "Oh, damn it," before he stormed out. Half an hour later, he returned and informed us they'd contacted Bhagwan and his attorney. His attorney said he would indeed surrender in three days. Well, that averted a senseless disaster!

I say disaster because we've had several of these events that didn't end well. And they didn't end well because we didn't do our job well. That single question, "Did anybody ask him if he'll surrender?" kept us from going in there, guns blazing, and potentially losing or taking lives.

As it turned out, the guru tried to flee one day before he was supposed to surrender. But they had him staked out, so when his plane landed in South Carolina to refuel, he was taken into custody and subsequently deported to India. But that was one of those moments when something good comes out of something bad.

I was impressed by how easy it is to make a mistake. All it takes is not having seasoned people where and when you need them, people who have current experience in the task at hand. In a political sense, each time a new administration takes office, many of the old political hands are held over until the new appointees can come up to speed. When that doesn't happen, when the new administration strips itself of all experience, the stage is set for havoc. I believe this is what transpired when the "Waco siege" took place during the Bill Clinton administration. At that point, the Attorney General was brand new, all her assistants were brand new, and they had no experience in negotiating with people from a religious sect. They elected to ram the building. In the ensuing fire 76 people perished, among them 20 children. I offer that horrible incident only as a comparison to what happened in our case. We easily could have ended up with the same sort of disaster.

Another story that has stayed with me from my days as the Deputy Director of Asylum Policy and Review involved a Chinese doctor and his wife. This was, by far, one of the weirder cases I ever encountered.

The Chinese couple, both medical doctors, fled the People's Republic of China and came to the United States. As they were both Christians, they applied for asylum on the basis that they were denied freedom of religion. They were articulate and educated. They managed to make their case and were granted asylum in Baltimore, Maryland. But before the approval documents could be prepared, the doctor, of his own volition, sent an additional document to the immigration service telling us that he felt he needed to provide more information about his job as a medical doctor in mainland China.

In those days, the "one child" policy was in full force in China. Abortion clinics were in abundance! If the state discovered that you were a pregnant single woman or a married woman, but you were under 23 years of age and pregnant, you would be taken to an abortion clinic immediately. If you were found pregnant with a second child, you would be taken to an abortion clinic. A macabre side-effect of that law was that suddenly they had a plethora of aborted fetuses, which the government elected to use for medical research and that's where the doctor comes in.

He and his wife worked together. Their job was to visit the abortion clinics and collect these fetuses in a way that didn't affect their use for medical research. In his report, the doctor said that, often, these abortions took place so late during the pregnancy that the baby (or fetus, or whatever you want to call it), was alive! It was making noise, crying. In these cases, he said, they would fill a syringe with alcohol and shoot it into its brain which would end the crying. Then the doctor and his wife could collect the fetus for medical research.

The Baltimore District Director was appalled by this revelation. He called it murder. In his opinion, the doctor and his wife did not qualify for asylum. In fact, he tried to get them out of the country as quickly as he could.

The doctor appealed his case. His appeal reached my office in due course. His argument was that the fetuses were, for all intents and purposes, dead. There was no medical way they could have revived them. To not help those with signs of life would have been against the law. In any case, the doctor argued that his occupation was separate and distinct from the claim of religious persecution that garnered a grant of asylum for him and his wife. The work he and his wife were doing, while it may have been repugnant to us, was lawful government employment in China. He had broken no laws nor had he performed any abortions. I don't know what the right call would have been in this case. I still think about it, to this day.

All I could do back then was to make a recommendation about whether the applicant qualified for a grant of asylum. I tried to put aside passion, religion, and my own personal bias to come to a decision that could stand legal scrutiny, wouldn't be hypercritical, and would be in the best interest of both the individuals and our government. I may not have liked what he was doing, or ever imagine myself doing something similar, but his work was part of what was going on at the time in China. That is how things were. He may not have made things better, but he certainly didn't make things worse. So, I recommended that the asylum not be revoked. I then went to the Attorney General with my recommendation.

Well, it didn't take him very long to say no. It was more like a "Hell no!" The guy had to go.

That was one of those decisions I was glad I did not have the last word on. I have often wondered whether not granting this couple asylum was the right call. Did we send them back to China when we could have given them a better, more ethical and moral life here, or did we condemn them to a death sentence back home?

The 1986 Legalization Program

As it may have become clear from all this, I've worked in many different postings during President Reagan's administration. I liked to think I was moved about because of my ample management skills. Although, I can see how some of my colleagues mused about my ability to hold a job. All the moving about only made me appreciate the President more.

To Ricardo Inzunza
With best wishes, Ronald Reagan

President Reagan was from California (although born in Illinois, he moved to California to pursue acting and, later his political career). I am also from California, so I knew we had that in common.

Unfortunately, I was not a resident when he was the Governor of California, so, until 1986, I did not know we also shared similar views on immigration.

In 1986, President Reagan signed the Immigration Reform and Control Act (IRCA) into law. For me, that development was the genesis of my long fight to help people in immigration distress.

At the time, I was posted with the former Immigration and Naturalization Service (INS), as Special Assistant to the INS Commissioner. Later on, I was assigned to duty on the Legalization Implementation Team. My responsibilities included supervising, designing, testing, implementing, operating, and closing out the 1986 Legalization program which permitted more than eight million qualified individuals, living here without an immigration status, to apply for a grant of lawful permanent resident.

IRCA was a wide-ranging reform of immigration law, and one of its components was a legalization program. It was created to help the estimated 20 million long-term residents living here without an immigration status. Many of these individuals had been living here for years, most for more than two decades. So, the idea was to allow qualified program applicants to move from no immigration status to that of lawful permanent residents if they could meet the same conditions that any immigrant would have to meet, with the exception of their non-immigrant status. That way, they could continue contributing to society and doing the things all other Americans do; pay their taxes, etc. (Of course, they were already doing those things, but not formally and without receiving any credit for those actions).

The Legalization program operated for one year. During that time, we received eight million applications. Now, an application could be from one person, or it could be from a family of 10. We didn't count people, just applications. At the end of that year, we closed the program and worked on the "after-action report." In government, when a major program closes, you prepare reports which focus on the lessons that were learned. These reports provide feedback on what went right and what went wrong. Actually, the reports are really to inform anyone else who may conduct a similar program in the future. So, of the 8 million applications filed, 3.5 million were rejected. That is a 40-percent rejection rate! In the civilian world, if you miss the target you've set by 40-percent, you cannot possibly say that the program was a success. However, in government, you declare victory and move on.

During development of our lessons-learned report, the extraordinary failure rate was carefully studied. Three major reasons for the failure emerged: the applications were either incorrect, incomplete, or lacked the necessary supporting documents to sustain them. The burden of proof was solely on the applicants. They were required to prove their claims through a preponderance of the evidence. For example, if the applicant claimed to have been in the United States for three years without an immigration status, he had to prove that residence on a month-to-month basis for the entire time of his residence. By itself, the word of these applicants was insufficient to sustain their claim. They had to provide pertinent documents that would give rise to the belief that it was more likely than not that they were being truthful about their residence.

Qualifying was not easy. It never has been. Many applications lacked sufficient supporting documents. Applicants didn't understand the instructions, and filled out the forms incorrectly, or failed to submit them in a timely manner. Although they had a year to submit their application, many individuals waited until the last minute to do so. We received over a million applications in that last month. Most of those applications lacked sufficient supporting documentation and were rejected.

And so, those 3.5 million applicants lost the opportunity to become lawful permanent residents of the United States. Not because they didn't qualify! But because they didn't take the time and actions necessary to prepare applications that would meet with approval. There was no appeal from a rejection. Applicants only had one bite at the apple, and that was that. They were stuck, and the only option open to them was to be placed into deportation proceedings. Fortunately, as Deputy Commissioner of the Immigration service in 1987, I was in a position to know that unless they broke the law, few, if any, denied applicants were actually deported. For some reason it never became a high priority.

I don't, for one minute, think all the blame for the program failure lies with the applicants. Remember what I said earlier about experience? This was the nation's first major legalization program. We should have sought more seasoned advice. We should have known more about branding our product, more about anticipating problems, and more about developing rapport with the applicants. We didn't do any of those things. We really weren't proficient at doing our jobs. We were more concerned about budget and putting good furniture in the office than we were about getting as many applicants across the finish line as possible.

Once the program started, we were receiving 70,000 to 80,000 applications a month. It was an enormous number to absorb on top of the existing INS workload. In the programs final months, the number of applications exploded into the hundreds of thousands. We didn't know how to deal with it. The service had 90 offices around the United States and we hired all new people that didn't have any in-depth experience. Well, I think we've already seen how lack of experience can lead to disaster.

I'm not ashamed to say that, personally, I almost buckled.

You know, they talk about the perfect storm. This might have been the perfect immigration storm for a project that was doomed to fail. I could have accepted perhaps a five or 10-percent failure rate, but 40-percent was a bitter pill to swallow.

I took it personally. I had put a lot of myself into the Legalization Program, a lot of hope of helping people who had already suffered far too long. I try to think if there was another thing we could have done for this program. There was also a political factor that played a part. It was a legalization program, but the people who were against it renamed it "amnesty." That is a misnomer. Amnesty is when your sins are forgiven. For instance, we have tax amnesties in America. If you haven't paid your taxes, a criminal act, we allow you to apply for tax amnesty because we want you to pay your taxes. If you complete an application, we will forgive your debt if you promise not to get behind again. Now that is an amnesty. The legalization program, on the other hand, was not really an amnesty, since folks here without an immigration status, a civil infraction, had to meet very stringent and onerous conditions in order to qualify. They also were fined and many were incarcerated for long periods of time. However, those opposed to the program started calling it amnesty anyway, and that turned a lot of people against the program.

One interesting note here: lawyers prepared about 80-percent of the legalization applications for a fee. The government paid non-governmental organizations to assist applicants to complete and submit their legalization applications (I think they were paid something like $15 or $25 per assist). Catholic Charities, the national network of charities organized by the Catholic Church, prepared and filed applications for free. Surprisingly, the rejection rate for these application preparation services was the same for all three entities. You would have thought that the lawyers would have had the lowest failure rate and the people who were doing it for free the highest, right? But it didn't turn out that way. At least to me, that meant the problem was not that the bar was set too high. The problem was one of understanding the rules and requirements. That was confirmed by the after-action report.

Sometimes failures are more important than successes because they contain the power to motivate us. The 1986 Legalization Program ignited my life-long quest to make a difference, to help with immigration. This frame of mind followed me into my next government posting as the Deputy Commissioner of the INS and hasn't stopped fueling me since. "How could I have made this better?" has echoed in my mind to this day.

Under the Obama administration, I thought we were on the verge of inaugurating a second immigration legalization effort, but Congress hasn't been able to agree on the form such a program should take. So, it looks like I'll have to wait for my answer. Hopefully, when the answer comes, I, as well as many others, will get a second chance.

Chapter 12

DEPUTY COMMISSIONER OF THE INS

The year was 1988. George H. W. Bush had just won the Presidency.

Despite any personal feelings I may have harbored regarding the 1986 Legalization Program being a failure, my career in Washington, D.C. flourished under the Reagan administration. When Bush was elected President, I was carried over with the INS, only this time, as the Deputy Commissioner. I had overall responsibility for all of the agencies' day to day activities.

I was responsible for the actions (or inactions) of more than 40,000 immigration personnel world-wide.

I took the oath of office on my 51st birthday (every important thing in my life always seems to happen around my birthday in April), and I quickly realized two things. First, how familiar I was with most of the agency's activities, and secondly, how little I knew about the type of decisions that fell to "top line" executives. All the equal opportunity interviews when I was working for the Department of Defense, all those briefings about the available resource of people that we drew our staff from, my stint as the Deputy Director of the Asylum Policy and Review Unit (even though that posting didn't last long), everything that happened in my life to that point, prepared me for this position (having grown up in San Ysidro, California, helped too, with the border patrol chasing me and regularly seeing people coming across the border who were referred to by a number of pejorative terms, including Mexican). I understood the border and the "border mentality." Because there is a border mentality, Americans in San Ysidro had more in common with the folks in Tijuana than they did with the folks in Sacramento, and the folks in Tijuana had more in common with those in San Ysidro than with those in Mexico City.

My background helped me build compassion and empathy regarding the nature of the problem, and the people involved in it. I also believed that as a sovereign nation we had the right to decide who could enter the country, for what purpose, how long they could stay, and what could be done if people violated the conditions of their admittance. However, nothing in my life prepared me for the esoteric decisions immigration executives have to make almost daily.

Vatican Nuns, a Divine Intervention

As I mentioned previously, I entered on duty as Deputy Commissioner on my birthday. Well, after the "gripping and grinning" was over, I sat at my desk to admire my new office and to contemplate a pile of papers sitting right before me. Apparently, the recently departed Deputy left some work for me. I asked the secretary to brief me on what was required. She meticulously explained what was required for each document except one, which she held in her hand until the very last moment. When she completed briefing me on the other documents, she handed it to me and said, "This one has a short fuse. The recommendation must be in the Attorney General's office by COB (close of business) today." Representatives from the offices of General Counsel and Detention and Deportation were standing by waiting to brief me on the matter. She shot me a stern look that said, well, hop to it, buddy, and I heard myself say, "OK, show them in." Apparently, she wasn't over the departure of the previous deputy yet.

After introductions and a few congratulatory comments, I was briefed. This was not a new case. It was first brought in 1983 but had languished in the court system for years. The case involved a removal order against four Cloistered Nuns from a Carmelite Monastery in Maryland. It had significant political ramifications and had reached the Office of the Attorney General, who was waiting for a recommendation about the political wisdom of staying the deportation order. I was stunned. Why on earth would we be trying to deport cloistered nuns? What could they have done in the monastery to merit deportation? A joke about a laundry man going to the monastery to pick up the nuns' dirty habits pushed into my conscious mind. I did not think that would help in this case, so I kept it to myself.

The monastery's roots were embedded in Maryland history, dating back almost two hundred years. Nuns from Belgium established the Carmelite Monastery in Charles County, Maryland, on July 21, 1790. It was the first community of religious women in the thirteen original colonies and the first Carmelite Monastery in North America. The monastery housed eighteen nuns and two postulants (aspiring members), women ranging in age from thirty-three to ninety-three. In this particular monastery the majority of the nuns were in the older-age range. The nuns' ex-professions included dentistry, nursing, education, and law.

The Vatican dispatched four nuns to the Monastery of Baltimore when three of the cloistered nuns passed in quick succession. Their job was to help out temporarily until replacements could be recruited. The spiritual focus of the Monastery was prayer. The Vatican Nuns were admitted for 120 days. They were assigned rooms and detailed to housekeeping duties in the monastery. When they were reaching the end of their stay, it was apparent that replacements would not arrive in time. The monastery applied for an extension of the nuns' stay. They were interviewed at the Immigration and Naturalization Service (INS) District office in Baltimore. During the interview, one of the nuns was asked how much she was paid. She answered that she was not paid. Then she was asked how much rent she paid, and she answered that she did not pay rent.

At that point, the interviewing officer, who was new to the job, for reasons known only to God, concluded that even though the nuns were not compensated monetarily, the fact that they were provided free room and board constituted payment-in-kind. So, their service was viewed as compensated work. Therefore, the nuns were working without authorization. This violated the conditions of their stay, so he canceled their visas and placed them into deportation proceedings. They were released on their own recognizance after posting appearance bonds and returned to the monastery. Besides being new to the assignment, the officer must have been some type of disgruntled atheist. The case had implications beyond the monastery, and the Vatican mounted a vigorous defense. As it turns out, many nuns posted here are foreigners who provide their service without compensation.

Over the years the case turned into a political football. At various times Republicans ran with it and at other times Democrats picked the case up and ran with it. Now, there was no place left to run. All this time the nuns remained at the Monastery. They became the replacements since other nuns could not be posted here until the work issue was resolved. Both parties were weary of the case and were looking for some type of divine intervention.

Growing up I was taught you must always protect your mother (in my case foster mother), nuns, the church (Catholic of course), the Vatican, the Pope, and my younger siblings. If I understood the briefing correctly, the government was trying to remove 4 Catholic nuns, sent here from the Vatican, for temporarily helping other nuns with housekeeping duties in a cloistered environment, while the Vatican tried to recruit replacements for the nuns who died. Our recommendation to the Attorney General was due by close of business, which in this case was 3 hours. I was torn. The government was trying to hurt one of my protected classes.

In 1989, Immigration Judges were assigned to the Executive Office of Immigration Review (EOIR), which was part of the Department of Justice and reported to the Attorney General. EOIR ordered the nuns deported. The only person who could save them this late in the game was the Attorney General. When I was briefed, I decided that the AG was looking for a way to help, but he needed political cover. Our recommendation had to put him in the most favorable light possible. In those days there was no set policy on who could revoke visas or place individuals into deportation proceedings. In some offices the authority was delegated down to the interviewing officer level. In others, it was not delegated below the supervisory level. In others, authority was not delegated below the District Director level.

Our recommendation was for the Attorney General to establish a standardized policy for visa cancellation cases wherein authority to revoke a visa could not be delegated below the District Director level. In so doing, a "de novo" review of the decision would be in order. This would stay the deportation order. We also recommended that INS be required to send the Attorney General a report, within 60 days ensuring that all relevant adjudication policy was compliant with the new directive. Finally, I assured the Attorney General that I would personally oversee implementation of the policy directive.

As a result, after a "de novo" review, the nun's visas were re-instated and extended. Further, the record reflected that the sisters did not accrue "unlawful presence" in the United States. This would permit things to return to normal, the Vatican could win, the nuns could win, the Attorney General could win, but most importantly, America could win.

I brought empathy, understanding, and all the lessons I had learned with me to my new posting, but apparently there was a side of immigration the public didn't often see. Here is another example.

A Nigerian in an Iron Lung

A few months into the job, I received a call from the District Director of the Dallas INS office seeking guidance on a sensitive issue. He had received a disturbing call from the Administrator of the Baylor University Hospital. The Administrator alleged that the hospital had a long-term Nigerian patient who did not have an immigration status and they wanted INS to move against him. I said, "You don't need my help for this, what's up?" He said, "You don't know the full story yet." The patient, a former medical student, was struck by an indigent driver in 1982, which left him a quadriplegic. He had to be maintained in an iron lung at all times. As inhumane as it may appear, the hospital board believed it unfair for Texas taxpayers to continue to foot the bill for the poor man. They wanted him out of the hospital. The District Director asked me what he should do. I told him to sit tight. I would get back to him.

I tasked the Associate Commissioner for Adjudications to come up with a plan. When we intend to deport anyone, we must obtain a travel document from the receiving country or we cannot proceed. The receiving country has to recognize the deportee as its own citizen before issuing a travel document. The adjudications branch called the Embassy of Nigeria to report the situation. The embassy accepted the fact that the student was, indeed, Nigerian, and they would receive him. However, they would need a bit of time to round up an iron lung. We agreed to put them in contact with Baylor Hospital to resolve that matter and to arrange for international aeromedical air transportation. I thought to myself, "Well done."

Adjudications determined that we were obligated to put the individual into deportation proceedings since his student visa had expired years earlier. The student found pro bono legal services which argued before the immigration judge that deportation amounted to a death sentence. He needed more time with rehabilitative services to see if he could attend to his own bodily functions.

Representatives from the hospital insisted he was never going to improve. The student's attorney argued that he required a stable and reliable source of power for his iron lung. The Niger River provided the hydropower to the student's hometown. But according to the student, even though the Niger is the longest river in Nigeria, it was a very unreliable source of hydropower. A representative for the

Nigerian government refuted that argument. He stated Nigeria possessed a power grid fully capable of constantly powering an iron lung.

The immigration judge ordered that the student be deported. The Baylor hospital was notified and indicated they would help brief the Nigerian medical team that would attend to the student's medical regimen and accompany him on his return to Nigeria. Baylor provided a list of supplies and equipment the receiving hospital would require. The embassy of Nigeria was notified so that a travel document could be issued for the student. The embassy was asked to provide particulars for the medical team that would accompany the student so visas could be prepared. All was in order. Problem solved right?

A week before the student was scheduled to be airlifted, the Nigerian Embassy called to notify me that they would be unable to provide a medical team, an air ambulance or an iron lung for the student. If we could provide those services and equipment they were still willing to receive their citizen. I told them to sit tight; I would get back to them. I notified Baylor. They did not think they could provide any of the support services or equipment required for the deportation. They ended the conversation by saying, "Deportation, in all of its manifestations, is a federal responsibility, but they would be glad to help us in any way possible."

Bill Clements, Texas Governor, wanted to resolve the problem quickly and discreetly, so he spoke to the Attorney General's Chief of Staff. Neither of them wanted to see the story in the "Washington Post." We fixed it. We bought the iron lung from Baylor, rented a medical team from Baylor to fly with the patient, borrowed an Air Force Air Ambulance, and off he went. We had to pull the expenses associated with this deportation from existing budgets. I was tempted to follow up to see how the student faired, but I was anxious about finding out.

When She Wakes Call Us

While I am talking about hospitals, here is another case that didn't go so well.

A middle-aged tourist from South Korea was visiting family in San Francisco in the early 1980s when she suffered a massive stroke. She ended up in UCSF Medical Center alive but in a persistent vegetative state. She had been in this state for over five years. The hospital called the District Director for the San Francisco INS office to report that the woman had over-stayed her visa and we needed to come fetch her. After due and thoughtful consideration, we decided to place her in deportation proceedings. We contacted the South Korean Consulate in San Francisco to fill them in on what we were doing with one of their citizens. They didn't object to the fact that she was in a coma. After an extended legal process, she was ordered removed from the country. We informed the Consulate so it could issue a travel document for the woman.

The Consular staff was quite courteous and helpful. They prepared the travel document, and when it was done said, "Now, the only thing remaining is to interview her to be certain she is not being returned to Korea against her will. Korean law requires it." Our staff said, "She is in a coma. You know, a coma where they can't speak." The Consular officer said, "Oh, OK. When she wakes call, and we will interview her. Without the interview there is nothing more we can do." When I left the administration, three years on, the woman was still in a coma, still in San Francisco, and still without an immigration status. You can't win them all.

On Breaking Glass Ceilings

I was the first Hispanic Deputy Commissioner, and from the get-go, it was obvious I was up against a "we versus them" mentality. This became crystal clear when I received my first border patrol briefing.

I believe the majority of management problems vexing field units are failures of leadership. After I was sworn in, I wanted to determine the health of the units under my command. So, I recalled all "Delegations of Authority" (DOA) issued by my office to field units. Each Director was tasked to personally provide me with a comprehensive briefing detailing the mission essential activities completed during the 6-month period prior to my arrival and the actions the Director contemplated completing during the first 6-months under my command. Additionally, the briefings were required to include the state of the unit's budget and a review of the unit's Equal Opportunity program.

If I was satisfied that the Director was up to par, I re-issued the DOA. If I believed leadership was sub-par, I would point out what I detected as a shortfall and provide the Director 90 days to get his or her unit in shape. During this probationary period Director's continued in charge. If they were able to whip the unit into shape, the DOA was restored in full force. If not, the Director would be replaced.

Not all Directors cleared the bar. It was against this backdrop that the Chief Patrol Agent of the Border Patrol briefed me. He cut a very soldierly figure in his border patrol uniform. He was a tall man and knew how to make himself appear even taller. I remember he opened his briefing by announcing he would provide me with a report on the status of illegal aliens in the United States. Then he went on to pepper his presentation with references to "those people," "their kind," and other references I viewed as border-line pejorative. He was not the first Director to brief me, so I had to believe the other Directors told him what to expect. Nonetheless, he came straight at me.

A portion of his briefing highlighted the fact that 70 percent of border patrol officers were Mexican American. This is not odd, considering it was the only job in the former Immigration and Naturalization Service where Spanish fluency was a condition of employment. What was odd, though, was the fact that all of our Hispanic border patrol officers were in the lower-pay grades. The border patrol was divided into 30 sectors, each with its own Border Patrol Chief and Deputy Chief, and there was not one Hispanic Border Patrol Chief. Never had been one, either! I asked if that seemed normal.

The answer I received was that these people are not interested in being Chiefs. They were happy being in Deputy positions. I seriously doubted the veracity of this statement because I knew over half of the sectors were staffed by highly regarded Hispanic Deputy Chiefs. When the Chief Patrol Agent concluded his briefing, I thanked him and gave him a 90-day conditional pass on his management based on several problems related to his budgeting.

I knew the answer to my concern and I also knew that a Hispanic Deputy Commissioner raising concern about Hispanics would be viewed with a jaundiced eye, especially when it was not coming from the field. I discussed my concern with our General Counsel and our Assistant Commissioner for Management. I asked them this question: after struggling so hard to get to Deputy positions, why would someone quit there? Why would they forgo a shot at Chief? Although the specific concern I raised was about Hispanic agents, there had never been an African American or Woman Border Patrol Chief either. The truth of the matter was that Hispanics had a proverbial glass ceiling too. They were convinced that applying for a Border Patrol Chief Position would be a waste of time. They knew they would never be selected. I was advised to tread cautiously. The General Counsel warned me that although the Chief was a career government employee, he had strong political connections. A "shoot out" at the OK Corral may not sit well with the President.

As luck would have it, an opening for a Border Patrol Chief came up unexpectedly. The promotion system works this way. Jobs are posted, interested applicants apply and the office of personnel compiles the applications and ensures applicants are fully qualified for the position. Then, a board meets and rates and short-lists five applicants in rank order. When the applicants were scrubbed down, vetted, rank-ordered, and ready to go, the promotion list was sent to my office for the candidates to be scheduled for interviews. Sadly, when the promotion list reached my office there wasn't a single Hispanic name on the list.

I called the Border Patrol Chief to my office to ask him if he had seen the list. He indicated he had, since he chaired the promotion board. I asked if he was comfortable with the process. He said he was. I expressed my concern that there were no Hispanics on the list. I asked again, "Is there any particular reason for this?" He seemed a bit irritated by my question and recited his previous narrative: Hispanics did not want to go higher. As I had been forewarned, I knew I was skating on thin ice politically for what I was about to ask the Chief to do, but I did it anyway.

I asked him, as a personal favor to take the list back to be absolutely certain there was not a single Hispanic Deputy Chief interested in moving to the top of the profession.

A few days later the Chief returned the list. Still there were no Hispanic candidates listed. He said, "I could not find anyone." I am certain he believed since I was Hispanic, I would select a Hispanic. If qualified candidates were on the list I might have.

At that point, I went ahead and interviewed the candidates and picked the one I thought was best suited. They were all qualified, so it wasn't as though I could make a bad call, but the issue still bothered me. I called the Chief back to my office and informed him that I wanted him to implement an "up or out" policy for the Border Patrol Deputy Chiefs. If there were individuals sitting in Deputy positions who had no desire to move up, they were standing in the way of someone who did. I said, "These are not lifetime positions. Either the incumbents try to move up, or I want you to move them out. They can retire or move to a lesser position."

The Chief looked shocked. He asked if I was serious. I assured him I was. These folks were not doing us any good if they behaved as if they were retired while on active duty. So, I wanted them out of those billets. I asked him to have an implementation plan on my desk in a week to initiate the new program.

As it happened, two months later, another Border Patrol Chief retired. The list of five applicants was sent to my office, a list that featured three Hispanic names that were rank ordered by personnel as one, two, and three. I was elated. I selected the number-one-ranked candidate. My secretary remarked sardonically, "Wow, how did this happen? I thought these people were happy as second-class agents?" Of course, I knew how it happened. The word was out that there was a real possibility of a promotion this time, so naturally they went for it.

Believing that a group of people, any group of people, has "naturally" less ambition (or less anything, for that matter) just because you have rigged the system against them, is propagating systemic racism.

In the system that existed previously, officers knew aspiring to further upward mobility was futile. The system had convinced them, up to that point, that it could not be trusted to be unbiased. For all intents and purposes, they knew this was the end of the road for their careers. Psychologically, they had thrown in the towel. The applicant I ultimately picked was a second-in-command, a Marine, Vietnam Vet and a Purple Heart, and Bronze Star recipient. When he retired, he ran and was elected to Congress. Once upon a time he showed his respect by calling me Commissioner; I ended up showing my respect by calling him Congressman.

But it goes to show that glass ceilings can and should be broken. It not only hurts individuals, but it deprives the organization of the best qualified leadership it deserves.

As expected, the talk whispered around the water cooler was that the Deputy Commissioner was a "Hispanic lover." (Actually, it had a nice ring to it.) By selecting a Hispanic, I validated the idea some had about me, and I was okay with that. I had to prime the pump, but once I did, the personnel system worked its magic. The personnel system, not me, screened, qualified, and sent the Deputy Commissioner a rank-ordered list of five candidates. I selected the candidate the personnel system said was the best qualified. I truly felt like I was doing what was best for the organization and for the affected personnel. On a personal level, I felt good because there is never a bad time to do the right thing.

Another reason folks might have thought less of me was because of what I did regarding the Chief of the Border Patrol. When his 90-day probationary period lapsed, he was not up to par and I didn't reinstate his authority. As a consequence, he decided to retire. There was a political intervention on the Chief's behalf, but fortunately the White House stood behind me. The Chief's staff threw a real nice retirement party for him and even asked me to preside over the retirement ceremony. Of course, I did.

Another personnel issue that bothered me was how quick the Border Patrol was to remove agents who failed the Spanish Language exam. Since Spanish fluency was a prerequisite for all Border Patrol Agents, a year after graduation and deployment to the field they were re-administered the Spanish exam. If they failed, they were ousted from the Border Patrol. This was lunacy. We invested hundreds of thousands of dollars in the officers teaching them how to be good law enforcement officers. We entered them on duty and provided them with a year of practical experience. Then we dismissed them because they failed a test? It was like we were training them for other law enforcement agencies who, by the way, snapped them up. But certain politicians didn't want the policy to change, so I received a great deal of push-back and ultimately couldn't alter the situation.

On Working with Refugees

Of course, internal issues had to be balanced against the many other responsibilities of the Deputy Commissioner. One major responsibility was helping refugees and asylum seekers.

I attended a lot of refugee forums around the world. I met with the United Nations High Commissioner for Refugees who, at that time, was Mrs. Sadako Ogata from Japan. (She had assumed the reigns of command from Thorvald Stoltenberg from Norway.) As the U.S. Representative, I played a substantial role in the development of our refugee policy. At this particular time, thousands of

Vietnamese were trying to flee Vietnam. When they tried to land in countries that bordered the South China Sea (Brunei, Cambodia, China, Indonesia, Malaysia, the Philippines, Singapore, Taiwan and Thailand) they were not allowed to come ashore. Some were given fresh provisions and fuel, but in all cases, they were pushed back into the sea. Consequently, they were at the mercy of pirates and the elements. Thousands of Vietnamese drowned when their rickety boats sank, and hundreds were raped and murdered by pirates from Thailand. The United Nations High Commissioner for Refugees convened an emergency meeting in Geneva for the 32 refugee resettling countries in order to try to find a resolution for the emergency. The plan we devised was called the Comprehensive Plan of Action (CPA).

Under this plan, refugees would be permitted to land in Hong Kong and Thailand. There, they would be placed in one of nine refugee camps. Some of the camps were in hostile areas. Whenever I visited Khao-I-Dang, a camp on the Cambodia-Thailand border, a minesweeper went before us to be certain the Khmer Rouge had not mined the road. Once the Vietnamese refugees were in the camps, they could apply for refugee status in one of the countries accepting refugees from Indochina. Refugee officers from the resettling countries then traveled to the camps to administer refugee interviews. Those who qualified were granted refugee status and moved to the accepting countries. When the crisis ended and it was safe to do so, the CPA program called for the folks remaining in the camps to be returned to Vietnam. When the CPA ended in 1996, all refugee camps for Indochinese boat people were closed and the program ended. Unfortunately, by that time, it was estimated that more than 72,000 Vietnamese perished in the South China Sea.

Worldwide, we had a large operation that dealt with other refugees as well. I visited processing sites just outside of Rome and in Cambodia, Mexico, Vietnam, Costa Rica, Moscow, Russia, and Havana, Cuba. I spent six months in Guantanamo Bay, Cuba, personally overseeing the refugee processing of Haitians. I divided my time between processing refugees on the Coast Guard cutters, between Port-au-Prince, and Guantanamo Bay, Cuba. We also handled adoptions, fraud, and foreign intelligence operations from our overseas offices. During those times I needed to be out of the country on business travel, there was one thing I knew for certain: when I returned my desk would be piled high with stuff that required my attention. Fortunately, I always had Joan MacKenzie on my side.

To get things done domestically, I had to manage through other people, so most of my staff contact was through Assistant Commissioners, each of whom had distinct responsibilities. We met weekly for executive staff meetings. That is where I received timely feedback on current conditions within INS component units and where I was able to offer executive guidance where I thought it appropriate. Although I had other things to do, I found the meetings productive. I enjoyed my personal interactions with the staff and learning directly (and sometimes indirectly) about what was going on in the field in a timely manner.

I remember one of those meetings where I learned something indirectly. The meeting hadn't started yet because someone was running late, so we were marking time, sitting quietly, waiting for that person to appear. The refugee officers who, as I recall, were sitting to my right, were mumbling about something I couldn't hear, so, I asked them, jokingly, what was up. I could see that they were startled. They thought I'd heard what they were talking about, but

I hadn't. Here is what they were talking about. If you saw it in a movie, you would say it was too far-fetched.

It was about a Vietnamese woman stuck at Khao-I-Dang refugee camp. She originally lived in Vietnam with her husband and her three children: two daughters who were just old enough to walk (I assumed they were perhaps two to three years old) and a baby boy she recently delivered. In an effort to flee Communism, she and her family boarded a fishing boat with other Vietnamese families and set sail into the South China Sea. After two days, they were overtaken by two Thai pirate boats, and she became the sole survivor of one of the most gruesome incidents in the long, troubled history of the so-called Indochinese boat people.

In her refugee application, the woman wrote how the two pirate boats divided the women and children between them and left the men on the fishing boat, which they then sank. She watched the boat sinking slowly below the surface, taking her husband with it. The thing which stood out in her mind, according to her refugee application, was the silence, how there was no noise at all as the boat went under.

When the pirates were certain there were no survivors, they took off. The woman was stripped of her clothing and sexually assaulted. She then had to watch as the pirates tossed her daughters overboard. She watched her little girls sinking below the surface without making a sound, like the boat that carried her husband. The next day, after the pirates raped her yet again, they threw her overboard, still naked, along with her son. Her refugee application included a grisly description about how she kept herself and her son afloat by clinging to a bloated corpse floating in the ocean. At some point, she didn't know how long it was she felt her baby slipping from her grasp and sinking below the surface of the sea, also in silence. That horrible deafening silence. That's all she recalled.

She was rescued by a Thai fishing boat. Despite her debilitated state, she wouldn't come out of the water until they gave her something to cover her naked body. That's how traumatized she was. Long story short, this poor woman ended up in the Khao-I-Dang refugee camp. Because her only living relative was a sister who lived in Seattle, Washington, she applied for the U.S. refugee program. Well, her refugee application was denied. She appealed the denial, and her appeal was denied. Mrs. Ogata, the United Nations High Commissioner for Refugees, heard about the case and was so moved that she intervened personally. She asked the INS District Director, whose office was in Bangkok, to help. The INS Director was a stand up-officer that I'd hired for the job, but Mrs. Ogata's request to help this poor woman was denied as well.

And that's what these two refugee officers in our staff meeting were talking about.

Naturally, I was shocked. I asked, "Is this some kind of sick joke?" When they said no, I asked them to get the Bangkok District Director on the phone ASAP. They reminded me that it was 3 a.m. in Bangkok where he lived, but after that story, I didn't care about pleasantries. They woke him, got him on a conference line, and I joined in.

The first thing he said was, "I know why you're calling, Commissioner, but there's nothing we can do for this lady." When I asked him why, he explained that he personally reviewed the case and the things that happened to her in Vietnam didn't qualify for a grant of refugee status. He was certain of that fact. She was an economic migrant. Additionally, she was the victim of crimes committed on the high seas that had nothing to do with Vietnam. She was a "victim of violence." The Director said, "We don't have a policy for victims of violence." I was shocked and said, "Well, we do now. I want her on the next thing smoking out of Thailand." Then, I told the refugee officers to write a policy for victims of violence immediately, if not sooner and bring it to me. I read and approved the policy and sent it to Bangkok that very day. Once that happened, the woman was granted refugee status and was scheduled to move to Seattle. I hope she was somehow able to heal from her terrifying ordeal and start a new life with her sister.

The problem of people asking for refugee status because of a crime perpetrated on them was a new problem for us. It certainly was the first time I heard about it. After we implemented the "Victims of Violence" policy, I heard another (thankfully less tragic) story. Some refugees from the Cook Islands were robbed and beaten on the high seas and sought relief through our "Victims of Violence" program. I was asked how the case should be handled. I responded that "Victims of Violence" cases should be interviewed like all other cases: if the applicants met the standard, they qualified. If they did not, we should tell them exactly why their application failed. I was nervous for a long time that someone would push back against my new policy. I certainly would have lost a legal battle since I took so many shortcuts when I created it. However, if the opportunity to help came up again, I know what I would do. There is no right way to do the wrong thing.

My people were not thrilled about this new policy. They felt that I had expanded their workload, that I was making things tougher for us and better for people who did not deserve better treatment. I rejected that analysis. I really wanted to scream, "So how badly damaged do you think someone must be before they can qualify for a grant of refugee status or to be declared a victim of violence?"

Of course, I did not scream. I remember the first time I went to Havana to process refugees. I learned that, to qualify, Cubans had to have been convicted of a political crime and have served at least two years in prison before they could apply for our refugee program. Four months earlier I was in Moscow setting up refugee processing. To qualify there, you simply had to have a well-founded fear of political persecution to qualify. The difference between the two standards was glaring. Believe me, it did not take me long to right that wrong.

In my opinion, the whole point of the Deputy Commissioner's job was to interpret and enforce immigration law enacted by Congress in accordance with the tone set by the President. Fortunately, for America, President Bush wanted the law enforced compassionately, and, to the maximum extent possible, he wanted us to pursue a philosophy of inclusion, not exclusion. In many ways, I was lucky that the President had his hands full with more important matters, so he relied on my judgment to do the right thing. I was grateful. There were so many people in need of help. We could help them and they would only know that it was America that helped to lift them in their time of need.

In 1990, Congress officially created "Temporary Protected Status" (TPS). I say officially since we hadn't been deporting individuals to countries beset with ongoing armed conflicts, environmental disasters, or extraordinary and temporary conditions for years. TPS has been a lifeline to hundreds of thousands of individuals already in the United States when problems in their home countries made their departure or deportation untenable. The word "temporary" has a hollow ring to it these days since many of the TPS recipients have been here for more than 30 years. TPS was supposed to be a stop-gap measure which would keep these individuals out of harm's way until Congress passed comprehensive immigration reform legislation that would fix these problems. That hasn't happened yet.

President Trump canceled TPS for individuals from El Salvador, Honduras, and Guatemala. There are about 700,000 people holding TPS status in the United States. These people now have to leave. Add them to the existing millions here without an immigration status, and it just doesn't make sense. It costs about $11,000 per person to deport them. That means if we're talking about 11 million people, it adds up to more than $120 billion in taxpayer dollars. How wise is that? There are folks without a permanent immigration status that have lived here for decades. It's not like they arrived yesterday. They have developed equities and set roots in America. Their children are U.S. citizens, as are their grandchildren. They have become an indispensable segment of the workforce, they pay taxes, they own businesses and homes, and they hire American workers. Where is the advantage to our country if we deport them? For all intents and purposes, these are settled immigrants. It makes more sense to find a way to legitimize their status, as we tried to do with the 1986 Legalization program.

On Children in Custody

A very thorny issue for Border Patrol Officers, that I constantly wrestled with during my time as Deputy Commissioner was: do children ever present a flight risk?

Imagine this scenario, which unfortunately happened way too often. Border Patrol Officers come around a corner and see a man, a woman, and two children walking. When the people realize that a Border Patrol vehicle is behind them, they scatter. The man runs north and the woman runs south. Now, the officers are left with two frightened, non-English speaking children without identity documents. For the sake of this scenario, let's say one of the children is three and the other is five years old. How much of a threat to the nation can they pose? Yet, they are detained as if they were criminals.

When I came on board, the existing policy called for unaccompanied children to be housed in homeless shelters. Then the embassy of the children's country of origin, if it could be determined, had to be notified. The homeless have priority in the homeless shelters. If the shelters are full, or if the staff anticipates they will soon be full, the children cannot be placed there. They must be taken to a juvenile detention facility. By previous contractual agreement, these facilities were obligated to accept the children, but their rules had to be respected. Juvenile delinquents could not be mixed with non-delinquents. That's the law. The only way mixing could be avoided was to place the immigrant children in individual cells in solitary confinement. This was the maximum-security section of these facilities, and they had strict rules. When anyone, even three-year-old children, was placed there, they had to undergo full cavity searches. If anybody visited the children, such as attorneys, family, anybody, they had to undergo another full cavity search when the visitors left. Yes, really.

I was conducting a staff meeting when I learned about this policy. I was dumbfounded! We're talking about a five-year-old girl or a three-year-old boy undergoing full cavity searches, for what? What law had they broken? What threat did they pose? When I asked for the policy to be explained, the Border Patrol Chief said, "Commissioner, you must understand these are the rules of the facilities where the children are detained and as draconian as they may seem, we have no control over them. We're a federal immigration agency, and they are state penal institutions. As long as we use their facilities, we must abide by their rules." "I get that," I said, "but why are we using their facilities in the first place?" The answer given to me was that this was the policy approved by the previous Deputy Commissioner some years earlier.

Well, I understood we had to abide by contractual rules. But I also understood I was the new Deputy Commissioner and our personnel had to abide by my rules, and my rules did not involve placing children in any type of juvenile delinquent facility. With me as the motivator, and with eager assistance from Catholic Charities and the Border Patrol, within two weeks the children were no longer sent to juvenile facilities. They were sent to Catholic Churches where volunteer families were waiting to care for them until they could be reunited with their families. You know the old saying, "Where there's a will, there's a way." I certainly had the will, and Catholic Charities certainly knew the way.

Another situation which involved INS playing fast and loose with the rules, was clearly illuminated by a Russian woman working on a Russian container ship that docked in Anchorage, Alaska. The ship's crew was inspected by INS officers and she was allowed to come ashore on a "D" visa which is for crew members working on commercial vessels. The woman had two children, aged five and six, aboard the ship, but the children were not authorized to come ashore. Somehow, she was permitted to come down the gangplank with her two children. Once she was on the dock, she sought out the nearest policeman and told him she wanted to apply for asylum. In those days we didn't have asylum officers posted in Alaska, so the District Director tried to hustle asylum seekers back on the ship as quickly as possible. Of course, you can't do that; it's against the law. Regardless, the practice had been going on for years (giving people who'd requested asylum a sham interview). Officers would explain to asylum seekers why they didn't qualify for asylum and load them back on the ship and fast. Otherwise, once the ship sailed, the INS district would be responsible for the expenses associated with detaining the asylum seekers, in this case the woman and her children.

I couldn't allow them to continue violating our policy and skirting the law. I was adamant that the woman should receive a real asylum interview from an asylum officer as the law required. I informed the Director of my desire and he informed me that she had already failed the interview and was back on board. I ordered him to have her and her children removed from the ship. If the ship had sailed, I wanted to be informed immediately so I could notify the Coast Guard to stop the ship so that she and her children could be removed. Fortunately, the ship had not set sail. The woman and her children were brought ashore and placed in a hotel with a guard outside the door to their room. I dispatched an asylum officer from the Seattle Washington office to Anchorage to interview the family. The officer was due to arrive within 48 hours.

I suppose the Anchorage District Director decided to teach me a lesson. He had the family moved from the hotel to the local jail for budget reasons. Anchorage didn't have a juvenile detention facility, so they placed the children in jail. Of course, the jail couldn't mix children with the regular population, so they had to segregate the children. I had the family returned to the hotel, and I thought it was time for the District Director and I to meet. I directed him to come to Washington, D.C., to explain his understanding of the law to me. As I recall, the family did win a grant of asylum and the District Director decided it was time to retire.

I was learning how some of INS conducted its business. It was a bitter pill to swallow. I cannot believe that somebody, somewhere along the line, didn't say "This is wrong; you can't treat children that way." Nowhere in the world should children be treated like that but least of all in America! With the help of Catholic Charities and many constituency groups, we put a stop to the practice of detaining children in penal facilities. The impetus to change the child detention policy already existed outside of INS. We just needed to create the same desire inside the agency. Once that happened, everything fell into place quickly.

I don't know whether the people who succeeded me have revived this practice, but our current policy of 100% detention of everyone here without an immigration status doesn't exactly fill me with hope. It is just astounding to me that anybody who has any sort of compassion or Christian ethic would think it is OK to put children in solitary confinement. I mean, according to the law, you can't charge a child with a crime before they are old enough to form criminal intent. The age varies from state to state but it is usually around the age of nine or ten. Entering the country without inspection, (and this is important to understand), is a civil infraction, not a criminal offense. It is like getting a speeding ticket. Children were being detained and undergoing cavity searches and INS was saying, "Gosh isn't it awful, but what can we do, it's the children's fault. They shouldn't have come here." The problem was not with the law; the problem was with our "us versus them" morality.

If you look around today and pick the top three problems affecting the world, one of them is going to be immigration. The world is in turmoil: refugees everywhere, a hundred million refugees world-wide suffering from starvation, separation, deprivation, murder, battery, assault, and all manner of abuse. I feel extraordinarily blessed to have been in this field and to have done my small part to help some people at least.

I am hoping my story will help keep hope alive. Mine is the story of someone who did not speak English and felt as though he was not integrated, who kept trying to tell people he was somebody that he was not. I am sure that immigrants, refugees, asylees, TPS people, those holding deferred enforced departure orders, and those here on parole, all these different classes of people, have stories more profound than mine.

The fact that I had a chance to work in a top position which permitted me to make policies, to make rules to help these individuals, means a lot to me. Nobody will ever know how many were helped, and those will never know I had a hand in it, and that's as it should be. My goal was not fame. I just wanted to do what I felt was the right thing. Over the course of my life, I have learned there is no right way to do the wrong thing. When you are doing the wrong thing and know it, stop it!

Chapter 13

ONE LIFE AT A TIME

Having a job as important as that of the Deputy Commissioner means you'll have to take chances. And if you take chances, you're bound to make mistakes along the way. Things can't and won't always break your way. As I look back over my life, I think it's equally important to acknowledge the bad as it is to celebrate the good.

As I've mentioned before, working in the government meant that along with our job application, we also had to tender our undated resignation letter to complete White House clearance. At least that was the case during the Reagan and the George H. W. Bush administrations. The White House personnel wanted to make it abundantly clear that, if you were cleared for a political appointment, you served at the will of the President. Make no mistake about it: if the President wanted you out, all they had to do was date your resignation letter.

There were a few instances during my tenure as Deputy Commissioner when I thought my (yet undated) resignation letter would catch up with me.

Thankfully, it didn't.

"The Deputy Commissioner
Had a Scorched Earth Policy"

As early as 1988, the year I started working as the Deputy, I managed to get myself in trouble and gain an infamous reputation at the same time.

If you are not from the West, you may not have heard of the Bureau of Land Management (BLM). The BLM oversees 245 million acres of public lands for the American people and takes its responsibility quite seriously. The agency manages about 12 percent of the landmass of the United States. The land is primarily located in the western states, including Alaska, California, New Mexico, Wyoming and Arizona. In Arizona, the BLM manages 12.2 million acres of land, and most of it is on or near the border with Mexico. Back in the day, there was a lot of drug smuggling going on across BLM-managed property. Drug smugglers used pack mules (real ones, not humans), to bring drugs into the United States. So the INS, with permission from the BLM and in league with Marine reservists serving their 2 weeks of active duty, set up listening posts along well-known drug transit routes.

According to information contained in Marine Corps intelligence reports, smugglers were going to be entering the United States along a well-traveled route at a date and time certain. We wanted to be ready to interdict them. The Marine Reservists were there solely to provide technical support for the operation. They were armed, but they could only deploy their weapons in defensive actions or on orders from the ranking INS team member. At least, that was the plan.

There they were, U.S. Marines and border patrol officers, sitting in the darkness on the border near Nogales, Arizona waiting to spring their trap. Suddenly, the sound of mules clip-clopping filled the night air. The story gets a little murky at this point, but for some reason, the Marines were spooked. Although they were only supposed to act on instructions from the senior immigration officer, the lieutenant in charge of the Marines shouted, "Put up some light!"

To Marines, this means "launch an illuminator." They fired an M-127A1 White Star Flare, which emits 50,000 candlepower when deployed. When it reaches its maximum height, a parachute pops open which retards the flare's descent. Instantly, night turned to day and everyone was momentarily blinded. As the flare descended, everybody, including the mules, were silhouetted against the night sky. That is when the shooting started. As most of the team members were still trying to adjust their eyes to the glaring 50,000 candlepower of light, two mules died from multiple gunshot wounds, but no humans were lost or injured. One mule was taken alive. How the drug smugglers escaped was never clear.

But the story doesn't end there. As the illuminator descended, a cooling breeze kicked up blowing it into a wooded area next to the smuggling route, where it immediately set the forest on fire.

The damage was extensive; a couple thousand acres of prime, old growth timber burned that night, all due to a botched operation. Well, it did not take long for the word to spread within the immigration service that, "The Deputy Commissioner has a 'scorched earth' policy." Suffice it to say, the Bureau of Land Management did not appreciate our way of doing business either. I was invited to visit the office of Mr. Robert Burford, BLM Director at that time.

After introducing himself to me he went on to say, "I have been briefed on your misfortune. Do you have other calamities you would like to spring on us?" I assured Director Burford that further drug interdiction missions were not contemplated on BLM lands. Then, of course, I placed blame for the entire debacle at the feet of the United States Marine Corps. I was not feeling any love from Director Burford, so I don't think he bought my explanation. The upshot of the whole incident was that the immigration service was barred from conducting further operations on BLM lands. Apparently, the Director gave credence to the deceitful rumor circulating around Washington, D.C. that the Deputy Commissioner intended to leave no tree standing as part of his scorched earth policy. Of course, the story was false. I love trees.

The Nanny Deportation

Another close call that comes to mind involved the deportation of a governor's nanny.

The nanny was from El Salvador. She had applied for asylum and was in the midst of the adjudication process. As the governor and his family were not inclined to seek special favors, I doubt anybody in the Miami asylum office knew the nanny case was working its way through the asylum process. My staff and I certainly didn't. When the process was completed, the immigration judge denied her asylum application and issued a deportation order, which the immigration court provided to INS for execution.

Perhaps we should take a moment here to explain how the deportation process actually works. Many believe the Department of Homeland Security has the power to deport someone on its own authority. Well, that's not the case. Homeland Security can only deport someone who has been issued an order of deportation by an immigration judge. If immigration officials determine that anyone they encounter is in the country without a valid immigration status the only option available to them is to ask the individual if they will voluntarily leave the country. If the person agrees to depart, they must do so at their own expense. In such cases, they are normally detained until they can arrange secure transportation for their departure. The advantage of voluntary departure, over deportation is, if the individuals force the U.S. Government to deport them, at government expense, they are barred from re-entry for 10 years. After that period of time has passed the chances of those individuals receiving a non-immigrant visa to the United States will be manifestly more difficult. Deported individuals are viewed as intending immigrants, as such, they are ineligible to receive non-immigrant visas.

In more difficult, long-term resident cases, the judge may offer voluntary departure in lieu of deportation. The judge might say, "I've heard your claim and the government's and you don't have a legal right to remain here. I also note that you are a long-term resident. If I permit you to voluntarily depart so that you will have time to put your affairs in order, will you leave when you're supposed to?" If you answer yes, the judge will issue a voluntary departure order with a deportation order attached. It is strictly the individual's responsibility to send the Immigration Service proof, from outside the country that he or she departed in a timely manner. If they fail to do so, the deportation order and the 10-year bar will take effect. If the individual hasn't departed, then and only then, armed with a properly executed order of deportation, will the Immigration Service have the authority to deport the person.

While individuals and families wait to make immigration court appearances, the Immigration Service has three options: they can detain you in an immigration detention facility, they can release you with some type of monitoring device, or they can release you on your own recognizance. Currently, the administration has elected to utilize 100 percent detention.

Deportation, not many people realize, is a wildly expensive endeavor. If you do not exit the United States on a voluntary departure order on time, the government has to locate you and then deport you. It also has to execute deportation orders. Last year, immigration judges issued 187,000 removal orders. In the grand scheme of things, the cost of putting deportees on a plane, often with immigration escorts, and sending them home is, in actuality, not that expensive. It's keeping individuals locked up that costs money, about $100,000 a year to detain one person! On top of that, the government must pay for sending that person home as well. When it comes to detaining children, it usually costs about $800 a day per person. Currently DHS detains 100% of the children which come into their custody which means that, on any given day, taxpayers are shelling out around $40,000,000 in unnecessary detention costs. Perhaps this puts these matters into perspective for people who are quick to spout things like "detain them" or "lock them up." I am fond of asking, "How much detention do you think America can afford?"

But let's get back to the governor.

The deportation order for the nanny was issued to the local asylum office and they turned it over to the Detention and Deportation Unit. Responsible for executing the deportation order were two young female Detention and Deportation Officers who, while new to immigration, were well-trained and knew what the law obligated them to do. So they drove to the governor's mansion at three o'clock in the morning intending to pick up the nanny. Of course, they were stopped by the governor's security detail. They explained that they were federal immigration officers executing a deportation order. The guards knew nothing about the pick-up, but after looking at the deport order, they allowed them to pass through to the governor's mansion.

When the officers knocked on the door the governor's wife answered. Because she was born in Mexico and had dual citizenship, the incident must have been quite scary for her. She called her husband downstairs to deal with the situation. Once the governor understood what was happening, he permitted the officers to execute the order without interference. The nanny was transported directly to the airport and permitted to return to her country of origin without immigration escorts. However, once aboard, the aircraft was surveilled until it lifted off on a non-stop flight to Central America.

When I came to work that morning, I had a message from the Director of the Asylum office that "The nanny was on a plane heading home." Well, that's odd, I thought. What nanny? And why would I care? When I returned the call to the asylum office and spoke to the Director, I got my answer to both these questions along with a healthy dose of dread.

See, the governor was someone very dear to the President of the United States. Normally, cases requiring special attention were directed to me personally, but for some reason that did not happen in this instance. The family could have easily complained to the White House that their nanny was being deported, and my job could very well have been on the line. So, I called the White House immediately, explained the gaffe, and asked if they wanted me to turn the plane around. I should not have been surprised by the answer. The President felt things had gone according to the letter of the law. Since the nanny had her day in court and did not qualify to stay in the United States, she had to be deported and that was that.

President George H. W. Bush, along with his whole family and the people who were near and dear to him (like that governor), was never one to bend the rules or to seek any special treatment. A true class act, that man!

President George H. W. Bush, me, and Barbara Bush, Washington DC, 1991.

But that was another one of those situations when the end of my career flashed before my eyes. Not that I would have broken the law to keep the nanny in the United States if I had known about it earlier. But I could have looked at the application to see if there was anything within the scope of the law that could be done to help.

It was not often that I felt unable to act during my time as Deputy Commissioner. Perhaps that is why I remember every single life I wasn't able to help or at least make better.

The Hypocrisy Regarding Some Russian Soldiers

Another instance, although not a personal failure or mistake of mine, has stayed with me because it made me aware, once again, in the words of Frank Zappa, "We are a nation of laws, poorly written and randomly applied."

Prior to the fall of the Iron Curtain, our last ambassador to the Soviet Union was a man by the name of Malcolm Toon. He asked to visit my office in Washington, D.C. which took me by surprise. Ambassador Toon was the chairman of a committee commissioned by the State Department at the behest of the former Soviet Union. The Russians were angered because too many of their soldiers were missing in action in the Afghan War. Their whereabouts could not be determined. Ambassador Toon's committee was tasked to see if they could make a connection in the United States which might help them locate the missing soldiers. So, he came to see us.

I assembled some of the adjudication officers that would handle any claims of that type, and we listened as the ambassador explained the issue. While he was talking, out of the corner of my eye, I noticed one of my officers looking worried, uncomfortable even. I had no idea why, but something told me I had to find out. So, I excused myself and asked that officer to join me in my office (which had an entrance to the conference room we were using). There, I asked the officer what seemed to be the matter. He said he recalled resettling Russian soldiers from Afghanistan some years ago.

Armed with that knowledge, we returned to the meeting and I assured the ambassador we would do everything we could to help. We would comb our files to see if we could find any information. Ambassador Toon thanked us and left.

After seeing him off, I rejoined my officers in the meeting. As it turned out, there were about 380 Russian soldiers who had either defected during the Soviet-Afghan war or collaborated with the Americans and the Afghans who didn't want to return to Russia. So, these individuals were relocated to the United States under a special visa program. I took this information to the INS Commissioner, and he and I went to inform Attorney General Barr. He thanked us for the briefing and asked us to sit tight. The AG then went to the White House to seek guidance on the matter. Several weeks later, he summoned the Commissioner and me to his office to tell us that after due and thoughtful consideration, we were to say nothing about the matter.

Initially, this did not sit well with me. I pointed out that the United States had a big MIA program and that we frequently accuse people of not telling us about our soldiers that are missing in action. But the position of the White House was that this is America. The individuals in question were fully able to contact their families or their government if they so chose. The fact that they hadn't made the effort meant they wanted their whereabouts to be kept private. And it certainly isn't the function of the U.S. Government to disclose the whereabouts of private individuals against their will.

So, the issue ended there. And while I felt uncomfortable with the decision, I could fully understand the logic underpinning it. This was truly a Hobson's choice. There was no good answer. Take it or leave it. Armed with all the facts, I believe I would have reached the same conclusion.

The Olympian Who Asked for Asylum

Which brings me to the next case that's stuck with me, one where I personally explored what it feels like to employ double standards and find myself in somewhat of a gray area.

First, I need to talk a bit about "parole" and the different meanings it has. In the penal system, parole is when you release someone from prison before their sentence is up (for good behavior or a variety of other reasons). In immigration, however, "parole" is a process where you allow individuals to enter the country without a visa for humanitarian reasons. For example, a family emergency requires a family member to come to the United States as quickly as humanly possible. Under appropriate circumstances, a humanitarian parole can be issued in a matter of hours. Although it permits you to enter without a visa, a parole offers no long-term immigration benefits. Many people don't know about this distinction, so when they hear the word "parole" uttered in an immigration context, it's easy for them to think we're talking about criminals. We're not.

With that in mind, here is the rest of this story.

In 1989, the Romanian gymnast and Olympic gold medalist, Nadia Comăneci, defected and asked for protection in the United States. Comăneci was in Rome and had gone to the U.S. Embassy to ask for protection. The embassy called the Department of Justice, and, since it was after normal duty hours, the call was forwarded to me. I remember I was having dinner at the "Prime Rib" restaurant on K Street in Washington, D.C., when the call came in alerting me that Nadia Comăneci had defected. I immediately went to my office to get on a secure, encrypted phone. I was patched through to the embassy, and the staff there filled me in on the details of the defection. I believed Ms. Comăneci's life was in immediate danger, so I approved a humanitarian parole, which permitted her to be moved at once.

In those days, there were many refugees in Rome waiting for admission to the United States (mostly Armenian Jews who were living in a refugee camp just outside of the city), but I made the decision to advance Ms. Comăneci over others who felt their cases were equally meritorious. Those applicants had a large constituency group in New York who wanted my head on a stake when they heard about it. I was in a lot of hot water, but, fortunately, the President supported my decision. The question was, of course, what made Nadia Comăneci more deserving than other refugees, all the people who were waiting in line? In defense of my position, after I listened to the full classified briefing, I felt her situation was extremely urgent. She had defected and the government of Romania was hell-bent on getting her returned. Did I exhibit a double standard in this case? I hope not. I believe I made the right call under the circumstances.

Years later, I was at an Immigration conference when an attorney (who was trying to help some people coming from India) wanted to talk with me. He mentioned he worked mostly with athletes, helping them to secure "P" visas. I found that interesting, so I told him that the only person related to sports I had been able to help was Nadia Comăneci, back when she'd defected. The lawyer looked at me and said, "Oh, so you're the guy, huh?" Laughingly, I responded, "yes." Apparently, I was "the guy," but I was not sure what he meant by that. It turned out that the attorney knew Nadia. She had told him that "some guy" had helped her come into the United States, and she never met him. I told him that if he ever saw her again, he should give her my regards. I believe she lives in the Great Lakes area now where she and her husband have a training camp for future Olympians.

It may be a recurring theme in this book by now, but it's one of my cornerstone beliefs that there is no right way to do the wrong thing and that when you're doing the wrong thing, 99.9 percent of the time you know it. So stop it! I've always stood by my inner moral compass. At the end of the day, helping Nadia Comăneci to start a new life, was the right thing to do. I wish more people would try it.

The Marriage Fraud of an Indian Man

Another case that seemed weird at first but ultimately felt good was one of the first cases I worked on.

Marriage fraud has been a big deal in the immigration business for decades because it is so easy to cheat. With any kind of fraud, we only catch the ones who are not good at it, who are not good liars. Every interview starts from this position. The burden of proof is solely on the applicants. We assume they are not telling us the truth, so, with a preponderance of the evidence, they must convince our officers that they are being truthful. Over the years we have improved our techniques. When someone tells us a story, they're either believable or not. If they're not, we'll test their story for internal or external consistency and then arrive at a judgment. If we believe the story, we'll grant the applicants the benefit they seek. If we don't believe it, we normally send the applicants a letter of Intent to Deny. They then have 30 days to overcome our objection. If they can't, we are bound by law to deny the application. If we are stuck on the fence, my policy was to try to find a way within the law to approve the application. If we couldn't, we denied the application.

Some cases are difficult because they don't lend themselves to an easy solution. The case I am about to relate, is one of those.

There was a student from India whose father and uncle already lived in the United States (both held American citizenship). The young man entered as a student, but his relatives wanted him to stay after graduation. Obviously, he accepted his family's offer to "handle the matter for him." In the finest Indian tradition, he listened to his elders, particularly his father, whose solution was to find a bride for him. After all, this was the easiest way to cheat the system. They made some inquiries and found a woman who, for $5,000, agreed to marry the young man. His uncle and father were pleased and arranged for the young man to meet his intended bride. The deal to marry was sealed.

The Indian family was not familiar with American marriage practices, so the bride agreed to find a justice of the peace to marry them. The Justice performed the ceremony, and they paid him the usual fee. The next thing was to submit their application to the Immigration service. So, with the help of the bride, they filled out the application and sent it in. While they waited for an interview date, the couple rehearsed their story. Surprisingly, the young man and his "wife-for-hire" received an interview date rather quickly.

During marriage interviews, we normally start by sitting the couple down to explain what is about to happen. The interviewing officers will remove their coats so you can see their guns and badges. They will then focus a video camera on the couple. What they're trying to do is intimidate the applicants, make them nervous; not for sadistic purposes, but because some people don't lie well when they get nervous. Then, they split the couple up to interview them separately. When things started, what the Indian family didn't know was that the woman was not a "wife-for-hire" at all. She was an undercover Immigration officer and so was the justice of the peace. As soon as the young man signed the application in front of the immigration officer and went through the part that says, "I swear that everything here is true to the best of my knowledge under penalty of perjury," he was practically doomed.

The young man was taken into custody on the spot. INS wanted to charge him with criminal fraud, a felony, before putting him before the immigration judge on the civil deportation charge. As the case had received a lot of political attention, I had been watching it closely. Every morning, I was provided with a listing of all INS adverse actions which took place or were underway the previous day. INS was out to make an example out of this young man, and I was being asked to sanction it. But my inner voice was cautioning me against it.

The way I saw it, the young man was a victim. He was basically set up. The socialization process he grew up with would not permit him to go against his parents' wishes, and if we're being fair, his parents should be the ones in custody, not him. We were visiting the sins of the parents on the son. His future was about to be ruined, so I decided against the criminal charge. I didn't think the government would gain anything from a criminal proceeding that we couldn't get in a deportation proceeding. I saw it as a waste of resources and time. I asked our attorneys to meet with the immigration court.

The immigration judge issued an order of deportation but also permitted the young man to voluntarily depart the country. The Immigration Service had flagged his record with the marriage fraud, which meant he couldn't enter the United States as an immigrant or non-immigrant without a waiver. After the young man exited the country, we readmitted him on a humanitarian parole. He was in his first year of college, which permitted him to complete his education, but he derived no immigration benefit from his time in the United States. When he finished school, he would not be able to work, and would have no incentive to stay. Once he left the country, for any reason, his parole would expire, and he could not return.

I've always felt good about that decision. I hope justice was served.

The young man was not out of the woods but at least the light at the end of the tunnel was not a train about to crash into him. I like to think that, somewhere along the line, he met a woman he actually wanted to marry. Perhaps they could build a better life here, although that would require an understanding immigration authority to issue him a waiver.

The Great Debt of Gratitude

Mrs. Leone, my foster mother, kept hammering into me that I owed America a great debt of gratitude because the foster system of this country took me in when I needed help. They gave me shelter when I needed shelter; they paid Mrs. Leone and other foster mothers to take care of my brother, my sister, and me. "You owe this country a lot," she would tell me in Spanish whenever she had a chance. That has always stuck with me. I joined the military with the mindset, that I owe this country not only allegiance but also a great debt of gratitude. I have spent most of my adult life trying to repay that debt.

In my life, my feelings toward service, be it military or civilian, has always been that it's something you do for your country, as a way to give back. That's also the mindset I had when I served in the position of Deputy Commissioner.

All in all, failures and tough calls and moral gray areas aside, I feel like we did a good job. If I could make a list of all the people who received green cards through a policy of inclusion instead of exclusion (all the people who were taken out of harm's way through TPS, refugee and asylum status; all the families kept intact through bonding out of detention; and all the people paroled into the country), I believe that number would be pretty substantial. Of course, these poor souls will never know I was helpful. They will only know that they caught a break in America. That's how it should be. President Reagan was fond of saying, "You would be surprised how many good deeds can be done when no one is interested in taking credit for them."

And that's okay. I don't need the credit. I recall myself, as I recall them, one life at a time.

Ricardo Inzunza
Deputy Commissioner
1990 - 1993
U.S. Immigration and
Naturalization Service.

Part III

THE LAND OF SECOND CHANCES

Chapter 14

A DECLARATION OF INDEPENDENCE

On November 2, 1992, Democratic candidate Bill Clinton won the presidential election. On January 20, 1993, he was administered the oath of office and became the 42nd President of the United States. As the administration changed hands, Republican political appointees were rapidly replaced with Democratic appointees. Suddenly we found ourselves on the outside looking in.

As the former governor of Arkansas, I thought President Clinton was a savvy and experienced sort of guy but dumping all the capable and experienced Republican appointees without allowing any overlap while the incoming Democratic appointees learned the ropes may not have been his best move. I attribute the haste to the fact that it had been almost 20 years since the Democrats were last in power. Unfortunately, it didn't take long for this error in judgment to manifest itself.

On February 28, 1993, federal law enforcement agents came face-to-face with the Branch Davidians, a controversial group whose followers described themselves as "students of the Bible." About 130 of them lived in Mount Carmel Center Ranch, an 80-acre compound just outside Waco, Texas. The Bureau of Alcohol, Tobacco, and Firearms (ATF) suspected the group of stockpiling illegal weapons and obtained a search warrant for the compound and arrest warrants for the group's leader, David Koresh, and a select few of the group's members. The ATF raid was botched and a standoff ensued. The standoff between federal agents and the Branch Davidians lasted for 51 days and dominated news headlines for months. The eventual siege left 76 people (including children) dead and changed the way many Americans felt about the federal government. Critics uniformly called what happened at Waco a massacre that resulted from lack of experience within the Department of Justice. I often say they were a bit too quick to drive all the angels out of heaven.

Certainly, we weren't angels. And if you've made it this far in the book, you already know I'm not shying away from my mistakes and failures either. But, after four years in the Deputy Commissioner's seat and eight years in the Reagan administration, the change in administrations still came as a stark reminder of the transient nature of political appointments. Given my circumstances, I felt it was time for me to become an independent business consultant instead of a political consultant. I was surprised, then, at how many people wanted to hire me. Despite being internally aware of its importance, I never knew there was such an external aura attached to having been the Deputy Commissioner of the Immigration and Naturalization Service.

So from 1993, I have had the chance to consult for the World Bank and the Millennium Challenge Corporation in most of Sub-Saharan Africa, South America and Asia. I also accompanied several congressional delegations to the People's Republic of China and consulted for The Great Wall and Jia Ming Groups in Beijing and Young Brothers Aviation in Hong Kong.

It was nice to see I could still help people, albeit in a different capacity. I was familiar with how immigration operated inside of government but I really had no idea how it was perceived in the outside world. Private sector consulting provided me with a vivid wake-up call. Moving around the world as a private consultant, I was surprised to see how little people knew about immigration and how much of what they believed they knew was wrong. Worst of all, I was painfully ignorant about how difficult the government made the external immigration process for everyone! Trying to help people standing outside of the system to get in had its unique challenges.

As always, I collected some interesting stories along the way.

It is Not All Chinese to Us

For years, whenever I was introduced as the former Deputy Commissioner of the INS, people seemed impressed. I don't know, maybe they were just being polite. But these introductions opened up new pathways for me.

Soon after I stopped working for the government, several friends invited me to the People's Republic of China (PRC), where I was able to meet many interesting people. I ended up consulting with private businessmen as well as some government entities.

After spending so many years working for the U.S. Government, being a business consultant in another country was certainly an unusual experience, especially in a place like China that wasn't considered a close friend to the United States. In those days, when you uttered the word "Taiwan" in Congress, people would cheer and get giddy. When you said, "People's Republic of China," they would boo and hiss "the communists." That was the prevailing sentiment. But I always felt that things couldn't be so black or white.

When an opportunity to share my thoughts with some members of the Chinese Ministry of Foreign Affairs came my way, and I was pleased to learn that they shared my feelings about the imbalance in governmental sentiment. In fact, they asked me to see if I could help arrange for congressional delegations to visit the PRC.

In short order, we successfully brought a CoDel (congressional delegations; both the government and the military sure love their acronyms) to China. Others followed.

It was interesting to see how nervous members of the CoDels were. They worried about what they would be permitted to say, and what they would be allowed to do and who they could speak to in China. In a way, they were wearing the same bias-colored glasses I was wearing on my first deployment to Southeast Asia. I knew I wasn't going to like Asians before I actually had a chance to meet any. But now I knew better, so I tried to explain to members of the CoDels that China wasn't as different as they imagined it to be. Of course, you were not permitted to enter military reservations or other restricted areas without prior approval, but that's true in most of the developed world. And there are probably places where taking pictures isn't permitted. But overall, you can talk to anyone you want to talk to, and you can move about the country freely. As in all cases, your behavior must be tempered with good judgment.

During our trips to the PRC, we had meetings with the mayors of the cities we visited. When we were in Beijing, we had meetings with the appropriate ministers of the committees the Congressmen and Congresswomen sat on, so they could exchange views and ideas. When we returned to the States, every member of these CoDels (and I mean every single one of them), expressed their surprise at discovering China wasn't quite like public sentiment led them to believe it was. They realized the point of view they were exposed to was rather biased.

I believed that the next time an issue came before Congress involving the PRC, it wouldn't get an automatic "boo, hiss, snarl" or a knee-jerk turn down from members of the CoDel. At the end of the day, they might still vote against the proposition, but I felt confident they would cast their vote after filtering it through their revised view of China.

During my work in the PRC, I enjoyed the opportunity to meet many Chinese individuals and families who sought my assistance in trying to understand American immigration policy. I mentioned earlier that my work as an independent consultant provided me with a giant immigration wake-up call, and China played a big part in that. I thought the non-immigrant visa process was professionally managed and transparent. Most importantly, I thought I understood it. Boy, was I ever wrong!

I remember one well-to-do businessman who came to see me in Beijing. His business had flourished in China, and he wanted to expand it to the United States. He applied for a non-immigrant visa so he could explore potential locations for his business. His visa was denied. Believing the embassy made a mistake, he re-applied and was denied again. When we met, he asked me what he was doing wrong, so I reviewed his application and could see that he was more than qualified for a business visa. When I asked him if he knew of any reason why his eligibility would be in question, he said, "No." I agreed to visit the embassy on his behalf to inquire about his case.

At the embassy, I met with the Chief of the Non-Immigrant Visa Section. After introducing myself, I told him that I had carefully reviewed the application and I couldn't understand why the businessman's visa was denied. I asked, "What don't I understand about this case?" The Chief quickly advised me that, two years prior to applying for the visa, the applicant was involved in an automobile accident that resulted in a fatality. He was found to be at fault in the accident but failed to disclose that fact in his application. The Embassy assumed he did not mention the accident because he thought it would disqualify him. In their opinion, he was concealing a material fact, which was grounds for visa denial. The Chief was beaming as he finished his explanation. I said, "Boy is my face red." I thanked him for the insight and departed the embassy with my tail between my legs.

When I met with the applicant again to report my findings, I was a bit out of sorts because I believed he had not been honest with me. When I asked him again if he knew of any reason why his visa should be denied, he again said, "No." Then I sprang my trap. I asked him if he recalled the man who was killed in the accident where he was found at fault, and he nonchalantly said, "Yes." He said it as if it was the most normal thing in the world. I knew then that I was missing something, so I asked, "Why didn't you declare that fact on your visa application?" He responded, "Why should I? That account was settled long ago."

What I didn't know was that in China, if you are involved in a fatal accident where no crime is charged (DUI, hit and run, fleeing a crime scene, etc.), the accident is managed as a civil, not a criminal matter. If you are found at fault, you must meet with the family of the deceased and arrange a financial settlement. When that is done, the case is closed. So the applicant was not concealing a material fact. He was simply not required to detail civil infractions on his application. Since neither the embassy nor I knew about that law and how the culture surrounding it worked in China, I met with the embassy again and explained what I learned. The visa was issued.

The take-away from this example is that consular personnel don't exchange "lessons learned" very well. I can't believe this was the first instance of a visa being denied for this reason.

On another occasion, a mother came to see me about a student visa for her 16-year-old daughter. A math prodigy, her daughter had received a graduate degree in physics, with honors, from Tsinghua University in Beijing. This is the most prestigious research university in China. She then applied to Stanford University to complete her PhD. As Stanford is a private research university with extremely high academic standards, only five percent of applications are accepted. Well, not only did Stanford accept her, but they also offered her a full research scholarship. She and her family were delighted. Because of her age, the girl's mother decided she would buy a home in Stanford, California, to live with her daughter while she was in school. The father was a high-ranking government official who owned a successful company that manufactured guidance systems for all Chinese Long March Rockets. The plan was for the daughter to take over the business when she received her doctoral degree and acquired the necessary experience. All was in order. The mother and daughter applied for their visas at the consulate in Guangzhou, China.

The mother's visa was approved but the daughter's was denied. The family was shocked. By any measure, the family qualified for their visas. Unlike visa denials by Homeland Security in the US, visas denied by the Department of State overseas do not provide a reason for the denial, nor can the denial be appealed. After debriefing the family, I agreed to make an inquiry on their behalf at the Guangzhou Consulate. The Visa Chief had the officer who interviewed the mother and daughter in his office waiting for me. The officer told me he denied the daughter because she was a single

Chinese woman who would, in all likelihood, not return to China after graduation. He said Chinese women had an extremely high over-stay rate. The officer indicated that he understood that the mother was applying for the visa so she could care for her daughter. He approved her visa because he didn't have a reason for denying it.

When applying for a non-immigrant visa, by law the applicant is presumed to be an intending immigrant and, therefore, not entitled to a visa. It's up to the applicant, through a preponderance of the evidence, to convince the interviewing officer that she intends to return to China. The daughter's application had more than enough evidence to support an approval. I asked the interviewing officer what led him to conclude that the sixteen-year-old was not going to return to her life in China. The officer became defensive and refused to discuss the case further. His denial stood. By law, the officer's decision cannot be overturned, not even by the President, unless the officer didn't properly weigh the evidence, didn't consider all the evidence, or made an error in applying the law.

I asked the Visa Chief if he would speak to his officer about the case, but he refused. He said he needed to support his officer. By then, I was frustrated and determined to right this wrong. I flew to Beijing to speak to the Deputy Chief of Mission. Like me, in my previous position, he was responsible for the actions of all consulates in China. After we reviewed the facts of the case, he agreed with me and called the Guangzhou Consulate to hear their side of the story. By that time, their position had softened considerably, and they quickly agreed to re-interview the daughter. This time they approved the visa.

I cite these two examples from China to make a larger point.

Immigration has many facets and many rules. The truth is that not everyone who wants a visa will get it. The government operates a vast and complex immigration system where many things can go wrong because no appeal can come from a consular denial. When I started private sector consulting, I was in the dark. I didn't realize that the State Department's visa issuing apparatus was still in the Stone Age. Since a consular decision cannot be appealed, the State Department operates with impunity. I encountered substantial and significant problems with immigrant and non-immigrant visa cases, adoption cases, refugee cases, marriage fraud cases, fiancé visa cases, and citizenship cases, to name a few. Much work needs to be done in these areas. Individuals seeking redress in immigration cases overseas have no collective voice, so they have no collective recourse.

In an effort to alleviate the problem, a few years ago we started conducting immigration classes for Chinese attorneys. We didn't think it was necessary for American lawyers to come to China to work those cases. Once Chinese attorneys understood the requirements of the Immigrant and Nationality Act, they would be fully capable of providing the help necessary. The classes usually consisted of 100 to 150 participants. We taught these classes in most of China's provinces. They were well received.

Nonetheless, there remains a great deal of work to be done.

Around the World for the World Bank

My next consulting job was with the World Bank. The World Bank is an international organization that is part of the United Nations system. It provides financing, advice, and research to developing nations to aid their economic advancement. The bank predominantly acts as an organization that attempts to fight poverty by offering developmental assistance to middle- and low-income countries.

Here's how the World Bank operates, in a nutshell. When a country requests a loan for a particular project, bank staff reviews the project application. If the World Bank thinks the application has merit, it sends a team of bank consultants to the requesting country to inspect the project. The consulting teams are composed of experts from each of the project's disciplines. Their job is to identify potential pitfalls that may hinder or cause it to fail. Members of the consulting team are required to prepare a report articulating their findings and recommendations. These reports are then compiled into a trip report for bank officials. If the consultants believed the project has merit, they would so indicate in their reports, as well as report any and all impediments they observed requiring remedial attention.

In my travels as a consultant for the Bank, I was sent to review the immigration and customs systems of many developing countries that requested bank loans. My job was to see specifically if there was anything in those systems that might impair or impede the success of the projects. For example, if the project required heavy machinery to be imported, would existing customs policies and procedures hamper or preclude the machinery from clearing customs? I had to be certain that existing import and export policies wouldn't negatively impact the project. Or, if expertise or technology (in the form of consultants) was required to support the project, I had to be sure the consultants and their families could clear immigration.

Even though many of the countries were poor, they did a great job of picking the projects and preparing the loan packages. Most of the projects dealt with infrastructure development or agribusiness creation. The defective element of most loan applications, however, was the customs and immigration component, so I would screen the projects and meet with the immigration and customs officials in each of the countries. It never ceased to amaze me how little project managers knew about the relationship between their projects and immigration and customs. It was also quite surprising to see how much overt (and covert) bias and opportunity for corruption was built into the loan applications.

One loan application riddled with opportunity for corruption came from Mozambique.

To give some context, Mozambique gained independence from Portugal in 1975, but it continues to suffer from the effects of a sixteen-year civil war that ended in 1992. Before the war ended, most of the country's infrastructure was destroyed. Tensions remain between the Frelimo Party and the former rebel movement Renamo Party that assumed power in 2014. Corruption, in all its manifestations, is a major concern. It was felt that the discovery of gas fields off Mozambique's coast in 2011 would transform the economy of one of Africa's poorest nations. The country has enjoyed meager economic growth, but more than half of Mozambique's 24 million people continue to live below the poverty line.

Back then, Mozambique requested a loan for a critical gas-fired power generation project the country desperately needed, so the bank dispatched us to qualify the project. I was in full agreement that the project carried a great sense of urgency; however, customs corruption was rampant countrywide. The size and scope of the project pointed toward substantial importation of heavy machinery, all the equipment that would ultimately generate the electrical power. The brain power to build, train and operate the equipment had to be imported as well. I feared customs corruption would cause the project to fail.

I could only see one way to recommend project approval. All of the customs personnel had to be replaced. All of them! The World Bank conditioned loan approval on a "buy in" for this drastic remedy. Initially, the Prime Minister was reluctant to agree. However, as the possibility of a bank loan began to fade, he dismissed all of the customs personnel. Of course, he was roundly criticized for this move. In conjunction with the housecleaning, the Prime Minister brought in a replacement consulting company from England, called Crown Agents. Their task was to temporarily replace dismissed customs agents and interview, hire, and train all new customs personnel. Once the new customs agents were ready, they would replace Crown Agents personnel and assume Mozambique's customs duties and responsibilities. To put the level of corruption that existed prior to the dramatic fix into context, within a month of the Crown Agents assuming responsibility for collecting fees, the customs income of the country increased by 300 percent. And it kept going up.

This corruption was not abstract or invisible. It didn't even have the decency to hide, as I experienced with my own eyes.

I still remember when I went to talk to the Customs Port Director in Maputo, the capital of Mozambique. When he learned that we were from Washington, D.C., he mentioned that his daughter was going to Georgetown Law School. Naturally, that started me thinking: how in the heck did he get the money to send his daughter there? As if to answer my question, during our meeting, a man showed up and wanted to talk to the Director urgently. The Port Director excused himself and stepped away but remained within our line of sight. He talked for a few minutes with the man who, eventually, reached into his pocket and took out something to give to the Director. I assumed it was money. Then the Director came back to us and continued our conversation as if nothing untoward (or even unusual) had happened.

As is the case in most countries, in Mozambique products requiring special inspections or fees in bond are held until they receive customs clearance. This means the fees have been paid. Apparently, the guy who approached the Director needed his product quickly for some reason or other. The Director told us that the guy "needed help getting his product cleared." And then he went on to attend to other matters. All the while, I was sitting there thinking that we just witnessed a pay-off and it was being treated as if it was the most natural thing in the world. Until the Crown Agents came on the scene, it was. That exchange also answered my question of how the Director could afford to send his daughter to Georgetown Law School, where tuition isn't cheap.

The upshot was that the project came in under budget and ahead of schedule, thanks to the new money the government was receiving. The Prime Minister, who was once reviled for his wholesale firing of the customs agents, was hailed as a financial wizard.

There is another case I recall vividly, mostly because it's part and parcel of today's immigration reality. I was consulting in Alexandria, Egypt, when I was approached by an American woman from Texas. The woman was in Egypt looking for help with her immigration problem and was referred to me by my client. Her case was unique because it had no legal remedy. When the woman was married to an Iraqi medical doctor in the United States she gave birth to a daughter. But around the time the daughter was 5 years old the relationship began to fray. The couple separated and later divorced. The mother was awarded sole custody of the child, and the father was permitted to have supervised weekend visits. Sometime after the divorce, the father decided to return to Iraq. However, he was determined to take his daughter with him when he departed.

Using subterfuge, the father managed to apply for and obtain a passport for his daughter without the mother's knowledge or consent. When he was ready to return to Iraq, he picked his daughter up for her weekend visit and went directly to the airport where they boarded a flight to Ramadi. By virtue of citizenship laws in Iraq, the daughter was a dual citizen. She was a full-blown Iraqi citizen and entitled to the full protection from the government of Iraq. She was also an American citizen.

Once the mother learned of the devious scheme, she was devastated. She had been struggling for more than a year trying to find a way to have her daughter returned, but the American government indicated their hands were tied. Her daughter was a citizen of Iraq and legally with her father in Ramadi. Case closed. Mother locked out.

I explained to the mother that this was an all-too-common problem. It had been going on for years without resolution. In her particular case, she had no travel document for the daughter. If she had had a valid passport, I explained, she would still need a way to get the child out of Iraq and onto a return flight to the United States. If she managed to do so, she would then have to ask the State Department to flag the daughter's passport so that the daughter would not be able to use it to travel without the mother's express consent. The mother's shoulders slumped, and she began to sob.

Even though I had seen these situations in the past, I was so moved by her passion and determination that I offered to help her formulate a plan. I was due to return to Washington, D.C. in a few days and she was bound for Texas, so we agreed to meet in Washington in two weeks. To keep her mind occupied, I provided her with a list of documents and items we would need. Meanwhile, I made some phone calls. When we met in Washington, I told her we needed to report her daughter's passport lost and apply for a new one. But we had to do it on a weekend and under emergency conditions. I had a friend who worked in passport services, and he was on weekend stand-by duty by himself. We went to see him on Saturday morning, filled out the necessary documents for the new passport, and filed a report to cancel the old passport. This gave him cover. (I had briefed him, so he knew exactly what we were attempting to do.) He issued us a new passport by Saturday afternoon and wished us luck.

I then told the mother that I had friends who provided the kind of rescue services needed here. On Monday we traveled to Columbia, South Carolina, to meet with the team which had already sketched out a rescue plan. Members of the team would go to Ramadi to outline the daughter's behavior pattern. The mother would travel to Ramadi in ten days. By then, the rescue team would know where to make the intercept and what the dispersal route would be.

The mother agreed with all this and arrived in Ramadi as planned. The team had already mapped out the route and the times of the school bus that picked the daughter up every day. They were ready to act. The bus traveled a route along a fairly isolated two-lane road, so they picked a section of the road where they could intercept the bus without arousing attention. They already knew that the daughter sat in the same window seat each day. When the bus was stopped and the team was boarding to make the intercept, the mother knocked vigorously on the bus window to let the daughter see her (so she would not be afraid). The daughter was removed from the bus without resistance, and the team drove north toward the nearest border crossing point which was on the route to Aleppo, Syria. This was a smoke screen. Ten minutes into the drive, the team switched modes of transportation. They moved the mother and daughter, who were now covered from head to toe in their hijabs, into an old truck and headed East toward Amman, Jordan. The hot vehicle was followed closely by a cover car, while the original vehicle continued on the road to Aleppo. On the way to the border crossing point into Jordan, they passed the bus. It was still stopped and surrounded by police cars.

The border crossing into Jordan was uneventful. The drive to Amman took the better part of seven hours. The team delivered the mother and daughter directly to the U.S. Embassy in Amman, where the mother asked for safe passage to the United States. They were then driven to the airport by embassy staff and U.S. Marine guards. On the flight home, mother and daughter slept soundly in each other's embrace. I'm happy to report that the daughter is now in her first year of college.

This particular story may have had a happy ending, but it is a story that is replicated far too often (and not always with such a positive outcome). Congress needs to come up with a way to extradite violators of custodial orders and return of kidnapped children.

Unfinished Business in the Land of Second Chances

When I was on Air Force deployments, I always loved meeting different people and learning about different cultures. I tend to like people no matter where I go. And those people and cultures that struck me as odd or clashed with my personal values, I've learned to accept and try to understand as a part of the cultural framework within which they exist.

No corrupt Customs Director, for instance, ever exists in a vacuum. Someone taught him it's okay, or even necessary for his survival, to behave in such manner. I've always tried to keep that in mind before I judge anyone from my not-so-high horse.

Regardless of the things I encountered while working with the World Bank, and even though my consulting assignments kept me on the move, a different sense of unease started creeping up on me. I never felt as though I'd done all I could with the 1986 Legalization program. I always yearned for a do-over. A second chance to help people acquire a documented status, to officially become the new Americans they had already spent years being.

So soon after becoming an independent consultant, I started working towards bringing a legalization program like the one contained in the 1986 Immigration Reform and Control Act (only better) to the attention of White House administrations. I haven't stopped since. And, hopefully, my efforts will bear fruit soon.

Chapter 15

A SECOND CHANCE TO HELP

I think I've made it crystal clear throughout this book that my true passion in life was always within immigration, with helping people get a second chance in life (like the second chance I was given when, as a juvenile delinquent, I was asked if I wanted to serve time or serve my country). For me, immigration is truly a personal matter. How could it not be?

I spent the majority of my childhood on both sides of the American Mexican border. I lived in San Ysidro, California a city marinated in immigration, home to the largest immigration port of entry in the world. It was also the largest entry point for spontaneous migrants. A large portion of San Ysidro's population were merchants who catered to cross-border Mexican customers. Another sizable group were employees of the Immigration Service who earned their living inspecting, detaining or removing Mexicans from the United States. I experienced almost daily examples of the heartbreak of immigration gone wrong and the boundless joy of immigration gone right. Because I was bi-lingual I was frequently asked to interpret immigration documents received by individuals anxiously hoping for grants of some immigration benefit. Sadly, in far too many cases I had to deliver the devastating news that applications had been denied.

In my early teen years I had a summer job working in Tijuana, Baja California at the Agua Caliente racetrack, as a stable hand. In those days, I was small enough to think I could be a jockey. I was painfully disabused of this notion after being thrown several times while exercising various mounts. While at Agua Caliente, I met plenty of young Mexicans who were planning to slip into the country. They wanted me to put the finishing touches on their decisions to immigrate by reinforcing their beliefs about the wonders of life in America. Of course, I did it because it made me feel important, but the warm fuzzies came with a price. It amplified the fact that I was not accepted by them as a real Mexican and I did not feel like I was a real American either. That sucked. I was a "Pocho!" a term used by Mexicans, frequently pejoratively, to describe Mexican Americans. We were in between the American and Mexican cultures; ergo, we were neither.

That being said, this program I've worked my whole life towards (in some capacity or other) was never just about me. It wasn't born in a vacuum. It was about the people, the passionate people who wanted to help make the world a better place. I couldn't have done it without them.

So I feel I should use this chapter to walk you through the different iterations of the RIA project I have been involved with for many years now. In that way, I can tip my cap to the people who helped me along the way and are still helping me to this day.

The Year Was 1977

I was living in Portland, Oregon. The first version of this project was CRIA, "Children with Rights in America," the program I started in order to join the fray for full civil and educational rights for children residing in America without an immigration status.

For me, the impetus for creating CRIA was a response to the 1977 attempt by the Tyler, Texas Independent School District (TISD) to oust the children of non-immigrated workers (farmhands, for the most part) from the school system. They did that by imposing tuition of as much as $1,000 per student to attend public schools.

Tyler ISD based its move on legislation passed by Texas lawmakers in 1975 that required the state to withhold funds to school districts that enrolled non-immigrated students. Vilma Martinez, MALDEF (Mexican American Legal Defense and Education Fund) President and General Counsel, sued in September 1977. While a federal court quickly granted a motion to block Tyler ISD from denying enrollment based on immigration status, the case underwent numerous appeals. It took four more years to reach the Supreme Court as *Plyler v. Doe*.

I knew the matter was far from resolution in 1977 and the outcome in the Supreme Court was uncertain. I felt I needed to do whatever I could to help. CRIA was going to be our vehicle for lending our voice to MALDEF's cause.

Joining me in CRIA was a professor at Portland State University, Beatriz Ortiz. Originally from Mexico, Beatriz got her U.S. citizenship after marrying her husband, whom she'd met when she was a student. When I made her acquaintance, she was teaching urban planning and shared my passion for immigration and for the "Dreamer" children who would be adversely impacted by an unfavorable *Plyler v. Doe* decision. She volunteered to help the CRIA group because she believed our cause was just. We were accompanied by another professor, David Gonzalez, who was from El Paso, Texas.

I feel that I have to make a segue here to explain what it means for someone to be from a place like El Paso, Texas, and how it affects one's worldview (as it did David's). Texas is such an immense state!

And when we're talking about El Paso, well, that's all the way down to the border. New Mexico, Mexico, and Texas converge in El Paso. It's such a weird feeling to fly there. You almost think you've been kidnapped. All you see when you look out the airplane window is sand. Then, all of a sudden, you land in this airport where, because it's so close to the border, everything is as much Hispanic and Mexican as it is English and American. And that's the case with any border town on our southern border.

Take San Ysidro, California, for example. When you leave San Ysidro to cross the border into Mexico the town you enter is Tijuana, Baja California. When you cross the border from Tijuana you enter San Ysidro, California. Well, I can tell you from personal experience, San Ysidro has more in common with Tijuana than it has with, say, Sacramento. Similarly, Tijuana has more in common with San Ysidro than it does with Mexico City.

Border towns in general have more in common with each other than they do with their own capitals, at least when it comes to the lives of the families living there. Many families are split by the international boundary, with different members living on both sides of the border. All too often, when there's a death, wedding, graduation, promotion, birthday, or birth in a particular family, and other family members or friends of the families need to cross the border to attend these events, it creates immigration problems. People who are originally from border towns, like David and me, understand that borders in real life tend to be more fluid (and arbitrary) than most people think.

All this to say, David had a lot of experience with immigration and immigrants, and a desire to help. He himself had two children, "There but for the grace of God go I," as he used to say. David was also a volunteer in CRIA.

When we started writing our business plan and outlining our vision, I knew the most urgent and immediate issue we were going to tackle was *Plyler v. Doe*. It was prominently covered in all the local newspapers. I knew we had to help raise awareness nationally about the plight of these children. Because our small group had unanimity of opinion, we had a lot of fun kicking ideas around and writing op-ed articles which we sent to newspapers around the country. I call it "fun" to highlight the thrill of the process, not to downplay the gravity of the matter.

I realized back in 1977 how much I liked working in a group environment doing things I felt made a positive difference. I know some people prefer to work alone, but I've always enjoyed a good group dynamic. I find it stimulating when I'm working with others and start throwing ideas around. One single idea can trigger 10 new thoughts in your head and then your response can trigger 10 thoughts into others, and that's how you get going. At least that's how I get going. If I sit by a computer by myself, my mind wanders a lot of the time, and I'm not as effective as I would like to be.

I think our first year with CRIA we operated on a very tight budget, not bigger than $50,000 ($20,000 of which was my own seed money). We operated out of our basement, where I had to put some desks and set some phones. But looking back, even that makeshift headquarters was exciting. In any endeavor, making the decision to leap into the abyss is the hard part. You hem and haw, you wonder about this and that, but once you decide yes or no it doesn't matter because your mind is free to move forward and engage. So when we were setting up that office, I really felt a sense of accomplishment. The motor had started. We were rolling.

All this was happening at a very trying time for me on a personal level. I'd just bought my then father-in-law's pest control company;

I was facing problems with my marriage and I was told about my health issue. Overall, I was discovering that I was a good business manager. I liked what I was doing in the pest control company, but my heart was never in it. It was just a means to an end, to support my family. As I look back now, all these years later, I remember my basement office and my volunteer friends at CRIA much more clearly than I remember that pest control company I bought from (and eventually sold back to) my former father-in-law.

Incidentally, in 1982 the Supreme Court ruled against *Plyler v. Doe.* The Court found that the Texas law was in violation of the Fourteenth Amendment, as non-immigrated children are people "in any ordinary sense of the term," and therefore, were entitled to protection from discrimination (unless a substantial state interest could be shown to justify discriminating against them). Our long vigil was finally over.

It pleases me to feel that CRIA might have played a small part in making the lives of these immigrant families better.

The Year Was 1993

I was in Washington, D.C. My second attempt to help with immigration was actually my third. It took place well after the 1986 IRCA program ended. IRCA's 40 percent failure rate never stopped haunting me.

By then, I was a different person with extensive knowledge in the field of immigration and customs. I was also enamored of Washington, D.C. That is why, when telling you the story of RIA, I need to take a step back and talk about my last day in office. I still remember it like it was yesterday.

The election took place in November 1992, but the President-elect wasn't administered the oath of office until January 20,

1993. This time gap provides the incoming administration with an opportunity to replace political appointees with those selected by the new administration. This process is accomplished through a transition team. Once the results of the election are confirmed, the transition team opens an office in Washington, D.C., to start accepting and vetting resumes from individuals who would like to become a part of the new administration.

The top two percent of government employees are political appointees who serve at the pleasure of the President. I was part of the Department of Justice, so the transition team set up shop in the main Justice Office building and started the process of deciding which political appointees were going to stay and which ones were on the way out. Normally, the first people out the door are those individuals holding cabinet level rank. The logic is to put the imprimatur of the new administration on the organizational chart as quickly as possible.

In our case, the first person scheduled to depart was the Commissioner of the Immigration and Naturalization Service. He was gone within a few weeks of the election. I was the Deputy Commissioner, so I was appointed acting Commissioner with abridged responsibilities. I was scheduled to serve in an acting capacity until the Senate confirmed the President's nominee to be the next Commissioner. (While in an acting capacity, temporary executives are not permitted to make major decisions. Their responsibility is to only do those things necessary to keep the operation going until the new leaders are seated.) Once the new Commissioner was confirmed by the Senate, I was relieved of command.

Incidentally, the next Commissioner was not confirmed until the first week of January, and he believed he needed a bit more time to come up to speed on the issues the INS was working on, so I stayed on until the inauguration. On January 20, 1993, I cleaned out my desk, turned in my badge and weapon, received my security debriefings, and I turned in the keys to all scrambled phones and classified lockers. It was time to ride off into the proverbial sunset.

There I was, after 12 years of working for the government of the United States. I didn't quite know what to do with myself. There was a restaurant in Washington, D.C., called the Prime Rib which was a political hang out for Republicans. I went there and I sat at the bar (it was 2:00 p.m., and the lunch crowd had already left). I remember sitting there, having a drink and thinking that I didn't have a job or anything to fall back on. The reality of being unemployed after all this time struck me. Other than in a negative way, since the people who came to see us were normally angry about something, I had no idea how people in the world viewed the INS. When they received the benefit they sought, of course, they were happy, but they didn't usually share that sentiment with us.

I knew I had to do something. My first thought was, "I can either work as an independent contractor or I can start my own corporation." That was a no-brainer. So I incorporated RIA International. In the beginning, RIA was just me, but that didn't last long. I don't know who talked to the World Bank on my behalf, but Dr. Ponavida, a senior officer there, called me within two weeks. She was heading up a World Bank Mission to review a project that the government of Ghana had asked the bank to fund. The project was to build a secure in-bond shipping facility for centralized import and export of products from Togo, Benin, Burkina Faso, Ghana, and the Ivory Coast. The facility would be located near the port of Takoradi in Ghana, which had a good deep water harbor. The in-bond process would allow imported merchandise to enter Ghana at a designated port of entry without appraisement or payment of duties. It would then be transported by a bonded carrier to the Ghana centralized facility and held there until it was delivered to the Port of Takoradi for export or shipped to other authorized destinations, provided all statutory and regulatory conditions were met.

Because this was a multi-national project which dealt with secure import and export of bonded products, the immigration and customs laws of five independent nations would have to be considered. Customs and Immigration was an area the World Bank had never touched until then. Dr. Ponavida said somebody mentioned me to her (she never told me who and I forgot to ask her, as the opportunity was exciting enough). This was the beginning of my consulting work for the World Bank, which, as you already know, allowed me to get a broader perspective of how immigration matters are being handled in different countries around the world.

It was also the beginning of RIA's journey to help bring forth immigration reform to the United States.

You see, the World Bank didn't hire Ricardo Inzunza as a person. They hired RIA International (as back then, the company was basically me). From there on, when I needed personnel to help me, I hired them ad hoc. For instance, when in Mozambique, we had to go to all the border posts to see how they operated and to observe all the customs and immigrations practices. I couldn't do all that by myself and still attend meetings in Maputo (the capital city), so I would hire two or three consultants who would work with me. At the end of the day, we would meet, discuss issues, and put our report together. When I came back to Washington, D.C., which was my home base, I already had my report drafted. I would just finalize it and send it to the World Bank, which provided for my salary and the salary of my consultants.

Soon after that, it looked like our government was inching toward immigration reform.

I decided to funnel my expanded knowledge about immigration and the resources I'd acquired thanks to my consulting work, into creating an enrollment program for the more than 10 million people residing here without an immigration status. It wasn't just my own passion to help people with immigration issues that made me decide to do so. The belief of most of the people in the know is that something must be done about non-immigrated residents. We can't just deport them. That's simply unrealistic. These are families and 80 percent of them have been here for more than 20 years. They're as American as one can be. This is their home. They have roots and they have established equities here. Over half of them have children who, as U.S. citizens, would be able to petition for them at the age of 21.

U.S. citizen children are able to petition for their family members to receive permanent resident status if they have lived here continuously for five years past the age of 17.

Of course, on a personal level, my participation in the 1986 Legalization program still weighed heavily on my shoulders. In my opinion, a 40 percent failure rate in a volunteer immigration benefit program is a failure of management. In this case, that was me. If the program had enjoyed a two percent failure rate, I certainly would have taken credit for the success. Accordingly, even though our government declared victory, even though we patted ourselves on the back and said what a great job we did, I believe I have to bear the weight for the failure. I know I did the best I could. But on a deeper level, I couldn't help but think, "I wish I could have done better." There were things that I didn't know that maybe I should have known, things that I didn't do that maybe I should have done to improve the program, to explain it better, to advertise it better.

You know, it's always easy to beat yourself up in hindsight. As they say, it's easy to be a Monday morning quarterback. I do a lot of that. And I think the reason is because this was supposed to be a one-time shot. 40 percent of the folks we were trying to help missed the boat because we didn't do our jobs as well as we could have.

The possibility that we could get a second chance at this really intrigued and enthused me. So I started working on this with a lawyer named David Fernandez, and a friend of mine by the name of Eric Lee. I also included Argen Loisiaga, Andrea Gonzalez, Yasmin Gonzalez Dedeaux and Amar Perumala. Some of them are still with us.

The Year is Now 2020

The latest iteration of RIA is what we now call the ESP, the Pre-Enrollment Service Program. We're hoping to really get it going by the end of this year.

On January 20, 2021 Joseph Biden was inaugurated as the 46th President of the United States. President Biden promised to send comprehensive immigration reform legislation to congress during the first 100 days of his administration. Although this certainly wasn't always the case throughout American history, Democrats are now the more liberal party and much more amenable towards comprehensive immigration reform. (However, it needs to be said, Republicans have a rich history of support for prudent immigration reform, too.)

Now that we know the Democratic Party will be in charge for at least four years, we'll be ready when a legalization type of program is signed into law. We've written the software, we've developed the forms, we've written the training manuals we've produced the videos, we know which states we're going to operate in and we've developed travel plans. We've put a lot of effort into doing this prep-work for the last five years. And we've had our share of "almost there" starts. During the Obama administration, we were actually one day from starting the program!

President Obama had signed an executive order creating the DAPA program, Deferred Action for Parents of Americans and Lawful Permanent Residents. According to this program, American citizens and lawful permanent residents whose parents resided here without an immigration status could apply for and be granted a quasi-legal status called "Deferred Action." This status would permit them to work and remain here without fear of deportation, in three-year increments, until a long-term solution to their immigration problem could be arranged. That really got us going. We started hiring people to help us do the work.

Unfortunately, one day before the program started, a court in Texas issued an injunction against the executive order, basically saying that it was unconstitutional. The administration appealed it to the Supreme Court, which, at the time, had eight members. The Supreme Court deadlocked four to four, so, by law, the Texas judge's injunction held and the program was stopped one day before starting. I believe Republicans and Democrats agree that some type of immigration reform is an imperative. What they are having difficulty with is what form the program should take. I remain optimistic about some type of immigration relief in 2021.

When the government ended the 1986 Legalization program, we conducted an extensive "Lessons Learned Investigation." This investigation revealed that three major mistakes accounted for most of the 40 percent failure rate. I know what those failings were, I know why they occurred, and I know how to fix them. For this reason, I have come up with a program that is designed to help applicants clear the bar. The ESP program will avert the pitfalls which caused so many applications to fail back then.

Here is one example of how we will be different.

One of the three major reasons for application failure was careless mistakes. Because denial of a legalization application could not be appealed, a mistake in the application was a kiss of death. The mistake was grounds for a denial. I want applicants to take their time completing applications. Our applications will be completed in the privacy of the applicant's home or another place of their choice. Our counselors will walk applicants through every step of the application preparation process and applicants won't have to pack up the children to come to our office. We will come to them. If the 1986 program has taught me anything, it's that people should be discouraged from completing applications themselves because it's just so easy to make a mistake that will ruin their chances. If applicants don't understand a question because English is not their first language, or if their handwriting is not perfectly legible, there should be no shame in that. This is why I believe applications should be completed in privacy, at the applicant's own pace, in a relaxed and comfortable environment.

I hope that, when an immigration legalization program is enacted, our Pre-Enrollment Service Program will become the nation's premier application preparation service program.

If You Are Reading This Book, You or Someone You Know May Be Interested in Our ESP Program

It is important for potential applicants to understand that when the U.S. Government offers a legalization type program for non-immigrated residents, their participation in such a program will probably be the most important thing they will ever do for themselves and for their families. When the program is offered, an appeal component may not exist. Applicants will only get one chance to do it right so I want them to put their best foot forward. It's in this spirit that I have created our applications and our software and have trained our primary staff. Everything is set. Now we wait and pray.

I am hoping that by telling this story, my story (but also, in a sense, America's story), potential applicants will be less suspicious than they were about the 1986 Legalization program. I remember that, for the first few months the program was in effect, applications just dribbled in. But during the programs last two months, the number of monthly applications rose from 66,000 to well over 150,000 monthly. The application failure rate almost doubled to 74 percent for the last two months. It seems people were waiting until the last minute to submit applications. By doing so, they didn't have enough time to properly complete the forms and submitted applications that were almost right. Unfortunately, there is a significant difference between right and almost right. Almost right didn't cut it.

If you think that you or someone you know would be interested in this program, please understand that we have the best interest of every applicant at heart. We've done a lot of public speaking, a lot of radio and television shows for the last five or six years. We're coming around the home stretch now. I hope we're headed for the finish line, where we can be American Together.

Chapter 16

THERE'S SOMETHING IN IMMIGRATION FOR EVERYONE TO DISLIKE

If you've made it this far into the book, you know there have been many interesting stories associated with my time as the Deputy Commissioner of the INS under George H. W. Bush's administration. I hope you'll allow me one more. It will be brief.

One afternoon near closing time at the INS, the call light on my office phone was blinking. My always vigilant secretary was uncharacteristically nowhere to be found (probably making photocopies or something of the sort). So I did something I didn't get to do very often. I answered the call myself. At the other end of the line was a woman who had an immigration question about her son. I listened to her question and assured her she had reached the right person. I explained that I was the Deputy Commissioner and I would have her answer in a few minutes. Then, I put her on hold and buzzed the Examinations Unit.

The Examinations Officer who answered my call was positive he could solve any questions I asked. However, the second I told him "I have a woman on the line inquiring about her son" he cut me off and I could hear him exhaling in exasperation. "What kind of son would that be, Commissioner?" he asked, almost sarcastically. I thought the question rather odd but answered it anyway. "It is a boy son," I said. Again, the exaggerated exhaling. "Is it a legitimate son? Is it an illegitimate son? Is it a legitimated son? Is it an orphan son? Is it a biological son? Is it a non-orphan son, is it an adopted son?" I was stunned. Apparently, these distinctions were important enough to affect the answer to her question. In his contorted way, the officer was simply telling me he needed more information to answer the question. Just "my son" wouldn't cut it. I took the officers name and told him to stand by, that the woman was going to call him in a minute. I handed her off to him.

I'm often reminded of this incident because of what it illustrates so vividly: nothing in immigration is simple or easy. It is an overly complicated discipline, filled with twists and turns. I can see why people get so frustrated dealing with it. Under normal conditions, things are complex and frustrating. They become more so when the Immigration Service adopts an exclusion policy rather than one of inclusion.

Throughout American History, Our Feelings and Policies about Immigration Have Changed Considerably

Here's a brief recap of what's happened on the immigration front since the 1980s, when Republicans started getting actively involved at the immigration policy level:

- In 1986, President Reagan signed the Immigration Reform and Control Act into law. It was euphemistically called IRCA. The Legalization Program, part of IRCA, was open for one year, during which INS received eight million applications and 4.5 million individuals became lawful permanent residents. However 3.5 million (40 percent) of those applications were rejected. Thus, the problem of long-term spontaneous migration was not solved. It has languished and grown for more than 30 years.

- During his administration, President Clinton extended a section of the Immigration and Nationality Act (INA). Section 245i of the Act stated that, if you were in America without an immigration status and a visa became available for you, you could agree to pay a $2,000 fine and adjust your status here without leaving the country. The advantage to this section of the law was that another section of the INA said if you had resided in the United States for more than one year and you left the country, for any reason, even to pick up your visa, you were barred from re-entering for ten years.

- In 2000, President George W. Bush promised comprehensive immigration reform and another extension to Section 245i of the Act. However, the events of September 11, 2001, put an immediate stop to all talk of immigration reform in America, and Section 245i lapsed.

- In 2005, the "McCain-Kennedy Bill" was introduced in the U. S. Senate, containing an Earned Legalization Program to solve the problem of non-immigrated residents. Fifteen Republican Senators signed on to the bill.

- During their 2008 presidential campaign, candidates Obama and McCain promised immigration reform with a legalization component. Obama won the election and was sworn into office on January 20, 2009. Almost immediately, Senator McCain withdrew his immigration reform bill and he along with the 15 Republican Senators who previously supported immigration reform lined up against reform chanting, "Now is not the time."

- In 2012, President Obama signed an executive order creating the *Deferred Action for Parents of Americans* (DAPA). This was a program which led to lawful permanent residence. A U.S. Circuit Court Judge, in Texas enjoined the program one day before it was scheduled to start. When the decision was appealed to the Supreme Court, SCOTUS deadlocked in a four-to-four-vote, which meant the decision of the Circuit Court prevailed.

- In 2017, President Trump issued an Executive Order canceling the Obama Executive Order which created the *Deferred Action for Childhood Arrivals* (DACA) program. President Trump was sued over his Executive Order and the Supreme Court will hear the case during its 2021 term.

- In 2019, President Trump signaled that, if the Senate sent him an acceptable comprehensive immigration bill, he would be willing to sign it. Legislation never reached his desk.

It's easy to see that immigration has adherents as well as detractors. It's also easy to see that the divide between the way the two major political parties approach immigration seems to be growing. For better or for worse, I remember a time when things were different.

The Republican Party Used to Be the More Inclusive Party

From Abraham Lincoln to Dwight Eisenhower to Ronald Reagan, Republicans historically represented the party of "the big tent," where there was room for everyone. This point of view was in vogue even as recently as George W. Bush's era, but it was forever changed by the tragic events of 9/11. But we'll get back to that later.

One thing not many people know about George W. Bush is that he was really open to immigration reform. His views on immigration were actually more progressive than people give him credit for. After I left office, I was able to campaign for George W. Bush in Texas, and we took 67 percent of the Hispanic vote. That happened because we were inclusive rather than exclusive in reaching out to voters. I really liked that about the Republican Party then.

You know, when they used to ask Ronald Reagan why he left the Democratic Party to join the Republicans, he famously said, "I didn't leave the party, the party left me." I didn't fully understand or appreciate exactly what he meant, until someone asked me the same question. I understand now how President Reagan must have felt. In my case though, it's the Republican Party that has left me. I feel like an outsider. Today's Republican Party no longer reflects my values. I am not alone in expressing this sentiment. With ever-increasing frequency, I hear Republican colleagues saying that they don't have a political affiliation. Now, they vote the issues or their conscience. At the end of the day, I think that's fair. I, for one, in any election, will vote for what I believe is best for America, not what's best for the Party. Since I no longer claim a political affiliation this is easy.

And speaking about what's best for America, despite my admiration for President Reagan and the progress that was made in immigration reform during his administration, I can see how one aspect of his administration suffered from unintended consequences that taint the way Americans view immigration to this day. That initiative was Reagan's "War on Drugs."

Back then, immigration hadn't been conflated with criminality yet. But the numbers on President Reagan's War on Drugs were lagging. His program needed a boost. In those days, the administration only collected drug statistics from the Drug Enforcement Agency (DEA) and the U.S. Customs Service. Both agencies had a small presence at the southern border. Customs inspected traffic at border crossing check points and DEA worked border counterintelligence. Most of the illegal drugs were entering across the expanse of our southern border and were mainly intercepted by the Border Patrol. In an effort to increase the drug war statistics, the administration started including Border Patrol drug arrest numbers with their own. The conflation of drug abuse and drug smuggling with immigration certainly raised the numbers. Initially, only statistics from major drug busts were counted. However, over time, numbers from individual drug incidents were included.

And so, it's not unfair to say that the War on Drugs was duping the American public into believing we were winning the war. Far worse, though, the public was being led to believe that drug smuggling and immigration were synonymous. Over the years, talk about immigration has always had pejorative overtones (and undertones). Fear of immigration has been instilled into the public psyche. This is why some Americans want to take a harder line against immigration.

Is it any wonder, then, that nowadays many Americans have learned to view cross border crime and immigration as the same thing? In significant part this is due to political immigration bluster. When politicians talk about immigrants, they use terms like "criminals," "narco-terrorists," and "rapists." Of course, crime happens on the southern border, but it's committed by criminals, not immigrants. Immigrants are not coming here to foment crime. They are just people, trying to get a chance at a better life. But unfortunately, even the word "immigrant" now has acquired a negative vibe.

Crime is crime, immigration is immigration. They're two separate and distinct activities that should never be conflated. Most folks who enter Walmart are shoppers, but thieves also go to Walmart. When individuals are caught pilfering, they are prosecuted in accordance with the law. However, it would be illogical to refer to all Walmart shoppers as "criminals." And yet, when it comes to immigrants, we refer to them as criminals all the time.

We've taken the words "illegal" and "alien" and strung them together. You may not know what an illegal alien is, but if you had to offer an opinion you'd be inclined to say it's not a good thing. So, politicians have demonized, criminalized, and put a negative aura around immigrants, to the point that Americans are confused, agitated, and divided about the proper course of action to take on immigration reform. Everything about immigration has taken on a pejorative connotation. I say it is high time politicians started telling the truth about immigration and immigrants. Immigration needs to be seen in its proper light.

If you think about it, the furthest thing from a criminal's mind is coming to America to live the American Dream in a gated community with a five bedroom home, a 3 car garage and a white picket fence around his home. Conversely, the furthest thing from an immigrant's mind is to come here to pillage and plunder. Immigrants come to make a living and support their families and to find happiness and security.

By painting criminals and immigrants with the same brush, we ensure that Americans will continue to be confused, agitated, and divided about immigration. And it makes it easier for politicians to sell the idea that immigration is against our nation's best interests.

9/11 Changed the Whole Perception of Immigration in America

Treating cross border crime and immigration like they are the same thing came about as an unanticipated consequence of President Reagan's War on Drugs. But our national attitude toward immigration wasn't always as harsh as it is now.

As I mentioned earlier, during the Clinton administration, Section 245i of the INA expired. It was this section of the Act that made it possible for eligible immigrants to receive a visa without departing the country. This was a great benefit to potential immigrants! President Clinton extended this section of the law. He also tried to push an immigration reform bill through a Republican controlled Senate but wasn't able to find the votes necessary to move the legislation forward. When George W. Bush's administration started, he was about to extend Section 245i, as he promised he would.

And then, 9/11 happened.

The tragic events which occurred on that day stopped all talk about immigration reform in its tracks. When President George W. Bush was unable to muster sufficient support for an extension of Section 245i, it expired. The conservative wing of the Republican Party then managed to pass a piece of "get tough" legislation, which President Bush signed, that modified Section 212 (a)(9) of the INA. This modified section said that, if you've been in the United States for more than 180 days but less than one year without an immigration status, and, if you left the country, you were barred from re-entry for three years. If you'd been in the United

States for one year or longer without an immigration status, you were barred from re-entering for ten years. This dealt a serious setback to proponents of comprehensive immigration reform.

September 11th created a paradigm shift in immigration. It made a bad situation worse by further criminalizing the terms "immigration" and "immigrant." People would say, "After all, wasn't it immigrants that caused the assault on the homeland?" The drug war had already tilted the concept of immigration toward pejorative terms. The term "illegal alien" morphed into "criminal alien." Anyone here without an immigration status broke the law; therefore, they were criminals. If this were true, every one of us that ever received a citation for some violation of the traffic code would be considered criminals, and we are not. So it does matter that entry without inspection is a civil, not a criminal offense.

The 9/11 paradigm shift changed the argument against immigration from being economy-related ("They're taking our jobs," "They're getting welfare benefits," "They're doing things Americans can't do because we're giving them special treatment," etc.) to being a national security threat ("They could have a dirty bomb," "Any one of them could be coming here to kill us," "Look at these guys; they're Muslim, we can't trust them"). The national security arguments are the ones that have gained the most traction.

September 11th made it easy to vilify, demonize, and criminalize immigrants. For that, I lay most of the blame at the feet of the political parties. We shouldn't stand with politicians who lie and use hyperbole or partial truths to score political points. It's not right. It wasn't right when Lyndon Johnson lied to us about Vietnam, it wasn't right when we invaded Iraq searching for weapons of mass destruction which were never there, and it certainly isn't right now.

I was talking to a Rotary Club recently, and the conversation shifted to the babies who were brought into the country without inspection in the arms of their mothers. As I've mentioned before, you can't even form criminal intent by American law until you are at least nine or ten years old. These children were much younger than that, too young to even walk. So I was talking about it and was faced with reactions such as "Those kids are criminals, they should be prosecuted" and "They broke the law; they're law breakers." I tried to explain the difference between breaking a civil law and a criminal law, since crossing the border is up until now at least a civil infraction and not a criminal one. I tried to explain that it's like getting a speeding ticket: you have been arrested, but by special arrangement, if you pay the citation or elect to appear in court, you are not arrested and not labeled a criminal. And yet, the Rotary Club members I was speaking to still stood by their conviction that these kids are criminals, and they deserve what they get. The politicians have done their job of dividing us well.

At that moment, I remembered seeing a "YouTube" video taken from a police officer dash cam, showing people who robbed a 7/11 store at gun point and were trying to escape in an SUV, while police were giving chase. At some point, the driver lost control of the SUV. It crashed and rolled on its side. When it turned upright, a baby was left lying in the street. Thankfully, the baby only received superficial wounds and was okay. One of the robbers, the baby's mother, is seen in the video picking up and embracing her child. I asked the audience, with a show of hands, to tell me who had seen the video. Quite a few hands went up. I explained the video for those who had not seen it and ended my explanation by saying, "You know, you are right. These children are criminals and must be punished to the full extent of the law. But then, so must the baby in this video be prosecuted to the full extent of the law. The baby was party to a host of major felony crimes." When I said that, I could see the reaction in the faces of the audience. They blanched! They looked at me like I was crazy for involving the child in crimes committed by the parents.

At that point I quickly said, "I have presented you with two scenarios involving children and their parents. One scenario involves a civil crime and the other several serious felony charges. In the scenario involving the felonies, you seem to recognize the need for compassion, mercy, and understanding for the child; however, in the civil infraction, you don't see it. Most of you don't know or have never seen immigrant children or the child in the video, but you believe the one in the video is good but the others are bad. I don't know how this happened, but I can see there is a bias operating here, a bias that is causing some of you to view the immigrant children as different. It's almost like you see them as children of a lesser God."

This meeting brought it home for me. People had been emotionally programmed and didn't even know it. They were good, Christian individuals who believed they were right. But, I left it at that because I wasn't there to start a fight. I was there to share my point of view on immigration. I feel certain most of the audience never thought there was bias in their thinking; but there it was, and it was real.

And herein lies the problem for me: we are being emotionally programmed by politicians. This is something all of us need to think about. Implicit bias is very real, it is happening right now, and it will continue to happen because, as humans, we are highly susceptible to implicit biases. An implicit bias refers to the attitudes or stereotypes that affect our understanding, actions and decisions in an unconscious manner. This is especially so when it comes from people we trust and believe in. Politicians constantly try to push their point of view by steering our minds in a certain direction. That's not always a bad thing. But we need to be confident that what our politicians are telling us is the truth, the whole truth, and nothing but the truth. Far too frequently, that's not the case. Truth matters.

We have to recognize when our politicians are lying to us and call it out. Let's not forget politicians lied about the Gulf of Tonkin incident to escalate the Vietnam War. This resulted in 58,000 Americans being killed. We attacked Iraq looking for weapons of mass destruction and there were none. Look at where Iraq is today, thanks to us. We may be able to gloss over it and say things like, "That was then, this is now," but it can happen again. Any day, on any event. But to get back to my point, the fact that we permit politicians to get away with lying bothers me immensely. Especially when it comes to lying about immigration.

Because there is no such thing as "illegal immigration."

If you want to get nitpicky, the website of the Department of Homeland Security and the law define an immigrant as "a person who has been lawfully accorded the privilege of residing in America permanently." If you have not applied for and the U.S. Government has not granted you this privilege, you are not an immigrant. You may be a resident because you moved here, but you are not an immigrant, period. There are no degrees of immigrant. The same way you can't be a little bit pregnant, you can't be a little bit immigrant. Ergo you cannot be an illegal immigrant. That is a bureaucratic oxymoron.

I prefer to use the term "non-immigrated resident" to define the individuals and families here without an immigration status.

Non-immigrated residents are people, without an immigration status, who are residing in the United States like immigrants even though the government has never accorded them immigrant status. So, the most accurate definition for this group is non-immigrated residents. It is also a term that is neutral in value shading. Currently, the Department of Homeland Security estimates this population to be 10.5 million strong.

The number of Mexican non-immigrated residents has been in decline since 2007, while the total from other nations ticked up. According to DHS statistics, Mexicans made up less than half of all non-immigrated residents in 2019. Their numbers dropped from 6.9 million in 2007 to 4.5 million in 2019. This shift was brought about by a combination of factors: The recession that began in 2007 made it more difficult to find work; enhanced border protection made it harder to slip into the country; and improved economic conditions in Mexico provided hope that economic parity could be achieved there.

During the Trump Presidency even more drastic "get tough" legislation was contemplated. They were mulling over the possibility of forced deportation of 10.5 million non-immigrated residents. President Trump argued that we are a nation of laws and that leaving the country would be the first step in making things right for this criminal element. He believed rewarding criminal behavior (by permitting them to adjust to a lawful immigration status in the United States) was a prescription for chaos and a de facto rewarding of lawlessness. The administration's argument held no water but it did attract quite a few adherents.

The part of the administration's removal proposal garnering the most support was the assertion that these residents were criminals and must be deported. Nationally, only one in five adult Americans

(20-percent) favored any type of forced deportation. Yet, most of them believed, these individuals broke the law.

If punishment is being considered for these long-term residents, then we need to plot a course of action which will provide the greatest national good. To do that, we need to know if long-term non-immigrated residents are really criminals.

So what are the facts? There are two statutes that may have been violated: For some this means improper entry (crossing the border surreptitiously) and for others it means unlawful presence (remaining in the country after their visa has expired); however, neither are criminal violations.

Civil laws, when violated, have a five-year statute of limitations which starts on the date of the violation. Consequently, non-immigrated residents who entered undetected more than five years ago and have never run afoul of immigration or local law enforcement authorities, cannot even be charged with a civil infraction. However, they can still be deported through an administrative process, but it's just plain deceitful to refer to them as "criminals." A criminal violation of law is a whole other thing.

Civil law seeks redress of wrong doing by compelling compensation or restitution from offenders. The offender is not punished but suffers as much redress as is necessary to remedy the wrong that has been committed. In this case, the Immigration and Nationality Act normally calls for a minimum of a $50 fine for first-time violations of this civil statute. On the other hand, when considering violations of criminal statutes, the main objective of the law is to seek retribution by punishing the criminal in a way that will provide a strong inducement not to commit another crime. In other words, to satisfy the public sense the punishment should be severe enough to deter future criminal behavior.

In ethics and law, there's a principle which calls for "letting the punishment fit the crime," a principle that means that the penalty for a misdeed or wrongdoing should be reasonable and proportionate to the severity of the offending behavior. Yet, today we see people seeking to create heavy penalties as the price to be paid for a path to lawful residence. They believe offenders must be harshly punished for entering (or remaining in) the country without an immigration status. Even babies! Like Shylock, in Shakespeare's The Merchant of Venice, these politicians are determined to extract their pound of flesh.

Forcefully deporting 10.5 million individuals (when 80 percent of them have resided here more than 20 years) for a non-chargeable violation of civil law should insult the American sense of justice and morality. It's totally out of proportion to the severity of the infraction being addressed. It's like using an atomic bomb to kill a mosquito. Yes, it will get the job done, but at what cost? My best explanation for the anti-immigrant vitriol is that we have been emotionally programmed to see immigration as something bad. Yes, I keep saying this, but politicians have done a great job of poisoning the immigration well.

The destruction of lives, families, and communities created by forced removal of long-term non-immigrated residents would be incalculable. And the worst trauma will be inflicted upon those children who have never known any home other than the one they have in this country. In 2021, we are holding 51,000 men, women, and children in government detention daily. Have you ever wondered why we call it detention and not arrest? As I mentioned previously, these individuals cannot be charged with a crime but they can be placed in deportation proceedings because they don't have an immigration status. That is an administrative procedure. They can be placed in administrative detention, not arrested, during this procedure but not charged with a criminal infraction.

Many Americans are OK with it because they have been taught to believe these are criminals. So far, six children have died in administrative detention. More than 28 adults have died in the custody and care of Homeland Security. Six children and at least 28 adults died because of that new policy of zero tolerance we have. One child dying in DHS custody is one too many!

Children don't belong in cages. We shouldn't be allowed to detain people in that way. We do it with immigrant children because politicians view public silence as assent.

And we're certainly not equipped for it. This brings me to my next point.

There's Something in Immigration for Everyone to Dislike

Most Americans support the idea of creating a path to lawful residence for individuals without an immigration status, and support for this proposition has been stable for more than a decade.

Polls have consistently indicated that nearly 70-percent of Americans favor a plan which will permit non-immigrated residents who have resided here for more than five years, have developed equities and set roots in America and have become lawful, productive members of society, to have a path to lawful permanent residence. Nearly all Americans believe to enroll the maximum number of people in a successful legalization program it must combine measured penalties with clear and achievable goals. The program should identify and remove the relatively few who do not belong here based on criminal activity and integrate as quickly as possible those who can contribute their talents.

I know that ICE officers would like nothing more than to be allowed to perform the jobs they trained for. They, like most Americans, want to prioritize enforcement against repeat immigration violators and those with criminal records who pose a threat to society. But a 100 percent detention mandate causes them to squander resources on detention and deportation of people who pose a threat to no one.

I also know we can't afford all of today's detention. Estimates from the Department of Homeland Security indicate that it costs taxpayers $475 per day, per adult individual detained in a contract detention facility. It costs $800 daily to detain children. This means that during the course of one year, U.S. taxpayers spend more than $8,000,000 daily to detain non-criminal individuals. I am certain it will come as no surprise that most of the taxpayer money used to pay for these detention services is going to a couple of private detention companies who are making a fortune. Compare this to alternative forms of control, such as "release on bond" or "own recognizance release," where the cost per detained individual ranges from less than 25 cents daily up to $1.70 daily, and the control rate is nearly 100-percent, and you'll see why our current detention policy doesn't really benefit the American people.

Throughout my time as a consultant for the World Bank, I had the opportunity to witness many mismanaged immigration systems in developing countries. And yet, I have to say, unnecessarily spending billions of dollars locking up hundreds of thousands of non-criminals yearly like the United States does, may just be one of the biggest mismanagements I've ever encountered!

Before the "catch and release" program was canceled, Congress was receiving pressure from the private contractors who provide the majority of our detention services to increase the number of mandatory detentions. Congress subsequently mandated that Homeland Security detain 34,000 criminal immigrants daily. The operative word here is "criminal." That number has now grown to 51,000 thousand, daily. ICE has never be able to find the requisite number of criminals to satisfy the detention mandate, so they are filling the quota with non-criminal immigrants. Does that sound familiar, given what we discussed earlier about padding the numbers during Reagan's War on Drugs? I think it should. Before "catch and release" was canceled, detention of non-immigrated residents was costing taxpayers more than four billion dollars yearly, and non-criminals represented more than 30-percent of the detained population. With 100-percent mandatory detention of all non-immigrated residents, the cost will rise to $1,700,000,000 (one billion, seven- hundred million) daily. We will have more than ten and a half million individuals in detention. How realistic is that?

And here's another problem with detention. Despite immigration detention's legal characterization as civil, individuals in immigration confinement are treated no differently than individuals in criminal confinement. With few exceptions, private contractors engaged by ICE to provide administrative detention services operate their facilities like prisons. ICE contractors primarily rely on the correctional incarceration standards of care, custody, and control protocols designed for convicted criminals. With the blessing of the Department of Homeland Security, these contractors impose criminal-style restrictions that carry far more costs and psychological damage than is necessary to effectively manage and care for the detained non-criminal immigrant population. The cold numbers by themselves show that what we're doing is wrong.

If only individuals who pose a danger to the community or a significant flight risk are detained, the taxpayers will save a lot of money. For the relatively few who require follow up monitoring, there are less expensive alternatives to detention which can be used. Taxpayers will save billions of dollars in needless and hurtful detention of non-criminal residents.

In 1967 at the Ebenezer Baptist Church in Atlanta, Dr. Martin Luther King Jr. gave a sermon in which he said, "There comes a time when silence is betrayal." For me, silence is consent. Let's not allow our silence to be our consent.

In 1987, Alan Bock wrote that our immigration problem is caused by the American Dream. "The Dream," he wrote, "although tattered around the edges and undermined by an accretion of rules, regulations, and conventions is still alive. Those of us who have had the privilege of living here all our lives may have complaints about many things, but for those who view us from afar, whether from across the oceans or from across a border wall, this is as close to the Promised Land as this troubled world affords." Just think how much richer America would be if we could re-discover our heritage of nourishing liberty, our heritage of opening our hearts to those seeking the same legacy!

This heritage hasn't come easy. America may be a nation of immigrants, but we have never really been comfortable with that notion. Not if we're being honest. Going all the way back, we were against all immigrants, Poles, Germans, Italians, Irish no matter what country they immigrated from. We were basically against everyone coming over here at some point. And yet, we had the good sense not to move against these immigrants. Today, if I randomly selected 100 Americans and asked you to point out the Germans or the Italians or the Irish in that group, you would be hard pressed to do so. We have become an undifferentiated mass of people called Americans. We are all Americans and that's the beauty of it. Will we be able to keep being like this? Will we be able to continue being American together? I don't know. I sure hope so. But as long as we keep focusing on what divides us instead of on the things that unite us, we can only show our mean-spirited selves.

And our mean spirit can be quite specific about the person or nationality it targets. Just ask the Japanese, who were American citizens of this country, Yet, after Pearl Harbor, we put them in concentration camps. We gave them 72-hours to dispose of all their property and then treated them like prisoners of war by forcing them into POW camps. Interestingly enough, this only happened on the West Coast. We did not intern Asians on the East Coast or Italians or Germans, for that matter, even though their countries of origin declared war on the United States. But on the West Coast, the bias against Asians was greater. It's the same bias and mean-spiritedness that, during the Depression, led us to deport about 400,000 Mexicans, many of whom were US citizens. It's the same kind of mean-spiritedness that holds babies responsible for their mothers bringing them into the United States. No one is born with a mean spirit. We have to be taught how to hate.

There's something in immigration for everyone to dislike. Consequently, it's being turned into a wedge issue that is dividing people. Whether the division is based on culture, color, race, religion, or ethnic lines, it is still a division. I refuse to believe this is the best we can do. We just need someone to make us realize that we are stronger together than we are fighting against one another. We need to learn there is something in immigration for everyone to like. Even if that something is just the common sense of avoiding costly deportation and incurring an astronomical national debt.

Chapter 17

THE NEW AMERICANS

You may have noticed that I'm using this term a lot: "The new Americans." Who are they? How long have they been here? How can they help America reach its full potential? Equally important, how can we help them successfully and quickly assimilate into the United States?

Whether you count yourself among these New Americans or simply want to understand more about this complicated but important matter, it's great to have concrete facts to support your conversations and to underpin your conclusions. Arguing from the facts is how we avoid operating on hearsay or bias. Knowing the facts will make it manifestly more difficult for anyone to divide us on the subject of immigration.

To that end, I have included some statistics provided by the Department of Homeland Security, the PEW Research Center, and the RIA International Group. I believe this data will help us stop thinking about immigration in abstract terms; it will help us see that it involves real people, not that different from you or me.

Let's start with the countries of origin for these New Americans. Because, like many of our perceptions about immigration, where these folks are emigrating from may surprise you.

Where Are the New Americans Coming from?

When we think about most immigration and migration, our visceral response is to immediately look south to Mexico. But that visceral response, while correct years ago, is incorrect in 2021.

When considering immigration and migration in years past more Mexicans were migrating to America than the rest of the world combined. This came about because in 1920 there were no two countries in the world which bordered each other that were more economically disparate than Mexico and the United States. As a consequence we exerted a tremendous pulling influence on Mexican citizens. The Mexican economy was poor, and state corruption was so crippling, people were willing to endure almost any hardship to get to the United States for a shot at improving their circumstances. That's no longer the case. Today, Mexico is the world's thirteenth-largest economy, and growing. It's our third-largest trading partner, and it has trade agreements with the United States and Canada. Fewer and fewer Mexicans believe they need to migrate to America to find salvation for their families. Several years ago, the PEW Research Center, a nonpartisan fact tank, reported that Mexico ceased being the major country of origin for immigration to the United States, and, in 2018, they ceased being the leading country for spontaneous migration.

According to the PEW Research Center, migration from Mexico today is, in fact, at net zero. This means more Mexicans are leaving the United States than are arriving. So, where are the New Americans coming from?

Before I get to that point let me touch on a couple of other issues. As I noted previously, non-immigrated resident is the term I use to describe long-term residents here without an immigration status. I use this term because it accurately describes who we are discussing and it is still neutral in value shading. Even though there is no such thing as an "illegal immigrant," almost daily references to them are made by people who should know there is no such thing as an illegal immigrant. Immigration is a lawful process. There are no types of immigrants. Either you are an immigrant, or you are not. Yet, the House, Senate, the President, and the immigration elite, so confused by their own misunderstanding of what immigration is, have even bifurcated immigration into legal immigration and illegal immigration. There is no such thing. Either you immigrate or you migrate. These are the folks that make the laws and drive the policies. The next thing they will come up with is legal crime and illegal crime. They and the media make daily references to illegal aliens, undocumented immigrants, illegal immigrants, as well as a host of other terms such as criminals, wet backs, rapists, border jumpers, and other terms with pejorative connotations. I don't for one minute believe that the media and these politicians don't know that what they are saying is factually incorrect. By keeping Americans confused, agitated, and divided about immigration, they score political points.

The second thing you might glean from the statistics about the New Americans is that this is a large population. Not only is it large, but it's stable and long standing. Mexicans make up 63-percent of this population, but according to PEW research they also make up the group of longest continuous residence. In fact, 80-percent (5,360,000) have resided here more than 20 years. Many Mexicans in that group have resided here more than 30 years. Three percent (200,000) have resided here less than five years. Seven years ago (2014), 14-percent had lived here less than five years. If, as we are asked to believe, this population is growing, the number of individuals here less than five years would be on the increase, but it's shrinking. This means spontaneous migration is on the wane.

Collectively, these non-immigrated resident families have set roots and developed equities in America. In 2018 the estimated size of this population was approximately eleven million. In 2010 they were estimated at fourteen million. Because the number of Mexicans returning to Mexico is constant, the Department of Homeland Security placed the official government number at 10.5 million in 2013. They have not increased that number in eight years.

These statistics speak directly to the fact that increasingly, younger Mexicans are concluding that they can reach economic parity in Mexico as easily and quickly as they can do it in the United States, and they would rather do it where they don't feel scorned. For this reason, many are emigrating.

For years, Mexicans dominated the non-immigrated resident statistics. However, that is no longer the case. Those numbers are being quickly diluted by a richer mix of arriving families and individuals. The increase from Europe and Canada (six percent), while small, is surprisingly significant and raises an interesting border security question. More Mexicans are leaving than are arriving, and the number of Canadians here without an immigration status is rapidly rising, so why are all of our enforcement resources clustered on the southern border? I don't think it's to fend off immigration. I think the southern border is militarized to intercept criminal activity.

We have about 6,000 miles of border with Canada. There we have more than 300 ports of entry and about 2,500-customs and border protection agents. Only 7 of the larger Canadian ports have 24-hour staffing, while the smaller ports close up at night. When it's time for the smaller ports to call it a day, the officer in charge lowers the "boom barrier," puts a padlock on it, and goes home. But you can still walk around or under the bar. There is no wall on our northern border because we understand there is little, if any, pulling effect by our economy on Canadians. Heck, most Canadians believe they can do better in Canada than they can here.

In stark contrast, our southern border is a militarized zone. We have 48 ports of entry along our 2,000-mile border with Mexico. We exercise control of the border with walls, fences and fortified barriers. We have drones, airplanes, helicopters, and aerostats (low-level airborne radar surveillance systems). We have underground sensors and infrared cameras. Our 23,000-customs and border control agents are supplemented by active duty and reserve military units. The only thing we don't have a lot of on the southern border is spontaneous migration! Let's face it, the build-up of defenses on our southern border exists to deter criminal activity, not spontaneous migration.

It has been reported by all major media outlets that economic turbulence coupled with poorly considered refugee policies are now pulling folks from the Northern Triangle region of Central America (Guatemala, Honduras, and El Salvador) to our southern border. Since the 1990's, these three countries have generated the majority of asylum and refugee flows.

Back in 1996, when this phenomenon started, there was only one column on the border patrol detention forms for the nationality of detained individuals, and that column was for Mexicans. Eventually, as the numbers of Central Americans increased, we were forced to add a new column and a new acronym to our detention forms: OTM. "Other Than Mexican." Yes, really.

DHS reports that 2018 was the first year in immigration history where more OTM's than Mexicans were detained trying to enter the country without inspection. Mexicans are also being outpaced in the area of immigration. Remember, immigration is a lawful process. Immigrants have been inspected and admitted as immigrants. This means they can reside and work here permanently. Yet, many people still believe that the largest group immigrating to the US comes from Mexico. Well, that is simply no longer true. According to DHS data:

- The Number 1 country of immigration to the United States is China.

- The Number 2 country of immigration to the United States is India.

- The Number 3 country of immigration to the United States is Mexico.

Another thing people believe: the largest group of visa overstays are from India and China. This is also not true. According to DHS, visa overstays are those who were properly admitted to the country but failed to depart when their visas expired. According to DHS, most visa overstays today are from Canada. They go to Florida during the Canadian winter and return during the summer.

As this population ages, fewer and fewer are making the return journey, but who will stop them? Canadians look exactly the same as Americans; they speak the same language. No police officer will question them. Plus, as we've already seen, crossing our northern border is basically a piece of cake. Canadians do not require a visa to enter the United States if they plan to stay within 25 miles of the border. Incidentally, Mexicans don't require a visa to enter Canada. If they wanted to, they could go to Canada and then walk in to this country. Once this word gets out, we may have to build a security wall around Canada.

Speaking of things people believe about immigration which are simply not true: DHS tells us most of the folks here today without an immigration status didn't slither across the border in the dead of night. Most were properly admitted at a designated port of entry by an authorized immigration inspector who saluted them and said, "Welcome to America, folks." So, the truth is that most non-immigrated residents today entered legally and then violated the conditions of their visas (many from Africa and the Middle East). Quite naturally, this raises the question about the need for a border security wall. If the folks who are giving us heartburn are being admitted through our airports and seaports, how will a great security wall mitigate the spontaneous migration problem?

This idea that we are being invaded just doesn't hold water. The PEW Research Center tells us, with the notable exception of the caravans that were arriving from the Northern Triangle due to the cancellation of refugee processing in Costa Rica, migration and refugee arrival numbers have been in decline for more than a decade.

What we are being told about current immigration trends is that America is being inundated by folks without an immigration status. We are told the country is full and cannot hold any more immigrants. When you consider the most recent non-immigrated arrivals, only three percent have been here less than five years. If being overrun were true, that three percent number at the bottom of the inverted pyramid would be ballooning because of recent arrivals. It's not. It's actually shrinking year after year.

In 2016, according to DHS, the number of apprehensions on our southern border were at a 40-year record low. So, one might wonder: what exactly happened from 2016 to the present, that suddenly caused thousands of refugees to form caravans and walk more than 2,500 miles with their families to our southern border seeking asylum? I doubt that this is a decision any family takes lightly. Civil unrest in the Northern Triangle region commenced prior to 2009. The U.S. Government didn't want refugees taking the dangerous trek to our southern border, so we implemented refugee processing in Costa Rica to stem the unnecessary flow of refugees from the region. Everything was under control until, suddenly, in 2017, we learned our border was under assault and we needed funding to build a 2,000-mile border wall to solve the problem. What changed? Why was an endless stream of refugees walking toward our southern border? The answer is, sadly, simple. Refugee processing in Costa Rica was canceled.

Why is that important? Because, as I pointed out earlier, a refugee must be outside of the United States to apply for refugee status and an asylee must be in this country to apply for asylum. That's the law. At the same time refugee processing was canceled in Costa Rica, foreign humanitarian aid to the Northern Triangle countries along with Temporary Protection Status (TPS) was canceled. It's not difficult to see why these refugees were left no other option than to trek to the U.S. southern border seeking refuge in the form of asylum.

If I were a cynical man, I might be inclined to think that the contrived "refugee invasion" had more to do with creating a need to fund a border wall than it did with spontaneous refugee flows. Create the flow to get the dough!

Demographics and Living Conditions of the New Americans

Now that we've seen where these non-immigrated individuals and families are coming from, it's time to get to know them a bit

322

better. The New Americans are mainly clustered in 10 different States and the District of Columbia (although they live in all 50 States).

The New Americans, while well dispersed, are still a shadow population living under a constant threat of deportation. They are not permitted to work legally, so many don't have social security numbers. Therefore, they can't get things like a line of credit, credit cards and, in some states, driver's licenses. The majority of the population which has resided here more than 20 years may have managed to get social security numbers years ago. The more senior members of the new Americans own homes and businesses, have American citizen children and grandchildren, employ other Americans and pay taxes

Most of the younger members of this population are under-employed. And yet, if you look at the numbers, remittances (aka the money immigrant workers are sending back to their families in their home country) to Mexico from the United States total more than 20 billion U.S. dollars annually. Of course, remittances come from immigrated and non-immigrated Mexicans.

It would certainly be to our benefit as a nation to empower these people. To give them the tools they need to succeed so that they can participate fully in the American Dream, be reunited with their families, and keep their money and allegiance here. To be American together.

Getting to Know IBP and ESP Programs

I believe it needs to be said: being granted refugee or asylum status is no walk in the park. The qualification standard is high and extremely difficult for most applicants to meet. Normally, more than 90-percent of all groups fail to meet the standard necessary to qualify.

From the current pool of applicants waiting to apply for refugee or asylum status, El Salvador has the highest approval rate, nine percent. Nine applicants out of 100! So, what happens to those applicants who are denied asylum status? They are placed into deportation proceedings and mostly held in detention camps.

I've mentioned earlier that only an immigration judge can order a deportation. Once the deportation order is issued, it passes to the immigration authorities to be executed. So, after being denied asylum, it could still take one or two years to receive a final order of deportation. Under the 100-percent detention policy, denied applicants will unnecessarily be held in detention. Why do I say unnecessary?

Recent adjustments to our refugee policy made it abundantly clear: migrants fleeing violence and poverty in Central America were not welcome here. These changes ushered in a regressive and hostile immigration climate when a cruel and inhumane policy change that would detain and criminally prosecute anyone without an immigration status was announced. This "one-size-fits-all" approach to civil immigration detention is out of touch with the concept of constitutional proportionality, offensive to our fundamental values as a nation, and contrary to common sense. Yet, it has supporters. They must be law and order folks who believe the policy of incarcerating criminals is the right thing to do. In this case it would be the proper thing to do if it were true. It's not. These individuals are not criminals.

Unlike everyone else in the custody of state and federal correctional departments for criminal convictions, individuals in ICE's custody are not there as punishment for having committed a criminal infraction. ICE has no incarceration authority over criminal proceedings. These families are in custody because the

Department of Homeland Security believes they might not have permission to remain in the country. Legally, these individuals are civil detainees, not arrested individuals suspected of criminal activities. The administration needs to spend more time being truthful by explaining to Americans that non-immigrated residents are not criminals. It needs to humanize, not dehumanize, their plight.

In order for the new 100-percent incarceration plan to succeed, the administration gambled that Americans would buy into this perverse scheme. They needed us to believe they were telling the truth when they claimed that parents who arrived here with their children seeking protection (a lawful act by the way) were a threat to our national security. They were not. We were expected to believe tearing children, including toddlers, away from their parents and incarcerating them separately was a proportionate and necessary response to a civil infraction. It was not. Our leaders needed us to believe that children were criminals. They were not. This policy reminded me of the adage, "The beatings will continue until morale improves." The administration was trying to scare us into believing the immigration problem in America was spiraling out of control. It was not. The crime problem may have been out of control but not immigration. Remember, individuals who are denied asylum are well known to us. We have interviewed them extensively, we have conducted background investigations on them, and we have observed them in detention. We know they are not flight or security risks.

So what are the facts?

The administration was utilizing the threat of causing immigrants pain to justify pulling in the welcome mat thereby dissuading potential asylum seekers from coming here. Sadly, immigrants were being used as "pawns" to achieve a political end rather than being seen as human beings in need. Carried to its logical conclusion, the 100-percent incarceration order held the potential to surpass President Roosevelt's internment of Japanese Americans in its scope and inhumane and cruel treatment of detainees.

During a 1988 bill-signing ceremony which included an apology from the American people and provided restitution for internment of Japanese-Americans, President Reagan remarked, "More than forty years ago, shortly after the bombing of Pearl Harbor, 120,000 American Citizens of Japanese Ancestry, including women and children, were forcibly removed from their homes and placed in makeshift internment camps. This action was taken without trial, without a jury. It was based solely on race, for these one hundred and twenty thousand were Americans."

Mass civil immigration detention has taken various forms throughout our nation's history, but we have never used it to break up families. In 1954, with the closing of Ellis Island, mass immigration detention was suspended. However, after the sudden influx of large numbers of Cuban and Haitian refugees in the 1980's, its use was reluctantly reinstated. Since then, despite a Congressional call for fiscal restraint in all areas of the federal budget, civil immigration detention has continued to see dramatic growth. Now, it is the mandated form of control. One sure symptom of a mismanaged immigration system is exorbitant spending by unnecessarily incarcerating hundreds of thousands of non-immigrated residents. I know I sound like a broken record, but these things are important.

In fiscal year 2013, the Department of Homeland Security reported for the first time in the nation's history that more than 430,000 individuals and families were incarcerated in civil detention, while they waited to learn whether they would be allowed to remain in the country. Remember, this is America, not China! This is in addition to the 2.3 million individuals we have incarcerated for criminal convictions. Think about it, we are four percent of the earth's population and we account for 25 percent of the world's incarcerated men, women and children in the land of the free and the home of the brave.

As we already know, Congress has mandated that 42,000 criminal immigrants must be detained daily. These are supposed to be people who have been convicted of a crime and are waiting to be removed from the country. Most of us would agree that this is a sound policy. ICE plans to increase that number to 51,000 daily criminal detentions this year. This requirement is known as the "bed mandate." ICE interprets the requirement to mean that 51,000 beds must be filled daily. Thus far, its agents have been unable to locate a sufficient number of criminal immigrants to fill the bed mandate, so they are filling the detention space with non-criminals.

When the new incarceration goal is reached, we will be spending more than $28 million daily to rip families apart, or more than $855 million a month on needless detentions. A close examination of the figures makes it clear the numbers behind civil immigration detention simply cannot be justified. They do not add up to sensible policy. Make no mistake about it; these "detention chickens" will come home to roost, and they will come with an invoice. Which raises another interesting question. How much of our national treasure can we continue to spend on needless detention when we don't have enough money to repair our buckling infrastructure?

In 2018, the Congressional Budget Office (CBO) predicted that this unprecedented detention policy would run up a trillion-dollar deficit by 2020. Well they were wrong. The new debt level reflects a rise of more than two trillion was reached by 2018.

The U.S. Government's public debt is now more than $22 trillion, the highest it has ever been. The Treasury Department data comes as tax revenues have fallen and federal spending continues to rise. The irony between the decision to end "catch and release" and the CBO's predictions that we are spending ourselves into oblivion should not be wasted on anyone.

As Americans, we share a common moral commitment to limit the range of acceptable detention policies we can allow as remedies. The destruction of lives, families, and communities created by mass administrative detention should never be acceptable. For example, I am steadfastly opposed to forcefully deporting "Dreamers" who have lived here their entire lives for non-chargeable violations of civil immigration law. It would not only insult America's sense of justice, but would be totally out of proportion to the severity of the infraction being redressed.

A more enlightened remedy is available. By creating an Immigration Benefit Program that provides a path to an immigration status for qualified applicants who have been living in the nation's shadow for decades, we will greatly enhance our national security posture. Bringing them into the sunlight will free up valuable enforcement resources for more pressing national security and law enforcement concerns. It will also significantly add to government revenues by adding millions of workers to our tax rolls. This can all be accomplished at no expense to taxpayers.

Erosion of trust in our political institutions, coupled with an absence of acceptable remedies for public wrongdoing, is expanding the nation's impulse to punish. We must seek a shared moral vocabulary that will unite us in our pursuit of justice with mercy for the "Dreamers." As Shakespeare reminds us in The Merchant of Venice, "We are most God-like when we are most merciful."

Making decisions and investing in policies based on flawed assumptions is simply bad leadership. Remember, if you get the assumptions wrong nothing else matters. The program will fail. The Department of Homeland Security replaced the existing "catch and release" program with a regressive policy based on concocted assumptions rather than managing from the facts.

Perhaps I should explain a bit more about "catch and release," as it was euphemistically called.

Under "catch and release," when ICE officers encountered persons who they believed were here without an immigration status, they were required to make a comprehensive threat assessment. If it was determined that an individual posed a national security risk or had a previous criminal conviction, they were mandatorily detained until they could be removed from the country. Most will agree that this was a prudent course of action. After all, we have enough criminals and security threats of our own. We don't need to import more.

Individuals who did not represent a national security threat or had no criminal conviction but who, in the opinion of the ICE officer, represented a flight risk, could be detained or released on an immigration bond. Then, if an individual released on bond didn't show up for a hearing, the breached bond would have covered the additional cost for ICE officers to round these individuals up.

Finally, those individuals and families who represented no security, criminal, or flight risks were routinely released on their own recognizance while awaiting a court hearing, not only as a humanitarian matter but also as a family and cost-saving measure. This is what the canceled program was all about.

But once the administration hung the "catch and release" moniker on this program, it made it easy to demonize it for political gain. If you want to know how it's working, six children and 20 adults have died in ICE custody in the last 24 months. Let that sink in.

The big criticism of the program was that after their release individuals would not show up for their hearings. Currently, immigrants enrolled in the deportation process that were released under "Catch and Release" show up for their hearings 94 percent of the time and comply with orders of removal 84 percent of the time. Under the 100-percent detention policy, all these folks, including children, in deportation proceedings must be detained. We've already seen how terribly cruel and expensive this process is. And can it really be justified when immigrants, currently in the deportation process, who are not detained, show up for their hearings and comply with orders?

Getting Americans to believe that criminal and civil incarcerations are the same thing dates back to President Reagan's War on Drugs. Since drugs were being smuggled into the country by foreign criminals, legislation was enacted which exposed an urgent desire, on the part of Congress, to use immigration detention as a tool in fighting the nation's proliferating war on drugs. Their legislative efforts intertwined criminal incarceration and civil immigration detention in such a way that they became indistinguishable.

Wittingly or unwittingly, an immigration detention apparatus was created that blurred the line between criminal incarceration and civil detention to the point where both classes of detainees are now viewed as criminal. I am not picking on President Reagan for this unintended consequence. I loved the man. I worked in his administration for eight years. But the facts are the facts.

Labeling immigrants as criminals to pave the way for their detention should never be used as the default approach for enforcing immigration laws. Reducing immigration enforcement to a one-size-fits all approach means stripping ICE officers of the discretion to determine who must be detained and who can safely be released. This illustrates a gross lack of knowledge for the human complexity of immigration enforcement. Moreover, the assumptions underpinning the cancellation of "catch and release" are specious at best. Peter F. Drucker, whose work contributed so much to the philosophical and practical foundations of modern business corporations wrote, "Get the assumptions wrong and nothing else matters. You will fail."

As reliance on automatic imprisonment escalates, policy makers are realizing that rapidly expanding civil detention is imposing heavy fiscal burdens on taxpayers and intangible social costs on the incarcerated families. Without thoughtful prior justification and leadership, exposing women, children, and infants to the harsh conditions of criminal confinement, loss of employment, family break up, and extreme financial hardships is patently wrong. In my opinion, it warrants a constitutional proportionality review pursuant to the Eighth Amendment's Cruel and Unusual Punishment Clause.

My major concern is not with the government's authority to detain anyone who represents a threat to national security or good order. Most Americans agree legal authority to detain is necessary. My concern is with how that detention power is wielded. Remember, civil immigration detainees are not guilty of any chargeable crime. However, immigration detention has devolved into a system that is routinely used to criminally punish civil detainees. For example:

- Incarcerating families without any form of due process in an effort to dissuade other refugees from attempting to seek asylum here.

- ICE's civil immigration detention system functions to deprive non-immigrated residents of social and physical liberty in the same way as criminal incarceration does, without any form of due process.

- Immigration detainees are incarcerated in the same jails and prisons and subjected to the same disciplinary regimen as convicted felons and criminal defendants.

- The lives of civil immigration detainees are regulated in the same way as the lives of those whose confinement results from a criminal conviction.

- Immigrants can be held in detention indefinitely without due process.

I believe the system is wrong. As citizens, we have a civil and moral responsibility to ensure that decisions of policy makers are firmly rooted in the Constitution. Policy makers shouldn't be able to wield the law as they see fit for political gain. Their decisions and pronouncements must be just, practical, and firmly-tethered to the truth. We must not allow any administration to lose sight of the fact that each non-immigrated resident here represents a human being who counts on us to treat them fairly and in accordance with our laws. A "silent" public is a consenting public.

Enrollment Service Programs (ESP) and Immigration Benefit Programs (IBP), are Important

Over the 30 plus years since I worked on the original 1986 IRCA, everyone who worked with me has retired. There isn't a single attorney or a senior government official left in government who worked on IRCA, only guys like me out there trying their best to do good. But for that very reason, I believe I have the depth of experience necessary to help, which will serve the best interests of individuals qualifying for an immigration benefit program.

We have already covered the facts and figures supporting the assertion that immigrants are flooding through our border fortifications. We've seen how arrests on the southern border have been declining for decades, how more Mexicans are leaving the country than are arriving, and how more Non-Mexicans than Mexicans were arrested trying to slip into the country surreptitiously. Finally, we know that the mix of individuals detained attempting unauthorized entry, include fewer and fewer first-time entrants. This is significant. The bulk of detainees are persons attempting to rejoin their families after brief and casual departures from the country. If we were really being overrun, it wouldn't be with husbands and wives returning to join their families. It would be with first time entrants looking for work.

Trust me when I say that members of Congress are intimately familiar with the problems of Dreamers, non-immigrated residents, persons denied asylum, and all the other classes of folks here without an immigration status. They know the dimensions as well as the urgency of the problem, and they are in accord that a comprehensive solution must be implemented. During the last administration, they were unable to agree on the form an immigration benefit program should take. I hope in the Biden Administration they will find a way to reach a consensus.

I remain convinced that an Immigration Benefit Program is a moral imperative. It will work wonders as an alternative to our existing chaos. But what should such a program look like? What type of program would be most helpful? Based on my experience with the 1986 IRCA Legalization program, I have outlined my thoughts on what the essential elements of a comprehensive benefit program should be. If these core concepts can be incorporated in an IBP, the major hurdles to finding relief for most qualified applicants will have been cleared.

An effective Immigration Benefit Program should:

- Permit qualified non-immigrated residents to apply for a lawful status and stop removal proceedings while applications are pending.

- Be the first step toward Lawful Permanent Resident status and admission to an IBP must cancel pending deportation actions.

- Anticipate an open IBP enrollment period of at least one year. Provide a path to an appeal process for denied applications.

- Operate IBP adjudication process on a policy of inclusion rather than exclusion.

- Promptly open the door to applications for employment authorization and social security numbers.

- Provide ample opportunity for applicants to prove they qualify. Burden of proof should fall on the applicant.

- Require passing rigorous background checks with an appeal process.

- IBP must operate at no expense to the government.

- Ensure all IBP program costs are absorbed through user fees.

Even though an IBP has not been voted on yet in either chamber of Congress, you can be certain that once it is, there will be no shortage of individuals who will want to provide applicants with IBP enrollment services. Since immigration is a federal program, as long as attorneys have been admitted to the bar in any state, they can practice immigration law anywhere in the United States. Applicants should be incredibly careful who they select to help them prepare their application when the time comes.

There will be many sole practitioners who will offer legalization services but they will add these cases to their existing workload. And here's my experience from IRCA: most attorneys like to take on as much work as they can to stay busy. That's normal, but it usually doesn't leave them sufficient time to properly focus on applications. Surprisingly, in 1986, there was no distinction in the rejection rate between cases filed by law firms, Volunteer Agencies (VOLAGS), or Catholic Charities who prepared and filed free applications. They all failed at the same rate. I think this came about because they all lacked experience on the new applications, and denials could not be appealed. In most instances, a professional without experience is not really a professional.

If you or someone you know is interested in this program, don't be afraid to do research on who you select to help you. This is one of the most important things you will do in this lifetime. Give it your best attention.

My belief is that providing IBP enrollment services must be a mutually beneficial program where the applicants get what they seek and the service provider receives a fair compensation for the opportunity to make things right for them. No matter what type of remedy the government selects for dealing with non-immigrated residents, you can bet an application of some type will be required. Like asylum, meeting the standard for approval of an IBP application will be strict. Below are some of the general requirements I believe will be contained in any IBP application.

To be enrolled in an IBP, Non-Immigrated Residents will most likely have to:

- Demonstrate continuous unlawful residence for the time that will be set by law. For example, if a law is passed in 2021, it will most likely require that the applicant have entered the country and resided here continuously for at least five years. The five-year residence must have started at least two years before the law takes effect. This means the applicant must have entered and remained here continuously since 2019.

- Undergo full Interagency Border Inspection System (IBIS) background checks.

- Demonstrate a steady work history. DHS will want to know where you have worked (usually five years to show you can support yourself or your family). Whoever provides you with enrollment services must be familiar with an "imperfect work history" in order to help you.

- Meet the same standards as all other immigrants.

- Convicted criminals (Aggravated Felons) will be barred from participation. Presently, a DUI is considered a serious misdemeanor and may disqualify you.

- Not subject to become a public charge. You must present a stable social and work history. Your service provider should know the requirements

- Be a person of good moral turpitude. Multiple moving traffic citations, spousal abuse complaints, child support delinquency, etc., could disqualify you.

- Cannot have a record of bad debt. Your tax responsibilities will have to be in order.

The enrollment service provider must be intimately familiar with each unique requirement, so it's important that applicants choose wisely. Let's take the first requirement for instance. If an applicant claims to have resided here for five years, he or she must prove it in thirty-day increments. Proof may take the form of any of the following documents:

- Any type of monthly receipt with the applicant's name and address on the correspondence.

- Envelopes mailed to them with their name, address, and a cancellation mark

- Notarized testimonial letters from friends or family members who can attest to one's presence.

- Photographs/ Videos of the applicant with dates created by the camera

- Billing statements from credit card, phone or loan companies.

If you are a potential applicant, you may benefit from starting to round up your pertinent documents now. It's not too early to start putting your case together. It might also be useful if you started thinking about how you might get your hands-on original birth, marriage, and divorce documents for you and your family. Don't make the same mistake applicants in 1986 did and wait until the last minute. Remember when opportunity knocks, that is not the time to say, "Wait, I have to go pack a bag!" Be ready.

I Remain Optimistic

There is a diverse group of women and men throughout the nation, ordinary citizens, who believe in the power of truth. They know you don't have to be in a formal leadership position to insist on honest leadership. Human history has known many moments when change happened, not because leaders led and people followed, but because people led, and leaders followed. These citizen leaders are among us, and they will provide us with direction during these troubling times.

While much has changed since the nation's founding, certain ideals have not. The United States is still a country with a mission and a desire for greatness on the world stage. America's openness to people who want to move here and make a better life for themselves is fuel for this greatness. There was a time when our political parties understood this concept. Today supporting your political affiliation has become more important than supporting the nation.

In the final analysis, if we are successful in creating an America that has fewer people, even though the population may be more homogeneous, the nation will not only be smaller and weaker but also poorer on a per capita basis. An America that is shrinking is a country that is going to be a lesser force in the world than an America that is growing.

For those of us who believe in the principles of the Declaration of Independence and the value of America's ideals, a future of economic decline and retreat in the name of uniformity and conformity should be unacceptable. More than 200 years of experience has shown us that this nation can best meet the challenges of the new decade by cleaving to the concept of unity without uniformity and to the concept of diversity without fragmentation. The lessons of history tell us that the nation as a whole will benefit by keeping Lady Liberty's torch lit, held high, and steady for all to see.

EPILOGUE

When I sat down to write this memoir, I asked myself what kind of book I wanted this to be.

Did I want it to be a conventional memoir? Did I want it to be a manifesto of my views on immigration? Did I want it to be an informative guide for prospective applicants who might be interested in an ESP type program? Did I want it to be funny? Somber? Useful?

In the end, I decided that much like my life itself, this book shouldn't be just one thing. It should be allowed to breathe, to change, to take turns (if not always elegantly) in different directions. But if I were to focus on one overarching quality, this book had to be optimistic.

I can't help it. I've always been an optimist, "a cup-half-full kind of guy." Even with the arguable wisdom that comes with age, even if a couple of jokers over the years have tried their best to prove me wrong, I've always opted to believe that our world is made up of basically decent human beings. (Sure, there are bozos everywhere, but eventually you learn how to ignore or navigate around them.)

I've always had an affinity for getting along with people. Even in places that were emotionally challenging for me, like the poverty-plagued, developing countries I visited during some of my consultancies. I don't like poverty and I know it sounds horrible when someone says something like that but if you've read this book, you know I've earned my right to say it. I grew up in poverty; in a debilitating, powerless state of being hungry and not being able to get enough food; of having to fight for and steal scraps to survive; of being seen as "a hopeless case." And the kind of poverty I witnessed in those developing countries was hard for me to face, not just because it brought up unpleasant memories, but because I knew there wasn't much I could do to help. I knew that for most of these people, barring some miracle, it would be impossible to escape the clutches of poverty in their lifetime. It would be impossible for them to turn their lives around the way I did.

I have to admit, I have been lucky enough to live in a country where it was possible to do so.

You know, after hearing my story, people usually comment on how unlucky I've been; about what a hard life I've led. I don't agree at all. I believe it was all supposed to happen that way. Every hardship and every bump on the road, prepared me for what I needed to do, for what I needed to be. Being born to immigrant parents, growing up poor and often unwanted, feeling that I didn't belong, having trouble communicating because of the language barrier, and getting in trouble with the law...all these experiences helped me become a better military man, a better civil servant, and ultimately, a better Deputy Commissioner.

I guess you could say I'm an optimist who also believes in destiny. I believe that things tend to happen for a reason. I see everything in my life as a part of the journey I'm on, and every day as a necessary step toward a better tomorrow.

I've been thinking a lot about that tomorrow, lately. What will it look like? Will America get over its internal divisions? Will this program, which I've been working on most of my life in some capacity or other, be able to help as many people as I hope? Will all my efforts bear sweet fruit? In the end, I'm reminded of Kahlil Gibran's words about parenthood:

Your children are not your children.
They are the sons and daughters of Life's longing for itself...
You may house their bodies but not their souls,
For their souls dwell in the house of tomorrow...

We cannot control what the house of tomorrow will look like. (Perhaps we can control what the White House of tomorrow will look like, but that's another story.) We can only do our best, and hope for the best. As Gibran so eloquently puts it, we can be the bows "from which your children as living arrows are sent forth."

So here I am, at the end of this book, doing my best and hoping for the best, as I've always done. I'm hoping that people will acknowledge my efforts; that they will say, "He contributed. He made things a little better, where he could." That's the goal, you know, to try and do the right thing. To be the bow.

Where the arrow of that bow will land, I don't know. But I'm nothing if not hopeful. And you know what? I think being hopeful is the most American quality a person can have.

This unequaled freedom we've been lucky enough to enjoy in America has filled us with a bounty of hope and pride. It has provided the nation with a harvest of blessings throughout our history. So yes, I do hope that we, the people, the old Americans and the new Americans, will commit ourselves to finding ways to stop the acrimony and lack of civility that is tearing away at the fabric of our democracy. Harmony and politeness have played such an important role in the making of our great nation, and it will be needed as a source of strength if we are to get past these turbulent times and remain a great people, American together.

In case you haven't figured this out about me yet, I believe we will succeed.

My wife, Carole, and me.

ACKNOWLEDGMENTS

Writing a book is harder than I thought and more rewarding than I could have ever imagined. Of course, none of this would have been possible without the help and endless support from a host of believers.

Let me begin this expression of gratitude with a smart doff of my cap to my generous and kind benefactor Barry de Paulo. He believed in me and in this project when few others did. Thank you very much.

I am eternally grateful to America and the State of California. They teamed up to take this street waif into their protective embrace when I desperately needed it. Thank you very much.

To my wife, Carole, my psychic leader and spiritual guide. She was as important to pushing this book across the finish line as I was. Thank you very much.

A special nod belongs to my Probation Officer, Mrs. Shelton. She never saw my race, my snotty attitude, my anxiety driven stuttering or my rudimentary command of English. She just saw a child hungry to learn, hungry to grow and hungry to succeed in life. Thank you very much.

To my three mothers. My godmother, Anita Sanchez, who started me off on the right track until one of life's aberrations ripped me from her bosom. My biological mother, Antonia Figueroa, who played her hand as best she could. She was loved through it all. And my foster mother, Emilia Leone. She persevered and loved as only a real mother can. Thank you very much.

Although my years in foster care were filled with ups and downs, Mrs. Leone's determination and love never faltered, not one time. She sustained me in ways that I never knew I needed. She taught me discipline, tough love, manners, respect, and so much more that helped me throughout my life. I have no idea where I would be if she had not put a roof over my head, a boot in my behind and become the family figure I so desperately needed. If only I understood about real love then as I do now. Thank you very much.

Special thanks to Nick Porter, my ever-patient book writing consigliere and his amazing cover designing team. A shout out also belongs to Danai Christopoulou, my book writing idea person, wordsmith and guide. Thank you very much.

Special gratitude belongs to Dr. Rosemary Frederickson. Her command of English coupled with her efforts to bring my story to life, in proper English, has provided me with a legacy where one didn't exist before. Thank you very much.

To Chris Angermann of Bardolf & Company for shepherding my manuscript through its final stages into book form with proficiency and ease. Thank you very much.

Finally, to all those dreamers who have been a part of my getting there: the world is a better place thanks to people like you who want to develop and help others grow. In that vein, I want to thank everyone who ever said anything positive to me or taught me something. I heard it all and it meant something. Thank you very much.

BIOGRAPHY

Ricardo Inzunza spent his career in the U.S military and government helping oversee the creation and administration of policies furthering fair treatment of women and minorities. He served as Director, Military Equal Opportunity Programs for the Department of Defense, and Deputy Director of the Asylum and Review Unit of the Department of Justice under President Ronald Reagan. As Deputy Commissioner of INS under President George H.W. Bush, he provided executive guidance on all agency matters to more than 40,000 personnel worldwide. He also worked behind the scenes reversing the cancelation of visas of nuns in a cloister, dealing with the deportation of tourists in comas, and facilitating the defection of Olympic gymnastics champion Nadia Comăneci to the United States.

In his current capacity as CEO of RIA International LTD, Ricardo has led several Congressional Delegations to the Peoples Republic of China, consulted for the World Bank in various African countries, and continues to work for Immigration reform.

A frequent speaker and lecturer, he has received numerous accolades, including:

- Peoples Republic of China, US Immigration Lecture Series, 127 presentations throughout China, 1993 to 2007.
- Member of Congressional Delegations to China (PRC), 1996, 1999, 2003, 2007. 2010 and 2013 (Delegation Leader).

- Key Speaker, Taiwan world Affairs council, Taipei, Taiwan, 2003
- Guest Speaker, Lesotho World Affairs Council November 2016, Kingdom of Lesotho.
- Guest Speaker, Starkville Rotary Club, Starkville, Mississippi, August 2016.
- Key Note Speaker, Mississippi State University, Immigration Reform, September 2018, Starkville, MS.
- Principal Speaker, Eupora Rotary Club, July, 2019, Eupora, MS.
- Immigration Guest Speaker, Maseru, Lesotho, 2018. Kingdom of Lesotho.
- World Bank Consultant, 1993 to present, analysis and recommendations on Immigration and Customs projects in 23 of Sub-Saharan Africa's 46 Countries.
- Principal Immigration Consultant to the Millennium Challenge Corporation in Sub-Saharan Africa, 2000 to 2010.
- Legal Corner Lecture Series Speaker, Keiser University Tampa FL Campus—12/12/2013.
- US China Educational, Economic, and Cultural Foundation, Appointment as President—10/6/2012, Houston, Texas.
- Commonwealth of Kentucky, Commissioned as Kentucky Colonel - 10/1/2000, Lexington, Kentucky.
- Commissioner of Immigration, Appointed Special Assistant to the Commissioner, Washington D.C.—10/2/1994.
- Immigration and Naturalization Service, Executive Management Team Leadership Award—1/1/1993, Washington DC.
- Journal of International Law and Practice and the Detroit College of Law, Recognition of Outstanding Contributions in the Field of International Relations—8/16/1992,Detroit MI.
- National Indian American Chamber of Commerce, Outstanding Service to the Indian American Community, Washington DC, 5/1/1992, Atlanta, GA.
- U.S. Immigration and Naturalization Service, Deputy Commissioner—1988 to 1993, Washington DC .
- U.S. Department of Justice, Senior Executive Service Outstanding Performance Rating—6/30/1991, Washington DC.
- City of Huntsville, Honorary Citizen of Huntsville, AL—3/25/1991, Huntsville, Al.

- Defense Communications Agency. Keynote Speaker DCA Hispanic Employment Program—10/1/1990, Washington DC.
- City of New Orleans, International Honorary Citizen, New Orleans LA, - 9/28/1990 New Orleans, LA.
- Cuban American National Foundation, Appreciation for Humanitarian concern on behalf of Cuban Refugees, Miami, FL— 5/19/1990, Miami Fl.
- U.S. Immigration and Naturalization Service, Director, Legalization Implementation Team—1983 to 1985, Washington DC.
- By the Attorney General, Commissioned Director, Asylum Policy and Review Unit, reporting to Attorney General, 4/15/1987, Washington DC.
- Immigration and Naturalization Service, Commissioner's Award for Excellence in Group Achievement—1989, Washington DC.
- Department of Justice, Dedication to the mission of US Immigration and Naturalization Service—11/14/1988, Washington DC.
- Immigration and Naturalization Service, SES Outstanding Performance Rating, 6/30/1985, Washington DC.
- Attorney General of the United States of America, Appointed Special Assistant to the Commissioner, Washington D.C, 4/16/1995, Washington DC.
- Commissioner's Unit Citation, U.S. Customs Service, Award for Diligent Efforts in supporting the South Florida Task Force, Miami Air Branch, FL—1/14/1985, Miami, FL.
- 1776th Air Base Wing, Guest Speaker during Hispanic Heritage Week, Andrews AFB, Maryland, 9/14/1984, Morningside, MD.
- USAF Armament Division, Guest Speaker During Hispanic Heritage Month Luncheon, Eglin AFB—9/13/1984, Valparaiso, FL.
- U.S Air Force, Outstanding Presentation, Hispanic Heritage Month, "Hispanics-A Part of America's Excellence," Wright Patterson AFB, Ohio—1984, Dayton, Ohio.
- Air Force Association, USAF Outstanding Airman of the year— 1976, Washington DC.
- United States Air Force Office Directorate of Personnel Plans Headquarters, Outstanding Airman, Washington DC, First enlisted Action Officer (Protocol Rank Lt. Colonel), Washington DC.